HUMAN RIGHTS
Concepts, Issues & Laws

HUMAN RIGHTS
Concepts, Issues & Laws

Edited by

S.C. Joshi

AKANSHA PUBLISHING HOUSE
NEW DELHI - 110 002 (INDIA)

AKANSHA PUBLISHING HOUSE
4649/21-B, Ansari Road,
Daryaganj, New Delhi - 110 002
Phones: 23263193, 9811582579
E-mail: ektabooks@yahoo.com

Human Rights: Concepts, Issues & Laws

First Published, 2006

Reprint 2007

Reprint 2008

ISBN 81-8370-031-4

Reprint 2011

PRINTED IN INDIA

Published by M.P. Misra for Akansha Publishing House, New Delhi - 110 002 and Printed at Tarun Offset Press, Delhi

To

Jurists, Social Scientists
and Social Activists,
who have contributed their lot
for upholding the cause of
Human Rights.

Contents

Preface ix

1. Evolution of Human Rights 1

2. Glimpses of Human Rights 15

3. Economic Development and Human Rights 42

4. Human Rights and Criminal Justice Administration 47

5. National Human Rights Commission (NHRC) of India 63

6. NGOs and Human Rights 94

7. Positive Action for a Humane Society 101

Appendices 104

Select Bibliography 299

Index 305

Preface

Since times immemorial man has longed for freedom and equality, for guaranteed human rights and for fraternal relationships in a society in which the people run and manage their own affairs. In the present times, a majority of States have inscribed these ideals in their Constitutions. And yet, these categories and notions appear to be ambiguous and susceptible to differing interpretations. The courts frequently give different verdicts. The human rights are also governed by different political Philosophies.

It is very much apt in this connection to quote, Rousseau, "Man is born free and is everywhere in chains". Countering the Sophists who preached that every individual was qualified to judge, according to his own beliefs and desires, what was right, the Greeks and the Romans built a society on the conception of the subordination of the individual to the community and of the citizen to the State. Plato and Aristotle regarded the positive furtherance of goodness as the mission and goal of the State. Plato went to the extent of rejecting democracy as a contemptible form of Government. The Romans separated State and individual, each having definite rights and duties. According to them the State was a necessary and natural framework for social existence, but the individual was made the centre of legal thought and the protection of the rights of the individual was the main purpose for which the State existed. The medieval theory of legitimate power propounded by the Romans depended upon both the Emperor and the Pope. People struggled even against this Royal absolutism. By the close of the sixteenth century, the medieval institutions where the king had become weak the State started disintegrating. The liberty of the subjects, said Hobbes, lay only in those things, which the Sovereign had permitted in regulating their actions, and nothing the Sovereign could do to a subject on any pretence whatsoever could properly be called injustice.

'Human Rights' as a phrase is rather new coinage which came in vogue with the Universal Declaration of Human Rights. A new consciousness emerged among all nations to protect and ensure basic fundamental rights of human being.

In India National Human Rights Commission (NHRC) was set up. Besides this States have also set up Human Right Commissions at state level. Though Constitution of India enshrines Fundamental Rights of citizens.

Despite that, we frequently come across cases of human rights violations. Mostly police and other forces are found responsible for this. Terrorism and militancy as is prevalent in many parts of the world add to violation of human rights.

This book addresses many issues pertaining to human rights in coherent ways. The information is gathered under seven chapters namely—Evolution of human rights; Glimpses of human rights; Economic development and human rights; Human rights and criminal justice administration; National Human Rights Commission of India; NGOs and human rights; and Positive action for a Humane society. Besides this many important' documents on Human Rights are reproduced for enlightening the relevant laws and other statutes.

In fact, the information is collated from the writings of different social scientists, human rights experts and legal experts. As such entire credit goes to them on whose literary exercises this endeavour is devised and developed. I owe a deep sense of gratitude to them all. Though all names appear in Bibliography, who missed mention is unintentional.

I am deeply beholden to Sri S.K. Muttoo, Secretary, Department of Social Welfare and Women Empowerment,

Govt. of Uttaranchal for his patronage and guidance. I owe a deep sense of gratitude to Dr. H.C. Upreti, (Retd.) Associate Professor, Dept. of Sociology, University of Rajasthan, Jaipur. I am thankful to my colleagues at NIPCCD for their constant moral support and inspiration. I am grateful to my family members especially my wife and children for providing congenial work environment at home. Finally, Mr. M.P. Misra deserves all appreciation for bringing out the book superbly within short time.

—Editor

1

Evolution of Human Rights

> **"The (fundamental rights) expressly seek to strike a balance between a written guarantee of Individual rights and the collective interests of the community."**
>
> ***—D.D. Basu***

Human rights are the fundamental natural rights which are the most precious possession of mankind and a world without them will have to face a perpetual risk of moral depredation. Human rights are also called fundamental rights or natural rights. As such these cannot be taken away by any legislative measure anywhere.

The new phrase "human rights" was adopted only in the 20th century from the expression previously known as "natural rights" of men. But systematic and conceptual changes have been taking over the period so far as fundamental rights are concerned. Consequently some more fundamental rights, which included the social and economic rights, have acquired wide recognition.

Being a human being one is entitled to have basic rights. All Human Rights derive from the dignity and worth inherent in the human person and that the human person is the central subject of Human Rights and Fundamental Freedoms. In simple terms, whatever adds to the dignified and free existence of a human being should be regarded as Human Right. Evolution and crystallisation of the concept took a long time. Initially there was confusion between the Natural Rights propounded by political philosophers in the bygone ages and the concept of Human Rights. The latter is an all-encompassing one.

Ample references and instances are found of Human rights in ancient scriptures and recorded history, though they were not referred to by that very name. Modern historians credit the origin of the concept to Magna Carta A.D. 1521. It would be seen that Magna Carta was a petition urging the King to concede certain rights to particular sections of the people. Its contents neither had the universality of application nor direct relevance to common man's basic freedoms.

For the first time, the term Human Rights was coined in the United States Declaration of Independence in 1776 and the U.S. Constitution embodied a Bill of Rights. French Revolution gave birth to the Declaration of Rights of Man and Citizen in 1789. In 1929, Institute of International Law, New York (U.S.A.), prepared a Declaration of Human Rights and Duties. In 1945, the Inter-American Conference passed a resolution seeking establishment of an International Forum for the furtherance of human rights.

The inhuman atrocities committed on political and ethnic minorities by the Axis Powers helped to usher in a world order for promoting respect for and observance of Human Rights and Fundamental Freedoms. The Charter of the United Nations Organisation (UNO) in its preamble declared 'We the Peoples of the United Nations determine to reaffirm faith in the fundamental human rights, in the dignity and worth of human person, in the equal rights of men and women and of the Nations large and small...'. The Charter also declared that the purpose of the United Nations is 'To achieve international cooperation in solving international problems of an economic, social, cultural or humanitarian character and in promoting and encouraging respect for Human Rights and for Fundamental Freedoms for all without distinction as to race, sex, language or religion.' The United Nations also proclaimed the Universal Declaration of Human Rights in 1948.

Coming to the case of India, the Constitution of India,

which came into effect in 1950, incorporated a Part on 'Fundamental Rights' of the citizens.

The United States defined Human Rights in a policy document in 1978 as follows:

> "Freedom from arbitrary arrest and imprisonment, torture, unfair trial, cruel and unusual punishment, and invasion of privacy. Rights to food, shelter, health care and education and freedom of thought, speech, assembly, religion, press, movement and participation in Government".

In India, the Protection of Human Rights Act, 1993, states, "Human Rights as 'the rights relating to liberty, equality and dignity of the individual guaranteed by the Indian Constitution as embodied in the Fundamental Rights and the International Covenants."

The relevant International Covenants are:

(a) Universal Declaration of Human Rights (1948),

(b) The International Covenant on Civil and Political Rights (1966),

(c) The International Covenant on Economic, Social and Cultural Rights (1966), and

(d) The Optional Protocol (1966).

With the progress of civilisation, the Human Rights boom is expanding day by day and the people all over the world are able to enjoy their basic freedoms and assured of dignified existence to some extent.

Classification of Human Rights

The Human Rights concept is gaining momentum and expanding day by day. Broadly, they fall into categories of:

(a) Civil and Political Rights, (b) Economic, Social and Cultural Rights, and (c) Group Rights.

Civil and Political Rights: The rights pertaining to the life, integrity, liberty and security of human person; the rights with respect to administration of justice; the right to privacy; the rights to freedom of religion or belief and to freedom of opinion and expression; freedom of movements the right to assembly and association; and the right to political participation are among the civil and political rights.

2. *Economic, Social and Cultural Rights:* The right to work; trade union freedoms; the right to adequate standard of living, including food, clothing and housing; the right to health care; the right to education; and the right to take part in cultural life are among the economic, social and cultural rights.

In principle, the United Nations Organisation (UNO) has been endeavouring to relate human rights to global issues and strenuously working to find solutions for human rights concerns affecting the millions of deprived, dispossessed, discriminated against and marginalised people.

This approach of United Nations was formalised in the Proclamation of Tehran (1968), known as the 'structural approach' having the following characteristic features:

(a) to identify root causes of human rights violations;
(b) to link human rights to major worldwide patterns and issues;
(c) to recognise the diversity of political and social systems, cultural and religious differences and varying levels of development; and
(d) to assess human rights in the light of concrete contexts situations.

This 'approach' also recognises the central position of the human person in the development process and links human rights with development.

The incessant efforts of the United Nations in the human rights area can be understood from the fact that there are nearly 90 (ninety) international covenants, declarations and other documents, known as 'Instruments of Human Rights'. These fall under the categories of general instruments, special instruments and legal instruments (treaties etc.). All these embody political commitments by member-States and also provide for the conduct of international relations in the field of human rights and bring the domestic policies in line with international code of ethics. There are elaborate international implementation procedures in the field of human rights. Broadly, these procedures serve advisory, assistance, correction, relief and remedy and preventive functions.

At times, to deal with individual countries and special situations, special procedures are also adopted. It may be borne in mind that the actual realisation of human rights by the people would depend upon the commitment of the member-States to the cause of Human Rights. The role of U.N.O. is moral in nature. In the ultimate analysis, Human Rights implementation is to be done at local and national levels.

The Republic of India ratified the International Covenants on Civil and Political Rights and on Economic, Social and Cultural Rights with certain declarations (reservations). A careful reading of these instruments would reveal the concern of the United Nations for Human Rights. All ratifying member-States including the Republic of India have accepted the values propounded in these covenants and are duly bound to bring their national policies and procedures in line with these covenants as required under International Law and Treaty. From the conceptual stage, the U.N.O. had marched to the operational stage with great vigour. An elected Human Rights Committee of the U.N.O. functions to consider communications from a State party alleging non-fulfilment of covenant obligations by another member-State. Citizens of those member-States, who are a party to the Optional Protocol, can directly petition the Human

Rights Committee, if do not their all available domestic remedies are exhausted.

International covenants and instruments are beacon lights showing the path of justice and humanity to the nations. The urge to implement and uphold Human Rights should come from within a nation. It takes time to transform international good intentions into national norms. In the meantime these give the national judiciary an opportunity to interpret national laws in the light of international obligations of the nation.

The position has been admirably summed up by the Supreme Court of India (in AIR 1980 SC 470 pp. 473-474):

> "The remedy for breaches of International Law in general is not to be found in the law courts of the State because International Law, per se or proprio vigore, has not the force or authority of civil law, till under its inspirational impact actual legislation is undertaken...the Declaration of Human Rights merely sets a common standard of achievement for all peoples and all nations but cannot create a binding set of rules. Member-States may seek, through appropriate agencies, to initiate action when these basic rights are violated, but individual citizens cannot complain about their breach in the municipal courts even if the country concerned has adopted the covenants and ratified the Optional Protocol. The individual cannot come to court but may complain to the Human Rights Committee, which, in turn, will set in other procedures. In short, the basic human rights enshrined in the International Covenants above referred to, may, at best inform judicial institutions and inspire legislative action within member-States, but apart from such deep reverence, remedial action at the instance of an aggrieved individual is beyond the area of judicial authority."

The Apex Court of India has referred often to the International Covenants while dealing with Human Rights violations. In the Prem Shankar Case (AIR 1980 SC 1535 p. 1537), the Supreme Court, while dealing with handcuffs and other humiliations inflicted on persons in custody, observed, "After all, even while discussing the relevant statutory provisions and constitutional requirements, court and counsel must never forget the core principle found in Article 5 of the Universal Declaration of Human Rights, 1948:

> 'No one shall be subjected to torture or to cruel, inhuman or degrading treatment or punishment.'

India is founder-member of U.N.O. and a signatory to all Human Rights Instruments. Thus, Indian Courts do take due note of the international instruments on Human Rights while dealing with cases of violation. Art. 51 of the Indian Constitution makes it obligatory for the State to foster respect for international law and treaty obligations.

Article 51: Promotion of International Peace and Security

The State shall endeavour to:

(a) promote international peace and security;

(b) maintain just and honourable relations between nations;

(c) foster respect for international law and treaty obligations in the dealings of organised people with one another; and

(d) encourage settlement of international disputes by arbitration.

As Article 51 finds a place in Part-IV dealing with Directive Principles of State Policy, it is not enforceable by a Court of Law. But it reflects the spirit of the Constitution and as such courts will take note of it while deciding matters before them. To have legal force in the country, a separate law has to be enacted to give effect to an international treaty under Art. 253.

A comparison of Universal Declaration of Rights (1948) and Fundamental Rights enunciated in Part-III of the Indian Constitution will reveal many similarities in content and form. Though the framers of Constitution of India would have been influenced by British Legal concepts and the American Constitutional traditions one cannot wish away the impact the Universal Declaration of Rights (1948) must have had on the minds of the Indian Constitution architects due to its contemporaneous character at that very time.

FUNDAMENTAL RIGHTS: A COMPARATIVE OVERVIEW

	Subject	Indian Constitution	Universal Declaration of Human Rights, (1948)
	(1)	(2)	(3)
(a)	Equality Before Law	*Art. 14:* The State shall not deny to any person equality before the Law or the equal protection of the Laws within the territory of India.	*Art. 7:* All are equal before the Law and are entitled without any discrimination to equal protection of the Law. All are entitled to equal protection against any discrimination in violation of this declaration and against any incitement to such discrimination.
(b)	Prohibition of discrimination on grounds only of religion, race, caste,	*Art. 15(1):* The State shall not discriminate against any citizen on grounds only of religion, race, caste, sex, place or any of them.	*Art. 2—Para(1):* Everyone is entitled to all the rights and freedoms set forth in this Declaration, without distinction of any kind, such as race, colour, sex, language, religion, political or other opinion, national or social origin,

	(1)	(2)	(3)
	sex, place of birth or any of them.		property, birth or other status.
			Art. 7—Sentence 2: All are entitled to equal protection against any discrimination in violation of this Declaration and against any incitement to such discrimination.
(c)	Equality of opportunity in matters of public employment.	*Art. 16(1):* There shall be equality of opportunity for all citizens in matters relating to employment or appointment to any office under the State.	*Art. 21 (2):* Everyone has a right to equal access to public service in his country.
(d)	Freedom of speech, assembly, association etc.	*Art. 19: (1)* All citizens shall have the (a) Right to freedom of speech and expression. (b) Right to assemble	*Art. 19:* Everyone has the right to freedom of opinion and expression;...... art. 20(1):

		peaceably and without arms. (c) Right to form Unions and Associations. (d) Right to move freely throughout the territory of India; (e) Right to reside and settle in any part of the territory of India.	Everyone has the right to freedom of peaceful assembly and association. Art. 23(4): Everyone has a right to form and to join trade unions for the protection of his rights. Art. 20(2): No one may be compelled to belong to an Association. *Art. 12(1)* Everyone has the right to freedom of movement and residence within the borders of each State.
(e)	Protection in respect of conviction for offences	*Art. 20(1):* No person shall be convicted of any offence except for violation of law in force at the time of the commission of the act charged as an offence, nor be subjected to a penalty greater than that which might have been in-	*Art. 11(2):* No one shall be held guilty of any penal offence on account of any act or omission which may not constitute a penal offence, under national or international law, at the time when it was

	(1)	(2)	(3)
		flicted under the law in force at the time of the commission of the offence.	committed. Nor shall a heavier penalty be imposed than the one that was applicable at the time the penal offence was committed.
(f)	Protection of life and personal liberty.	*Art. 21:* No person shall be deprived of his life or personal liberty except according to procedure established by law.	*Art. 3:* Everyone has the right to life, liberty and security of person. Art. 9: No one shall be subjected to arbitrary arrest, detention or exile.
(g)	Prohibition of traffic in human-beings and forced labour.	*Art. 23(1):* Traffic in human beings and 'Beggar' and other similar forms of forced labour are prohibited and any contravention of this provision shall be an offence punishable in accordance with Law.	*Art. 4:* No one shall be held in slavery or servitude; slavery and the slave trade shall be prohibited in all forms.

		Note: 'Beggar is a form of forced labour under which a person is compelled to work without remuneration.	
(h)	Freedom of conscience and free profession, practice and propagation of religion.	*Art. 25(1):* Subject to public order, morality and health and to the provisions of this part, all persons are equally entitled to freedom of conscience and right freely to profess, practise and propagate religion.	*Art. 18:* Everyone has the right to freedom of thought, conscience and religion; this right includes freedom to change his religion or belief, and freedom, either alone or in community with others and in public or private, to manifest his religion or belief in teaching, practice, worship and observance.
(i)	Protection of interests of minonties.	*Art. 29(1):* Any section of the citizens residing in the territory or any part thereof having a distinct language, script or culture of its own shall have the right to conserve the same.	*Art. 22:* Everyone, as a member of society, has the right to social security and is entitled to realisation, through national effort and international cooperation and in accordance with the

	(1)	(2)	(3)
			organisation and resources of each State, of the economic, social and cultural rights indispensable for his dignity and the free development of personality.
(j)	Right of minorities to establish and administer educational institutions.	*Art. 30(1):* All minorities, whether based on religion or language, shall have the right to establish and administer educational institutions of their choice.	*Art. 26(3):* Parents have a prior right to choose the kind of education that shall be given to their children.
(k)	Right to constitutional remedies.	*Art. 32(1):* The right to move the Supreme Court by appropriate proceedings for the enforcement of rights conferred by this part is guaranteed. *Note:* 'By this part' refers to) Part-III—Fundamental Rights.	*Art. 8:* Everyone has the right to an effective remedy by the tribunals for acts violating the fundamental rights granted to him by the Constitution or by Law.

2

Glimpses of Human Rights

"There is no better test of excellence of a government than the efficiency of judicial system."

—*Prof. Bryce*

Since times immemorial man has longed for freedom and equality, for guaranteed human rights and for fraternal relationships in a society in which the people run and manage their own affairs. In the present times, a majority of States have inscribed these ideals in their Constitutions. And yet, these categories and notions appear to be ambiguous and susceptible to differing interpretations. The courts frequently give different verdicts. The human rights are also governed by different political Philosophies.

To start with Rousseau, "Man is born free and is everywhere in chains". Countering the Sophists who preached that every individual was qualified to judge, according to his own beliefs and desires, what was right, the Greeks and the Romans built a society on the conception of the subordination of the individual to the community and of the citizen to the State. Plato and Aristotle regarded the positive furtherance of goodness as the mission and goal of the State. Plato went to the extent of rejecting democracy as a contemptible form of Government. The Romans separated State and individual, each having definite rights and duties. According to them the State was a necessary and natural framework for social existence, but the individual was made the centre of legal thought and the protection of the rights of the individual was the main purpose for which the State existed. The medieval theory of legitimate power propounded by the Romans depended upon both the Emperor and the Pope. People struggled even against this Royal absolutism. By the close of the sixteenth century, the medieval institutions where the king had become weak the State started disintegrating. The liberty of the subjects, said Hobbes, lay only in those things, which the Sovereign had permitted in regulating their actions, and nothing the Sovereign could do to a subject on any pretence whatsoever could properly be called injustice.

Locke stated that "Man being born with a little to perfect freedom and an uncontrolled enjoyment of all the rights and privileges of law of nature, equally with any other man.... hath by nature a power not only to preserve his property, that is, his life, liberty and estate, against the injuries and attempts of other men, but to judge and punish the breaches of law in others...." Locke considered this to be the basis of the existence of a political society. He justified the Glorious Revolution of 1688. He thought that a Natural Law was rooted in the reasonable nature of man and political power was merely a trust for the benefit of the people. Locke influenced Rousseau, who considered the sovereignty of the people to be inalienable and indivisible. Many significant developments took place in Europe and elsewhere in the 17th and 18th centuries. The struggle for liberty and fundamental freedoms continued. The chains which were put around the peoples neck did not break.

Institutionalisation of Human Rights

Claiming that one has a right (what we can call "propositional claiming" as opposed to "performative claiming") is another sort of thing one can do with language, but it is not the sort of doing that characteristically has legal consequences. To claim that one has rights is to make an assertion that one has them, and to make it in such a manner as to demand of insist that they be recognised. In this sense of "claim" many things in addition to rights can be claimed, that is, many other kinds of proposition can be asserted in the claiming way. I can claim, for example, that you, he, or she has certain rights, or that Julius Caesar once had certain rights, or I can claim that certain statements are true, or that I have certain skills, or accomplishments, or virtually anything at all. I can claim that the earth is flat. What is essential to claiming that is the manner of assertion. One can assert without even caring very much whether anyone is listening, but part of the point of propositional claiming is to make sure people listen. When I claim to others that I know something, for example, I am not merely asserting it, but rather "obstruding my putative knowledge upon their attention, demanding that it be recognised, that appropriate notice be taken of it by those concerned. . . ." Not every truth is properly assertable, much less claimable, in every context. To claim that something is the case in circumstances that justify no more than calm assertion is to behave like a boor. (This kind of boorishness, I might add, is probably less common in Nowheresville). But not to claim in the appropriate circumstances that one has a right is to be spiritless or foolish. A list of "appropriate circumstances" would include occasions when one is challenged, when one's possession is denied, or seems insufficiently acknowledged or appreciated, and of course even in these circumstances, the claiming should be done only with an appropriate degree of vehemence.

To have a right is to have a claim against someone whose recognition as valid is called for by some set of governing rules or moral principles. To have a claim in turn, is to have a case meriting consideration, that is, to have reasons or grounds that put one in a position to engage in performative and propositional claiming. The activity of claiming, finally, as much as any other thing, makes for self-respect and respect for others, gives a sense to the notion of personal dignity, and distinguishes this otherwise morally flawed world from the even worse world of Nowheresville.

The essential connection between the notion of a right and the justified limitation of one person's freedom by another may be thrown into relief if we consider codes of behaviour which do not purport to confer rights but only to prescribe what shall be done. Most natural law thinkers down to Hooker conceived of natural law this way; there were natural duties compliance with which would certainly benefit man—things to be done to achieve man's natural end—but not natural rights. And there are of course many types of codes of behaviour which only prescribe what is to be done, e.g., those regulating certain ceremonies. It would be absurd to regard these codes as conferring rights, but illuminating to contrast them with rules of games, which often create rights, though not, of course, moral rights. But even a code which is plainly a moral code need not establish rights; the Decalogue is perhaps the most important example. Of course, apart from heavenly reward human beings stand to benefit by general obedience to the Ten Commandments; disobedience is wrong and will certainly harm individuals. But it would be a surprising interpretation of them that tried them as conferring rights. In such an interpretation obedience to the Ten Commandments would have to be conceived as due to or owed to individuals, not merely to God, and disobedience not merely as wrong but as a wrong to (as well as harm to) individuals. The Commandments would case to read like penal statues designed only to rule out certain types of behaviour and would have to be thought of as rules placed at the disposal of individuals and regulating the extent to which they may demand certain behaviour from others. Rights are typically conceived of as possessed or owned by or belonging to individuals, and these expressions reflect the conception of moral rules as not only prescribing conduct but as forming a kind of moral property of individuals to which they are as individuals entitled; only when rules are conceived in this way can we speak of rights and wrongs as well as rights and wrong actions.

In the wake of the World War II and the defeat of

fascism many States realised the necessity of establishing a general international organisation based on the principles of sovereign equality of all peace-loving States for the maintenance of international peace and security. The Charter of the United Nations was signed on 26th June, 1945, to promote universal respect for and observance of human rights and fundamental freedoms for 'all without distinction to as to race, sex, language or religion. The Universal Declaration of Human Rights passed by the UN General Assembly on December 10, 1948 recognised the dignity of the human family and equality of its members as the foundation of freedom, justice and peace in the world, contempt and disregard of which had resulted into barbarious acts outraging the conscience of mankind. The question arises whether during the several decades, since the Declaration and the subsequent International Covenants on Human Rights were adopted by the world body, they have been realised anywhere.

The United Nations General Assembly adopted the Universal Declaration of Human Rights. During this period the declaration has become considerably more than was claimed for it when first presented to the General Assembly by Eleanor Roosevelt. A number of legally binding international conventions and Congresses on human rights have incorporated direct reference to the declaration. Nearly twenty one of the new African states, as well as a number of States in other parts of the world, include references to the declaration and its provisions in their constitutions. The declaration has clearly inspired human rights provisions in the constitutions of a number of other African states and such new non-African states as Cyprus, Jamaica and Trinidad and Tobago. Even national courts have frequently made reference to the declaration and in several instances have juridically applied it. No one, if he looks with a clear and honese eye, can fail to see close at home as well as in distant places far too many manifestations of man's inhumanity to fellowmen. On every continent there is an ever ready tendency to divert attention from transgression at home by crying out at the signs of neighbours. Various governments everywhere have been persistently inept in finding ways to express national interests in terms of cooperation to advance individual human welfare.

Progressive nations on the national level at the most guarantee the fundamental rights under the classifications of (1) Right to equality, (2) Right to freedom, (3) Rights against exploitation, (4) Right to freedom of religion, (5) Cultural and educational rights, (6) Right to property, and (7) Right to Constitutional remedies. A declaration of fundamental rights in a constitution may not be of much use if there is no adequate machinery for their enactment. In the United States this function was assumed by the Supreme Court. In France and other countries following the French tradition, the courts have no power to hold an Act of legislature invalid, though it may violate a fundamental right. In India, the courts have power to determine if a fundamental right guaranteed by the Constitution has been infringed. To ensure that the fundamental rights are properly protected, the constitution has conferred on the Supreme Court of India, concurrently with the High Courts, the power to grant most effective remedies whenever such rights appear to be or are being violated. It may thus issue the great writs of Habeas Corpus, mandamus, prohibition, quo warranto and certiorari. The right of a citizen to invoke jurisdiction of the courts for the enforcement of fundamental rights cannot, save in a declared emergency, be suspended. There are so many economic rights which are guaranteed by different governments. An independent and impartial judiciary is said to be the first condition of liberty. It is the Custodian of the rights of the citizen. In a federal constitution, it plays another important role; it determines the limits of the powers of the Centre and its constituting units.

Further Developed countries play a very important role in the protection of human rights in the developing countries that need foreign exchange sufficiently to speed up their rate of development in various fields. There are four ways of increasing the flow of foreign exchange to the developing countries, (i) by paying more stable and higher prices for commodities, (ii) a faster growth of exports of manufacturers (iii) a bigger transfer of public capital and a bigger transfer of private capital (iv) by reducing excessive price fluctuations. Developed countries have great influence on the formation of economic and social policies and in some developing countries even the political policies. The greatest export opportunities of the developing countries lie in the field of manufacturers. But this presupposes that the developed countries are ready for an unrestricted transfer of technology. Here again—their should be no discrimination. As Genscher, Foreign Minister of West Germany remarked: "the high priority that must be attached to human rights must be guaranteed. The industrially advanced countries strongly feel that the rights of the public were not ignored. The offenders should get a fair trial and the human rights must be protected in social, economic and cultural fields. The society needs protection and it is the responsibility of the government to safeguard the interests of the individuals and the society. A democracy cannot succeed of human rights are not protected in a country.

Despite the almost universal commitment to a host of international covenants and national laws upholding their inviolability, in large parts of the world human rights remain an area of darkness. Indeed, judging by the annual report of Amnesty International, there is virtually no country where human rights have not been violated. In El Salvador several thousand men and women, old and young, have been tortured and killed by government death squads. The record in Iran has scarcely been better. The Amnesty report has many such cases of "deliberate political killings".

As in the past India also receives mention for "the use of preventive detention to detain critics of the government, reports of police brutality, torture and deaths in custody, and continued killings in various states of political activists in so-called 'encounters' with the police". The report quotes the Ministry to say that over 1,500 people had been detained under the National Security Act (NSA) in the two years after it came into force in September 1980, and expresses equal concern about the Essential Services Maintenance Act "which might allow the imprisonment of prisoners of conscience".

Definition

Human rights are sometimes called fundamental rights or natural rights. As fundamental rights they cannot be taken away by any legislature or any act of government.

Human rights have a long history, but it was in the eighteenth century that the law of nature had begun to assert itself to protect the individual against the power of state. This culminated in the great general declarations of the Rights of Man in France in 1789 and in the United States Constitutional Amendment of 1791. By the World War I the idea of human rights had come to be concentrated on conflicts between the individual and the state, and between minorities and the large communities in which they lived. The post-war settlement extended the protection of human-rights through the Minorities Treaties, and establishment of the Mandate system and the International Labour Organisation.

According to the International Convention of the Elimination of All Forms of Racial Discrimination, 'racial discrimination' consists of any distinction, exclusion, restriction or preference based on race, colour, descent, or national or ethnic origin which has the purpose or effect of nullifying or impairing the recognition enjoyment or exercise on an equal footing, of human rights and fundamental freedoms in the political, economic, social, cultural or any other field of public life". The convention on the political

Rights of Women urges parties to the convention to give women the right to vote, to be elected to office, to hold public office and perform public functions, on equal terms with men.

The Universal Declaration of Human Rights has no binding legal value, but it has great political and moral authority and has had a definite impact on the thinking and practice of the United Nations itself and governments, when dealing with problems relating to human rights. Through public debate on many issues in the United Nations and through publicity in many countries the Declaration has worked as a political stimulant, an educator and a moulder of conscience.

It is necessary to stimulate an informed discussion of the theme of Human Rights and contribute to a practical and realistic development of the doctrine of Human Rights and its implementation in human affairs. One may well ask the question, as to what role the doctrine of human Rights plays, in the human affairs today. Mr. Roosevelt had said in 1948, while commending the Universal Declaration of Human Rights to the General Assembly of the United Nations, that It might well become the international Magna Carta of all mankind Thirty-three years back when this statement was made, it must have sounded as an exaggeration The experience of the world shows, that in the first post-war decade many countries used the U.N. Declaration of Human Rights for their political reconstruction, embodying the provisions of the Declaration in their own national constitutions. India, Nigeria and West Germany are leading and living examples of this. Fifteen European states gave to parts of the U.N. Declaration the force of International Law and made provisions for its vindication in European tribunals by concluding the European Convention on Human Rights in 1950. With the decline in the authority of the United Nations in 1950's and 1960's the Universal Declaration of Human Rights receded in the background on the international scene. In 1966, the U.N. Commission on Human Rights prepared two draft International Covenants translating principles of Universal Declaration into international treaty obligations. By 1978 more than fifty states of the world became solemnly bound in international law to observe the obligations arising out of the U.N. Declaration of Human Rights. After the Helsinki Conference of 1975, he doctrine of Human Rights emerged as one of the most prominent pre-occupations in the political debate across the world.

Human Rights is a twentieth-century name for what has been traditionally known as natural rights or, in a more exhilirating phrase, the rights of man. Perhaps, the best definition of natural rights begins with the claim which everybody naturally makes. Nobody wants to die a violent death, or suffer an injury and to be without treatment, or undergo an arrest and imprisonment without fair trial and defence and being heard, or to be deprived of expressing his thought and publishing his opinions and views and protesting against any action of the authority. Neither anybody wants to be prevented from practising any legitimate livelihood or occupation of his choice, or pursuing any religion, political and cultural development and selecting any place to live in, or pursuing any path to ensure his happiness, i.e., in one word, self-determination of human beings.

These aversions are so universally and so intensely felt that we speak of them as "natural" as they are the outcome of natural impulse. Again, these rights are inherited by man from the very dawn of civilisation simply because he is a man and therefore he is reasonable and rational and also moral. These rights are therefore also called "fundamental and moral".

The language of rights now dominates political debate in the United Nations. Does the Government respect the moral and political rights of its citizens? Or does the Government's foreign policy, or its race policy, fly in the face of these rights? Do the minorities whose rights have been violated have the rights to violate the law in return? Or does the silent majority itself have rights, including the right that those who break the law be punished? It is not surprising that these questions are now prominent. The concept of rights, and particularly the concept of rights against the Government, has its most natural use when a political society is divided, and appeals to cooperation or a common goal are pointless.

The debate does not include the issue of whether citizens have some moral rights against their government. It seems accepted on all sides that they do. Conventional lawyers and politicians take it as a point of pride that our legal systems recognises, for example, individuals rights of free speech, equality, and due process. They base their claim that our law deserves respect, at least in part, on that fact, for they would not claim that totalitarian systems deserve the same loyalty.

Some philosophers, of course, reject the idea that citizens have rights apart from what the law happens to give them. Bentham thought that the idea of moral rights was 'nonsense on stilts'. But that view has never been part of our orthodox political theory, and politicians of both parties appeal to the rights of the people to justify a great part of what they want to do.

The Amnesty International devotes itself to very specific objects—reminding the world of what most governments do to those of their citizens who step out of line on matters of conscience, finding out who are being held as prisoners of conscience, and trying to do something to improve their lot. Its task is, in other words, to tell us that there are certain rights which all human beings have, and work towards the restoration of those rights to citizens who have been deprived of them.

This type of belief can be—and is—held by individuals

of many kinds of political and philosophical persuasion who can work happily together to further Amnesty's aims, partly because those aims are practical and partly because the organisation is primarily concerned with rights about which there is little' controversy. It is possible to have very decided views on, for example, the right to property, which might impede or prohibit cooperation with those who disagreed. But Amnesty's main aims are those of Articles 18 and 19 of the Universal Declaration of Human Rights of 1948, relating to freedom of thought, conscience and religion, and freedom of opinion and expression. These of course may also generatic disagreement, but more, perhaps, at the level of reflection than of action. When it comes to action there is likely to be spontaneous agreement that certain situation are wrong. Thus, it is possible to hold any of a number of different views about the extremely complex questions of what exactly we mean by human rights, what those rights are, what we mean by conscience, and so on, and yet work with people who have quite different convictions. For at the practical level of working to get people out of prison it makes little difference if one man believes that the right to, let us say, freedom of speech is conferred by God, and his colleague at the next desk thinks it is a right acquired by the citizen through some form of social contract.

However, as Fawcett has aptly said (in his contribution to *Political Theory* and the *Rights of Man*, edited by D.D. Raphel): 'But this classical framework of civil and political rights, while it provides society with some essential securities, can leave it morally immobile. The man who stole bread was sure of a fair trial and was free to speak out in public against the Law that condemned him, but he was still hanged. Not only do moral perceptions change; cultural conditions change too. In a society where no one could read or write it would be nonsense to claim the right to a free press, but as resources increase, so do our expectations. Nowadays, therefore, in addition to the traditional rights, different in kind from the traditional ones.

Self-sacrifice is not always a sign of servility. It is not a duty always to press one's rights. Whether a given act is evidence of servility will depend not only on the attitude of the agent but also on the specific nature of his moral rights, a matter not considered here. Moreover, the extent to which a person is responsible, or blameworthy, for his defect remains an open question. Nevertheless, and conclusion should not be minimised. In order to avoid servility, a person who gives up his rights must do so with a full appreciation for what they are. A woman, for example, may devote herself to her husband if she is uncoerced, knows what she is doing, and does not pretend that she has no decent alternative. A self-contemptuous person may decide not to press various unforfeited rights but only if he does not take the attitude that he is too rotten to deserve them. A black may demand less that is due to him provided he is prepared to acknowledge that no one has a right to expect this of him. Most people, if they fully acknowledged their rights, would not autonomously refuse to press them. An even stronger conclusion would emerge if we could assume that some basic rights cannot be waived. That is, if there are some rights that others are bound to respect regardless of what we say, then, barring special explanation, we would be obliged not only to acknowledge these rights but also to avoid and appearance of consenting to give them up. To act as if we could release others from their obligation to grant these rights, apart from special circumstances, would be to fail to respect morality. Rousseau held, for example, that at least a 'minimal right to liberty cannot be waived. A man who consents to be enslaved, giving up liberty without quid pro quo, thereby displays a conditioned slavish mentality that renders his consent worthless. Similarly, a Kantian might argue that a person cannot release others from the obligation to refrain from killing him: consent is no defense against the charge of murder. To accept principles of this sort is to hold that rights to life and liberty are, as Kant believed, a rather like a trustee's rights to preserve it.

Even if there are no specific rights which cannot be waived, there might be at least one formal right of this sort. This is the right to some minimum degree of respect from others. No matter how willing a person is to submit to humiliation, by others, they ought to show him some respect as a person. By analogy with self-respect, as presented here, this respect owed by others would consist of a willingness to acknowledge fully, in word as well as action, the person's basically equal moral status as defined by his other rights. To the extent that a person gives even tactic consent to humiliations incompatible with this respect, he will be acting as if he waives a right which he cannot in fact give up. To do this, barring special explanations, would mark one as servile.

Mr. Y.V Chandrachud, the former Chief Justice of India said that the theory that poor nations could not afford the luxury of basic rights was a bogey created by those having a vested interest in authoritarianism. Human rights are the most precious possession of mankind and a world which is without them will have to face a perpetual risk of moral improvement. Human rights can be demanded without "shame, embarrasment or gratitude."

The right to freedom from violation of the integrity of person, the right to the fulfilment of the bare minimum needs like food, shelter and health care and the right to the enjoyment of civil and political rights are Indispensable for attaining the barest civilised existence.

The more the world talks about human rights, the more it tramples on them. Whether it is Pakistan, Philippines, Nicaragua, El Salvador, Chad or Chile, human rights are wilting away in the scorching heat of cynicism and political manipulation. All governments are morally obliged to take political action on behalf of human rights in countries where they are violated. And every State should act in a way that would at any time permit the maxim of its own will to become universal law. But, as in all politics, this area too is marked by conflicts between morals and interests. In a world of declining moral values and vanishing ethos, what holds the field in political interest. Human rights are a partial aspect of this overall strategy and cannot lay claim to priority over politics as a whole. The responsibility for human rights in the world, according to political analysts. has unfortunately remained an illusion and it will be unrealistic to think that an international reconciliation of interests could be brought about.

Only a country's own potential and its own interests determine its options and the limits of that which is possible. "In any event a responsible government", so runs the German thesis, "must not forfeit political position for the sake of humanity if this were to endanger the foremost humanitarian objective: the preservation of peace." Naturally, there will be moral crusaders who will ask challengingly "Peace but, at what price? To which the sovereign States' undeclared reply is: "At any price so long as it does not impinge on our security and vital political interests." Very cynical, but very true!

Amnesty International has published its Report for 1982 on abuses and violations of human rights. The 367-page Report covers 121 countries and is based on the information collected for the year 1981 by the Amnesty "though secrecy and censorship often prevented free flow of information."

In general terms the Amesty's findings are:

- The political killings by governments in many countries continued unabated in 1981.
- The techniques of repression and human rights violation varied from country to country.
- As the year ended, thousands of men and women were in prison because of their beliefs, many were still held after years without charge or trial.
- Prisoners were subject to torture, and people had

been executed or were under sentence of death in a number of countries, often for politically-related offences still others were put to death without any pretence of judicial or legal process, selected and killed by governments or their agents.

- In many countries men, women and children remained unaccounted for after being taken into custody, often violently by security forces or abducted by agents acting with the complicity of governments. They had "disappeared" and their families and friends could get no information about their fate or where-abouts.

The Third World has become accustomed to being patronisingly lectured at by those who, for no apparent reason, are generally considered to belong to the "First world." The presumptuousness with which this is done is seldom more painfully apparent than in the annual report by the American State Department alloting marks to various Asian and African countries for their track record in the observation of "Human Rights."

India, the latest survey says, is not too bad but is also not expected to do much better. Pakistan is very bad but should learn how to get on by getting rid of martial law. Bangladesh, poor thing, has "economic problems" and in fairness one should note that despite the regime's Draconian powers, they have been used with restraint. Sri lanka merits faint applause for "adhering to Democracy" against the severest odds. And so the report drones on, smugly, complacently, loftily, drearily, pointlessly with every trace of an enormous self-satisfaction. What exactly in this supposed assessment of "merit" intended to achieve? There is nothing to suggest that it has any bearing on the conduct of American foreign policy or that a failure in "Human Rights" will affect bilateral relations. Pakistan's low marks will not evidently affect the flow of sophisticated plans to that country, and the severity of American disapproval, one suspects, fluctuates according to considerations that have little to do with individual rights and liberties. In the merit of being convincing on its own terms.

The Helsinki Accords of 1975 gave the U.N. Declaration a new momentum and a new direction, the 35 countries participating in the Helsinki meeting promising to "encourage the effective exercise of civil, political, economic, social cultural and other rights and freedoms". These rights are now broadly categorised as:

Personal: No arbitrary arrest and no imprisonment of any individual without a fair public trial, and no invasion of privacy. Torture or inhuman treatment of any person by governmental authorities is also banned.

Economic: The right to work, the right to education, the right in adequate medical care, and the fulfilment of basic needs like food and shelter.

Political: Guarantee of civil and political liberties like freedom of speech, expression and religious worship, and unhindered participation in political activities.

To have a right, Bentham held, is to be the beneficiary of another's study or obligation. This theory, one of the more attractive and plausible suggestions about the nature of rights, appears supported by innumerable cases. It is reflected in the notion common to laymen, lawyers, and philosophers that someone with a right is on the advantageous side of a legal or moral relation. It promises to explain why rights are such valuable and important commodities. And it seems bolstered by a variety of facts, for example that compensation or reparation is often required, and might always be required when one's rights are violated or infringed.

It requires no long examination of the Charter of the United Nations to ascertain that the promotion and advancement of human rights and fundamental freedoms is one of the pillars on which the international organisation has been raised. This is evidenced by the prominence given to human rights in the Preamble, by the specification of promoting human rights as one of the purposes of the Organisation in Article (3), and by the extent to which organs of the United Nations are vested with responsibilities in the field of human rights under Article 13 (1) 55 (c) 56, 62 (2) 68 and 76 (c). The latter clause relates to obligations assumed by Member States to promote human rights for inhabitants of non-self-government territories.

The articles contain clear directive to the Organisation to make promotion of human rights a primary activity. Thus Article 55 states that the United Nations shall promote universal respect for, and observance of, human rights and fundamental freedoms; Article 13 provides that the General Assembly shall initiate studies and make recommendations; under Article 68, the Economic and Social Council shall get up commissions in economic and social fields and for the promotion of human rights. This is consistently mandatory language.

The objective of this mandate is the actual achievement of human rights and fundamental freedoms. This is started variously but clearly. Thus, the purpose is "to achieve international cooperation in promoting and encouraging respect for human rights and fundamental freedoms:" the General Assembly has the concrete function of furthering this purpose by initiating studies and making recommendations in order to assist "in the realisation of human rights and fundamental freedom"; under Article 55 the entire Organisation is directed to "promote universal respect for; and observance, of human rights and fundamental freedom". In Article 56, "All Members pledge themselves to take joint and separate action in cooperation with the Organisation for the achievement of the purposes set forth in Article 55".

There is no doubt that the Charter involves a commitment to the furtherance of human rights more extensive than any comparable inter-national endeavour. However, while the comprehensiveness of the United Nations commitment is unprecedented, it is built upon a considerable body of precedent extending over several centuries for international concern with human right.

International concern with human rights may be traced as far back as the stipulations of religious liberty incorporated in various treaties in the period following the Reformation, as elements in the settlement of religious wars. Subsequently, protection for members of religious and national minorities was included in the treaties drawn up at the Congress of Vienna in 1815. During the latter part of the nineteenth century, in the era of disintegration of the Ottoman Empire, numerous treaty provisions were adopted which sought to ensure religious freedom for Christians and Jews either within the Empire or in the newly established States of Serbia, Montenegro and Roumania.

Treaty provisions of this kind resulted from specific solutions of particular situations as they arose. They were not the product of a systematic scheme of international relations. Nevertheless, they had a cumulative effect which led Georges Clemenceau, President of the Council of the Peace Conference, to assert in 1919 that they had created an "established tradition" which amply justified imposition by treaty of guarantees for the protection of minorities. In his explanatory letter of June 24, 1919, addressed to Polish Prime Minister Panderewski, which accompanied the transmittal of the Polish minorities Treaty, Clemenceau stated:

> It has for a long time been the established procedure of the public law of Europe that when a state is created, or even when large accessions of territory are made to an established state, the joint and formal recognition by the Great Powers should be accompanied by the requirement that such a state should, in the form of binding international convention, undertake to comply with certain principles of government. This principle for which there are numerous

> **precedents, received the most explicit sanction when, at the last great assembly of European Powers—the Congress of Berlin—the sovereignty of Serbia, Montenegro and Roumania were recognised.**

The reassertion at the end of World War I of the tradition of international concern for the treatment of individuals in the form of Minorities Treaties concluded between the Principal Allied and Associated Powers and the several now and enlarged states which emerged after the War, likewise did not arise in the context of a general international principle of promoting human rights. Efforts to include in the Covenant of the League of Nations international pledges of religious and racial tolerance proved unavailing. However, under the League of Nations system there was a marked expansion of international involvement in the protection of human rights mainly as a result of the Minorities Treaties, but to a lesser degree also from the supervisory functions of the League's Mandates Commission.

To be sure, the Minorities Treaties were not designed to secure the observance of human rights and fundamental freedoms generally to nationals of the countries subject to the minorities obligations, but to guarantee equality to members of minority groups and mind meet their special needs in an attempt to avoid international friction occasioned by the revision of boundaries after the War. However, while the treaty obligations were concerned chiefly with the special protection of national; racial, religious and linguistic minorities, in their definition of rights to be accorded to members of minorities, the Treaties enunciated standards which were based on the acceptance of certain fundamental rights of the individual.

The subject of justice in holdings consists of the three major topics. The first is the original aquisition of holdings, the appropriation of unheld things. This includes the issues of how unheld things may come to be held, the practices, or processes, by which unheld things may come to be held, the things that may come to be held by these processes, the extent of what comes to be held by a particular process, and so on. We shall refer to the complicated truth about this topic, which we shall not formulate here, as the principle of justice in acquisition. The second topic concerns the transfer of holdings from one person to another. By what processes may a person transfer holdings to another? Row may a person acquire a holding from another who holds it? Under this topic come general descriptions of voluntary exchange, and gift and (on the other hand) fraud, as well as reference to particular conventional details fixed upon in a given society. The complicated the truth about this subject (with placholders for conventional details) we shall call the principle of justice in transfer. (And we shall suppose it also includes principles governing how a person may divest himself of a holding, passing it into an unheld state.)

If the world were wholly just, the following inductive definition would exhaustively cover the subject in holdings:

1. A person who acquires a holding in accordance with the principle of justice in acquisition is entitled to that holdings.
2. A person who acquires a holding in accordance with the principle of justice in transfer, from someone else entitled to the holding, is entitled to the holding.
3. No one is entitled to a holding except by (repeated) applications of 1 and 2.

Amnesty's founder Peter Beneson was a Londoner, a product of Eton and Oxford who bad long been interested in defending the victims of oppression. In 1950's he often left his commercial law practice for trips to Hungary, Cyprus, South Africa and Spain to serve as either a legal observer or defence counsel. In 1959 he gave up his practice and devoted himself entirely to his chosen cause.

Launched in May 1961 Amnesty proved the effectiveness of moral indignation linked with mass publicity. The organisation has compaigned for the release of some 1360 political prisoners and some 330 were freed.

Amnesty's basic technique is to dramatise individual case of injustice. Abdul Gaffar's case was typical. His offence was typical. His offence was purely political. He wanted regional autonomy for the 40 lakh Pathans. Khan was Gandhiji's follower—but Pakistan feared the old man's popularity among his people. Amnesty's representatives visited Pakistan and named Khan Prisoner of the year a designation that always inspires great publicity. The notoriety reaches a climax at public ceremonies commemorating Human Rights Day. These efforts finally elicited a commitment by Pakistan Government to review Khan's case. The old leader was set free in January 1964.

Considerable and impressive human rights jurisprudence was evolved by the European Commission and the European Court of Human Rights under the European Convention. National courts or constitutional courts of different countries which have written Constitutions with a Bill of Rights, also developed their own domestic human rights jurisprudence. The fact is that human rights jurisprudence has evolved and is firmly established. We now have an International Law of Human Rights.

What does this law consist of? What does it mean in practical terms? Where and how can it be, or is it, enforced? These questions and other related aspects are admirably dealt with in Paul Sieghart's book The Inter-national Law of Human Rights (Clarendon Press, Oxford, 1983). It is an outstanding work which provides an illuminating insight into "the substantive content of this new corpus of law" and that, too within the confines of a single volume running into about 570 pages.

The scope of the work is vast. In the first place, Sieghart covers the historical background, the formal structure and the enforcement procedures of the principal international instruments, namely, the U.N. Charter; the Universal Declaration of Human Rights; the International Covenants of Civil and Political Rights, and on Economic, Social and Cultural Rights; the European Convention on Human Rights; the European Social Charter; the American Declaration of the Rights and Duties of Man; the American Convention of Human Rights and the American Convention on Human Rights and the African Charter on Human and People's Right.

International human rights law is still young and is bound to display a certain frailty. The real achievement however lies in the recognition that human rights arc legal concepts capable of enforcement, not mere abstractions. No government rejects the ideology of human rights nor can any government dare claim the right to violate the human rights of its citizens. Governments may not obey the rules. But today we can point to certain minimum standards and put these delinquents in the dock and tell them that they have broken "the fetters against doing evil" which no decent government should ever do.

REFERENCES

1. Action, H.B. (1950), Symposium on rights. *Proceedings of the Aristotelian Society,* Supp. Volume 24, pp. 107-8.
2. Agarwal, R.S. (1978), *Human Rights in Modern World.* New Delhi, Chetna, pp. 122.
3. Ahmad, I. (1980), International efforts in the field of human rights: An evaluation. *Indian Journal of Politics.*
4. Alston, P. (1979), Human rights and the new international development strategy. *Bulletin of Peace Proposals.*
5. American Jewish Committee (1946), *World Charter for Human Rights.* New Delhi.
6. *Amnesty International Handbook,* London, Annual Publication.
7. *Amnesty International Report,* 1983. London, 1983. pp. 351.
8. Arendt, Hannah (1959), *Human Conditions.* Garden City. New York, Doubleday.
9. Barnes, Leonard. Rights of dependent peoples. In *Human Rights.* Ed. by UNESCO. London, 1950; 242-45.

10. Batra, T.S. *Human Rights—A Critique.* New Delhi, Metropolitan, 1979. pp. 350.
11. Beckett. Human rights. *Transactions of the Grotius Society,* 34, 1949.
12. Benn, Stanley. Rights. In *Encyclopedia of Philosophy.* Vol. 7, New York, Macmillan, 1967; 195-99
13. Benn, Tony. 1986: The end of the Magna Carta. *Telegraph,* 7 Dec. 1983; 7
14. Bhagat, B.R. Human rights: A survey of recent developments. *Foreign Affairs Reports* 32 (6-7) Jun-Jul. 1983; 86-122.
15. Big power rivalry in human rights. *Statesman,* 28 Jun. 1982; 10.
16. Bilder, R. Rethinking international human rights: Some basic questions *Wisconsin Law Review,* 1969; 171-217.
17. Bókser, Ben Zion. Ethics of the Fathers. In *Great Expressions of Human Right's.* Ed. by R.M. MacIver. New York, 1950; 43-50.
18. Brown, Stuart M. Inalienable rights. *Philosophical Review* 64, 1955; 192-211.
19. Buckley,. Ken. *All About Citizens' rights.* Melbourne, Nelson, 1976.
20. Buergenthal, Thomas. International and regionál human rights law and institutions; Some examples of their interactions. *Texas International Law Journal,* 12, 1977; 331-50.
21. Bull, H. University of human rights. *Journal of International Studies,* Aug. 1979.
22. Carr, E.H. Rights of man. In *Human Rights.* Ed. by Unesco. London Allan Wingate; 1950; 19-23.
23. Cartwright, Hilary. International action for the protection of human rights. In *Rights and Wrongs.* Ed. by C.R. Hill. Middlesex, 1969; 146-80.
24. Castel, J.G. International year for human rights. *Canadian Bar Review,* 46, 1968.
25. Chan, Wing-tsit. "Within the four seas all are brothers.". In *Great Expressions of Human Rights.* Ed by R.M. MacIver New York, 1950; 19-28.
26. Chandrachud, Y.V. Range and rationale of human rights. *Akashvani,* 14 Feb. 1982; 2-4.
27. Chattopadhyaya, Amal. Human rights—some ominous signs. *Amrita Bazar Patrika,* 11 Dec 1979.

28. Claude, Richard P. ed. *Comparative Human Rights.* Baltimore, 1976.
29. Coffan, Alfred. *National self-determination.* Chicago, 1944.
30. Cranston, Maurice. *What are human rights?* New York, Taplinger, 1973.
31. Croce, Benedetto. Rights of man and the present historical situation. In *Human Rights.* Ed. by Unesco, London, Alan Wingate, 1950; 93-95.
32. Cushman, Robert Eugene. *Excess Condemnation.* Doctoral dissertation. New York, Apleton, 1917. pp. 323.
33. Daube, David. Rabbis and Philo on human rights. In *EHR;* 234-46.
34. De Chandin, P. Teilhard. Some reflections on the rights of man. In *Human rights.* Ed. by Unesco, London Alan Wingate, 1950; 105-7.
35. De Madariaga, Don Salvador. Rights of man or human relations? In *Human rights.* Ed. by Unesco, London, Alan Wingate, 1950; 47-53.
36. Dimbleby, Jonathan. Acts of man. *New Statesman,* 94, July 1977.
37. Dominguez, Jorge I. Assessing Human rights conditions. In Jorge I. Dominguez. *etc. Enhancing Global Human Rights,* New York, McGraw-Hill, 1979; 21-116.
38. Dominguez, Jorge I. ed. et al. *Enhancing Global Human Rights.* New York, McGraw-Hill, 1980.
39. Eide, Asbjorn. *Human rights in the world society.* Earl M. New York, Coleman, 1980.
40. Hassan. P. Word arbitrary as used in the universal declaration of human rights Illegal or unjust? *Harvard International Law Journal.* 10, 1969.
41. Henkin, Louis (1978), *Rights of Man Today.* Boulder, Westview Press.
42. Hill, C. R. (ed.) *Rights and Wrongs; Some Essays on Human Rights.* Middlesex, Penguin Books, 1969, pp. 188.
43. Holcomb (1948), A. *Human Rights in the Modern World.* New York.
44. Hondius, Frits (1979), *Second Generation of Human Rights.* Strasbourg.
45. Human rights in the *World Community.* Washington, U.S. House of Representatives, 93rd Congress, 2nd Session, Committee on Foreign Affairs. n.d.

46. Human rights: *Madhya Pradesh Chronicle,* 5 April 1983; 4.
47. Human rights: International perspectives. *International Studies Quarterly,* Jan. 1979.
48. Human rights mauled. *National Herald,* 15 December 1983; 7.
49. Humana, Charles (1983), *World Human Rights Guide.* London, Hutchinson, pp. 224.
50. Huxley, Aldous (1950), Rights of man and the facts of the human situation. In *Human Rights.* Ed. by UNESCO. London.
51. *Impact of the Universal Declaration of Human Rights.* New York, UN Department of Social Affairs, 1951.
52. International Commission of Jurists (1977), *Report of Activities,* 1971-1977. Geneva.
53. Joyce, James Avery (1976), Human rights: A new dimension. *Contemporary Review.*
54. Khanna, H.R. (1983), Human rights preserve basic dignity of man. *Sentinel,* 17 December 3.
55. Lakshmana Rao, V. (1982), Is man really free? *Akashvani,* 14 Feb. 4-5.
56. Lamout, William D. Rights (1950), *Proceedings of the Aristotelian Society,* Supp. 24, pp. 83-94.
57. Laquer, Walter, Issues of human rights. *EHR;* 5-20.
58. Leuis, Job (1950), On human rights. In *Human Rights.* Ed. by Unesco. London. Alan Wingate. 54-71.
59. Lien, Arnold J. (1950), Fragment of thought concerning the nature and fulfilment of human rights. In *Human rights.* Ed. by Unesco, London, Allan Wingate, pp. 24-30.
60. Lillich, R. and F. Newman (1979), *International Human Rights: Problems of law and policy.* Boston, Little Brown.
61. Lyons, David (1978), Apology for rights. *Corneil Review,* 3 Spr pp. 24-32.
62. Lyons, David (1969), Rights, climants and beneficiaries. In Rights. Belmout, 1979; 58-77, *American Philosophical Quarterly* 6, Jul. pp. 173-85.
63. McKeon, Richard. Philosophic bases and material circumstances of the rights of man. In *Human rights.* Ed. by Unesco. London, Alan Wingate, 1950; 35-46.
64. Moskowitz, Moses (1975), *International Concern with Human Rights.* New York, Oceana.
65. Mukherjee, Dhurjati (1980), Human rights in the present world. *Searchlight,* 17.

66. Nariman, F.S. (1980), Recent trends in the field of human rights. In *Seminar on Human Rights*. Allahabad, pp. 124-37.
67. Owen. David (1978), *Human Rights*. London, Jonathan Cape, p. 154.
68. Painter, Sidney (1948), Magna Carta. *American Historical Review,* 53.
69. Parashar, S.L. (1982), What is amnesty? *Madhya Pradesh Chronicle,* 30 Nov., 4.
70. Roosevelt, Eleanor (1948), Struggle for human rights. *Department of State Bulletin 19 (484)..*
71. Rosenbaum, Alan S. (ed.) (1981), *Philosophy of Human Rights: International prespectives.* London, Aldwych Press, p. 288.
72. Rousseau, Jean-Jacques (1950), Discourse on the origin of inequality among men. In the Social *Contract and Discourses.* Ed. by G.D.H. Cole, New York.

3

Economic Development and Human Rights

In the sense, the concept of Human Rights, incorporated into several declarations and documents, is part agenda and part utopia. Human Rights incorporates a vision and seeks to spell out the major components of humanness. The historical contexts in which the notion was developed and articulated have imparted their mark on it, but some of them—the French Declaration of Human Rights and the Rights of Citizens (1789) and the Universal Declaration of Human Rights (1948), in specific—have elements of universality and timelessness about them. Some of these documents are country-specific, such as the US Declaration of Independence (1776) and the French Declaration (1789), some are region-specific, such as the European Convention on Human Rights, the American Convention on Human Rights, and the African Charter on Human and People's Rights; while some are theme-specific, such as the Convention on the Prevention and Punishment of the Crime of Genocide, the Convention on the Elimination of All Forms of Racial Discrimination, the Declaration on the Elimination of Discrimination against Women, the UNESCO Convention against Discrimination in Education, and the Charter of the International Labour Organisation.

The focal point of fundamental rights, in the main, have been on prohibition of slavery or servitude; prohibition of torture or inhuman or degrading treatment; equality before law for all: prevention of racial, religious and gender discrimination: right to respect for private and family life as well as home and correspondence; and freedom of the press. These rights are circumscribed by considerations of social responsibility, conditions of war and national emergencies, and domestic arrangements within individual countries. International processes do have some influence, but they are generally involved and time-consuming. Those in authority often get away when they defy human rights; the victims are too weak and vulnerable to resist or to seek redress. Development and the rights of the poor and the weak do not figure prominently in most of the declarations. The values implicit in them, however, point in the direction of equality and justice. The Universal Declaration of Human Rights (UN) is more explicit and covers a wide range of rights and value affirmations. Particularly important are its affirmation of "human dignity, equality and the right to freedom from discrimination and exploitation", "the right to social security, to an adequate standard of life and to the opportunity for the free and full development of the individual's personality". It also refers to the duties of the individual to his community, in which alone the free and full development of his personality can take place. The "right to development" is a relatively new idea, although it is gaining strength in the emerging contexts of the world.

There is an air of unreality about human rights, particularly in the developing countries. Because of destitution, a large section of people are compelled into servitude. The more vulnerable among them are subjected to torture and inhuman and degrading treatment. Equality before law, for them, is notional; justice is expensive, and it is often weighted in favour of the rich and the powerful. They encounter discrimination at every step. The poor have little "private" life: in the culture of poverty their life is an open book. Freedom of the press means little to them. The benefits of development bypass them; the grandiose plans and projects make practically no dent in the volume of poverty. In a world of rapid change, in the developing world poverty remains stationary. How can the people assert their human rights? This characterisation does not point only to a racist and apartheid state, it can also be witnessed in different kinds of democracies throughout the developing world.

The ideology of development, attractively packaged and persuasively sold to the developing world, has proved to be a misadventure. Mass hunger, illiteracy, and disease persist tenaciously. The quality of general social services remain poor; of course, for those who can afford the price, top quality services are available. Societies are polarised; the thin upper crust of society gets the best of everything; the masses have to remain content with crumbs or stale left-overs. The record of some four decades of development effort has been dismal, if we look at it from the point of view of the bottom two-thirds of the less developed societies.

The strategies of development continue to place their faith in the "trickle down effect" and the operation of "the invisible hand". The paradigm shift emphasises satisfaction of basic needs and improvements in quality of life, and takes note of new problems claiming attention—food, security, ecological balance, environmental quality, upgraded social services, and so forth. But there is little evidence of this shift making an impact on the praxis of development. The confusion regarding the real target groups of development still persists. Development has not been doing much to improve the lot of the poor and the marginalised, the weak and the vulnerable. One may rightly ask: Are human rights possible without the right kind of development of the majorities in the poverty sector of the developing countries?

Some affluent countries consume a disproportionate share of the world's resources-raw materials, energy, and even skilled manpower. They have unusually high consumption levels. Besides high personal consumption, they accord high priority to the technology of war and not to projects of peace and development. Their aid has invisible and visible strings attached to it; the technology transfers, often obsolete, cause environmental degradation and consume a great deal of energy. Their trade with the developing countries is on unequal terms, generally to the detriment of the poor. What they buy from them often results in diverting inputs to be made into basic needs of the people into inputs for earning foreign exchange. With some exceptions, foreign development aid increases dependency relations. A point has now been reached where to service the accumulated debt burden, still more foreign debt is needed.

Development strategies followed by the developing countries have also been detrimental to the interests of the poor. The benefits of development have not adequately percolated to the deprived and the disadvantaged. They were cornered by a small parasitical elite. Many large projects have led to development disasters. Several of them have caused considerable atmospheric pollution and have depleted non-renewable natural resources. Several irrigation and hydel projects—approved and funded by the World Bank, IMF and other donor agencies—have been ecologically unsound and have led to massive migration of people without proper and adequate rehabilitation support. Dense forests have been sought to be cut down to promote commercial forestry. High-input agriculture has often been out of the reach of the marginal and poor farmers. New technology has rendered many jobless to benefit the 'Kulak' peasants.

Development is necessary to promote human rights. But the paradigm of development needs re-thinking and its strategy needs retooling. Pursuit of GNP, it has been observed, can involve tremendous social costs with relatively little gain to the neediest. The goals of development will have to be retargetted: they should now be spelled out in terms of equity, basic needs, and quality of life, giving priority to the weak and the vulnerable. For them social security and an adequate level of social services will have to be guaranteed. Imaginatively-drawn plans of compensatory discrimination could fortify them to stand up and assert their rights. For ethnic and cultural minorities, collective rights will have to be contemplated. In any case, development must not be allowed to cause or result in cultural ethnocide.

No doubt, human rights declarations are great and noble documents in spirit, but the convolutions and perversions of the world order have rendered them into empty rhetoric. Only through a new strategy of development can the affirmations, ideals and values incorporated in these documents be materialised and realised.

In nutshell, unless we achieve the goal or at least divert the fruits of development towards the poor and weaker sections of society, no so-called 'Human Rights' are meaningless for the majority of have-nots (i.e. deprived). First at least provide them or make provisions for mere survival of human live—than comes the right for.

4

Human Rights and Criminal Justice Administration

> Untouchability is abolished and its practice in any form is forbidden. The enforcement of any disability arising out of untouchability, shall be an offence punishable in accordance with law..."
>
> —*Art. 17, Indian Constitution*

Since yore days in India, Vedas and other sacred scriptures provided the basis for Hindu jurisprudence and criminal justice administration. Village assemblies and the king with the assistance of select villagers and townsfolk, administered justice. People directly participated in adjudicating guilt and awarding punishment. The emphasis was on the good of the society, and the impact of punishment on the individual was of no relevance. Punishment served the purpose of retribution and as an example to deter and prevent others to take to crime. On some occasions, punishment served the purpose of compensating the victim. During Muslim Rule, Islamic Law formed the basis for jurisprudence and criminal justice administration. The offender was viewed as a sinner against the society, who deserved to be socially deprived. Punishment was severe and cruel and was meant to serve as a warning to others.

To maintain order and peace in society and to prevent, detect and check crime, the state provides its law enforcement machinery, particularly the police, with wide ranging powers. If used arbitrarily, these powers could impinge on the dignity and liberty of the individual. To preserve the Human

Rights of the citizens, it becomes necessary to build in safeguards in the criminal justice administration. Concern for Human Rights of individual in the criminal justice administration is of recent origin.

British Rule in India, for the first time, introduced egalitarian principles of Anglo-Saxon jurisprudence and the criminal justice system assumed the modern day role of reformist character. Though British adopted double standards in the administration of criminal justice—Whites always had many special privileges—it should be said to their credit, that justice was dispensed with even handedness World War II saw human behaviour at its worst and what were considered as Natural Rights of people came to be fine tuned into Human Rights. United Nations took upon itself the role of the crusader for Human Rights. As the preamble of United Nations Charter declared it was determined "to reaffirm faith in fundamental Human Rights, in the dignity and worth of human person, in equal rights of man and women and of the Nations large and small. . . .". Universal Declaration of Human Rights was adopted in 1948 followed by Covenants on Political and Civil Rights and Social, Economic and Cultural Rights in 1966. India, adopted its Republican Constitution in 1950 and included a special part on Fundamental Rights.

Indian Constitution, in tune with international endeavours, provides four basic principles to govern the criminal justice system.

I. Presumption of Innocence

As in Human Rights, the emphasis is on basic human dignity the basic principle that an individual is presumed to be innocent till the contrary is proved against him, has been enshrined in Article 21 of Indian Constitution (vide judicial interpretation by the Supreme Court) and in Article 14(2) of the International Covenant of Civil and Political Rights 1966.

II. Prevention of Ex-post Facto Operation of Criminal Law

The second principle is that no person can be accused and convicted of an offence for an act which was not an offence under the law in force on the date when it was committed. This is a guarantee against *ex-post facto* operation of Criminal Law. This principle has been enshrined in Article 20(1) of the Constitution of India and Article 11(2) of the Universal Declaration of Human Rights.

III. Protection Against 'Double Jeopardy'

The third important principle in ensuring Human Rights is the 'Protection against double jeopardy'—that is, no person can be punished for the same offence twice. This has been enshrined in the Indian Constitution in Article 20(2) and also in the Criminal Procedure Code.

IV. Due Process Concept

The most important principle that no person shall be deprived of his life and liberty except according to the procedure established by law has been enshrined in Article 21 of the Constitution, whose scope has been extended by judicial interpretation by the Supreme Court. It gives protection not only against executive action but also against legislation. This principle is also contained in Article 9 of the International Covenant on Civil and Political Rights 1966.

In criminal justice administration, police through their restrictive and coercive authority, effect arrests, interrogate, search, seize, and detain people prior to trial. All these actions affect individual's liberty and when done arbitrarily, individual's dignity. To prevent arbitrariness, following safeguards have been provided:

(1) Right to Freedom from unwanted arrest;
(2) Right to reasonable investigation, interrogation, search, seizure, etc.
(3) Right to legal defence;

(4) Right to a fair pre-trial detention; and

(5) Right to an open (public) and speedy trial.

I. Right to Freedom from Unwanted Arrest

The right to personal liberty of an individual is a basic Human Right. Arrest signifies apprehension of an individual by legal authority depriving him of his liberty. The decision to arrest a person has serious implications and cannot be indulged in lightly. Article 21 of the Indian Constitution and International Instruments stress on this. In our country, arrests can be made with a warrant or without one. In the former case, there is already application of mind by a judicial authority, and in the latter case, the person should be brought before a judicial authority immediately as ordained in Article 22(2) of the Constitution.

Grounds of Arrest to be Informed

Article 22(1) of the Constitution lays down that the arrested person shall be informed of the reasons for his arrest. This is to enable the arrested person to seek judicial redress. The Supreme Court has held that—

"Article 22(1) embodies a rule which has always been regarded as vital and fundamental for safeguarding personal liberty in all legal systems where the rule of law prevails.... The two requirements of clause (1) of Article 22 were meant to afford the earliest opportunity to the arrested person to remove any mistake, misapprehension or misunderstanding in the minds of the arresting authority and also to know exactly what the accusation against him is, so that he can exercise the second right, namely, of consulting a legal practitioner of his choice and to be defended by him" (1969 Cr.L.J.1440).

The Code of Criminal Procedure also provides for the same. The judicial magistrate should enquire from the accused (Cr.P.C.167) whether he has been informed of the grounds of arrest.

Right to be Brought Before a Judicial Magistrate

Article 22(2) enjoins that the arrested person shall be produced before a magistrate within 24 hours. Criminal Procedure Code also contains similar provisions and also forbids detention of the person anywhere else other than a police station.

The Right to Bail

The aim of provision of bail is to restore the individual his liberty pending adjudication of his guilt by the court. It protects unconvicted persons from the hazards of incarceration by granting them the presumption of innocence. Courts have held that bail is a Right which should be informed to the arrested person and the same should be granted without imposing unreasonable conditions.

II. Right to Reasonable Investigations, Interrogation, Search, Seizures etc.

F.I.R. Detailed legal requirements prescribed under the Code of Criminal Procedure including provision of supply of a copy of the F.I.R. to the person lodging the information ensure that the rights of the individual are safeguarded. From the time F.I.R. is issued, the activities of police are under judicial scrutiny and all further steps in investigation are to be as per prescribed legal procedures.

Right to Silence: Article 20(3) of the Indian Constitution says that no person accused of any offence shall be compelled to be a witness against himself. This principle is also contained in Article 14(g) of the International Covenant on Civil and Political Rights. Thus, while the Cr.P.C. enjoins a person to answer truthfully the questions put to him by an investigating officer, this Constitutional Provision gives him protection against self-incrimination.

Right to Protection from Unlawful Search and Seizure

As a coercive search violates the principle of right to live freely, the law provides safeguards in the procedures to be followed in respect of search and seizure. The

Constitution does not prohibit searches *per se* but the searches and seizures are to be legal and in accordance with legal procedures.

III. The Right to Legal Defence

Article 22(1) of the Constitution directs that no person who is arrested shall be denied the right to consult and to be defended by a legal practitioner of his choice. This legal right is also available in the Code of Criminal Procedure, Section 303. The courts have held that from the time of arrest, this right accrues to the arrested person and he has the right of choice of a lawyer. The accused may refuse to have a lawyer but the court has to provide an *amicus curie* to defend him in serious cases. The courts have also held that the indigent accused have a right to legal aid. This requirement is to ensure that poverty does not come in the way of any one getting a fair trial.

IV. Right to Fair Pre-Trial Detention

When accused person is in custody, pending trial for any reason, human dignity should be accorded to him. The Supreme Court has laid down legal dicta that the accused in pre-trial detention are entitled to fair and decent treatment by way of comforts, medical attention etc., so that their humanity is not degraded and dignity offended.

The Supreme Court has also frowned upon violations of Human Rights during pre-trial detention and has ordered compensation for unlawful detention. Courts have recognised the right to compensation in respect of unlawful detention though legislation is yet to be enacted to give effect to these rulings.

V. Right to a Public and Speedy Trial

The principle of openness of judicial proceedings acts as a check against caprice or vagaries and builds up confidence of the public in judicial administration. The right to public trial is implicit in Articles 14, 9(1)(a) and 21 of the Constitution and in the Criminal Procedure Code.

Justice delayed is justice denied. Though there are no specific provisions for a speedy trial in the Indian Constitution, by judicial interpretation, the Supreme Court has held that Article 21 of the Constitution confers this right on the accused. The Cr.P.C. contains many provisions to ensure speedy trial.

Human Rights of the accused as well as the victim, find frequent mention in the Constitution and in various enactments.

Human Rights of Accused Person

1. Protection against arbitrary or unlawful arrest [Article 22 of the Constitution and Section 41, 55 and 151 Cr.P.C.];
2. Protection against arbitrary or unlawful searches [Sections 93, 94, 97, 100(4) to (81) and 165 Cr.P.C.];
3. Protection against "Double Jeopardy" [Article 21(2) of the Constitution and Section 400 Cr.P.C.];
4. Protection against conviction or enhanced punishment under ex-post facto law [Article 20(1) of the Constitution];
5. Protection against arbitrary or illegal detention in custody [Article 22 of the Constitution and Sections 56, 57 and 76 Cr.P.C.];
6. Right to be informed of the grounds, immediately after the arrest [Article 71 (1) of the Constitution and Section 50 Cr.P.C., as also Sections 55 and 75 Cr.P.C.];
7. Right of the arrested person not to be subjected to unnecessary restraint [Section 49 Cr.P.C.];
8. Right to consult a lawyer of his own choice [Article 22(1) of the Constitution and Section 303 Cr.P.C.].
9. Right to be produced before a magistrate within 24 hours of his arrest [Article 22(1) of the Constitution and Sections 57 and 76 Cr.P.C.];
10. Right to be released on bail, if arrested [Sections 436, 437 and 439 Cr.P.C.: also Sections 50(2) and 167 Cr.P.C.].

11. Right not to be a witness against himself [Article 20(3) of the Constitution];
12. Right to get copies of the documents and statements of witnesses on which the prosecution relies [Section 173(7), 207, 208 and 238 Cr.P.C.];
13. Right to have the benefit of the presumption of innocence till guilt is proved beyond reasonable doubt [Sections 101-104 Evidence Act];
14. Right to insist that evidence be recorded in his presence except in some special circumstances [Section 273 Cr.P.C.; also. Section 317 Cr.P.C.];
15. Right to have due notice of the charges [Section 218, 228(2), 240(2), etc. of Cr.P.C.];
16. Right to test the evidence by cross-examination [Section 138 Evidence Act];
17. Right to have an opportunity for explaining the circumstances appearing in evidence against him at the trial [Section 313 Cr.P.C.];
18. Right to have himself medically examined for evidence to disprove the commission of offence by him or for establishing commission of offence against his body by any other person [Section 54 Cr.P.C.];
19. Right to produce defence witnesses [Section 243 Cr.P.C.];
20. Right to be tried by an independent and impartial judge [The Scheme of Separation of Judiciary as envisaged in Cr.P.C., also Sections 479, 327, 191, etc. of Cr.P.C.];
21. Right to submit written arguments at conclusion of the trial in addition to oral submission [Section 314 Cr.P.C.];
22. Right to be heard about the sentence upon conviction [Section 235(2) and 248(2) Cr.P.C.];
23. Right to fair and speedy investigation and trial [Section 309 Cr.P.C.];

24. Right to appeal in case of conviction [Sections 351, 374' 379, 380 Cr.P.C. and Articles 132(1), 134(1) and 136(1) of the Constitution];
25. Right not to be imprisoned upon conviction in certain circumstances [Section 360 Cr.P.C. and Section 6 of the Probation of Offenders Act];
26. Right to restrain police from intrusion on his privacy [Article 31 of the Constitution;
27. Right of release of a convicted person on bail pending appeal [Section 380 Cr.P.C.];
28. Right to get copy of the judgement when sentenced to imprisonment [Section 363 Cr. P.C.].

Human Rights of Victims of Crime

Human Rights ensure that the victims are:

— to be free from intimidation,

— to be informed about the availability of financial assistance and legal assistance,

— to get back stolen or other personal property which is no longer needed as evidence, and

— a speedy investigation and trial of the case.

The Council of Europe for Improving Victim Protection has Emphatically asserted that

— The victim should be treated in the police station in a sensitive manner so that he is not subjected to any additional emotional damage.

— The victim should be appraised of the possibilities of receiving financial, medical and psychological help.

— He should be advised about the restitutional claims and compensation from the State.

— The victim should be protected from secondary victimisation i.e., additional damage during the process of criminal justice.

— The family and friends of the victim should be protected from further victimisation and threat.

Compensation to Victims

Section 357(1) of Criminal Procedure Code provides that when a court imposes a sentence which includes a fine, the court may direct that the fine amount should be utilised:

(a) in defraying the expenses of prosecution

(b) in making payment in the loss caused to the victim

Section 357(3) of Criminal Procedure Code provides that the court can award compensation even in cases where fine does not form part of the sentence.

The Model Scheme for Victim Assistance in India

Considering the present status of crime victims in India, the need to have a comprehensive victim-assistance policy is obvious and requires no restitution. Acceptance of this policy should start with the recognition of certain basic rights of the victims, such as:

(1) The Right of Protection from Criminal Victimisation

This is the right to know about the protective measures which a person may take to avoid possible victimisation.

It is for the law enforcement agencies to educate the public about crime prevention measures and also to take necessary steps to improve the community's self-protection ability.

(2) The Right to Preparation for Consequences of Criminal Victimisation (physical injury, loss or trauma)

This right is aimed at ensuring physical, psychological, social and financial well-being of the victims. Consequently, the victims of crime should have:

(i) The right to have access to professional services and other support from the relevant agencies.

(ii) The right to Government compensation for physical injury.

(iii) The right to punish the offender through civil and criminal proceedings for the loss and damages suffered by the victim.

(3) The Rights Pertaining to the Agencies of Criminal Justice System

The victim must also have:

(i) The right to be informed about the procedures and practices of the Criminal Justice System in simple language.

(ii) The right to have information about the progress of investigation, arrest of the culprits, case status in the court etc.

(iii) The right to fair treatment from the agencies of criminal justice system.

(iv) The right to privacy, dignity and respect.

(v) The right to legal advice and assistance.

(vi) The right to ask for a speedy disposal of the case.

(vii) The right to have his recovered property returned early.

(viii) The right to receive fair treatment when testifying in the court.

(ix) The right of protection from any intimidation, threat or aggression from the accused side.

U.N. General Assembly Resolution 40/34 of 29 November, 1985 lists out the Basic Principles of justice for Victims of Crime and Abuse of Power.

Declaration of Basic Principles of Justice for Victims of Crime and Abuse of Power

Recommended for adoption by the Seventh United Nations Congress on the Prevention of Crime and the Treatment of Offenders held at Milan from 26 August to 6 September,

1985, and adopted by General Assembly resolution 40/34 of 29 November, 1985

A. Victims of Crime

1. "Victims" means persons who, individually or collectively, have suffered harm, including physical or mental injury, emotional suffering, economic loss or substantial impairment of their fundamental rights, through acts or omissions that are in violation of criminal laws operative within Member States, including those laws prescribing criminal abuse of power.

2. A person may be considered a victim, under this Declaration, regardless of whether the perpetrator is identified, apprehended, prosecuted or convicted and regardless of the familiar relationship between the perpetrator and the victim. The term "victim" also includes, where appropriate, the immediate family or dependents of the direct victim and persons who have suffered harm in intervening to assist victims in distress or to prevent victimisation.

3. The provisions contained herein shall be applicable to all, without distinction of any kind, such as race, colour, sex, age, language, religion, nationality, political or other opinion, cultural beliefs or practices, property, birth or family status, ethnic or social origin, and disability.

Access to Justice and Fair Treatment

4. Victims should be treated with compassion and respect for their dignity. They are entitled to access to the mechanisms of justice and to prompt redress, as provided for by national legislation, for the harm that they have suffered.

5. Judicial and administrative mechanisms should be established and strengthened where necessary to enable victims to obtain redress through formal or informal procedures that are expeditious, fair, inexpensive and accessible. Victims should be informed of their rights in seeking redress through such mechanisms.

6. The responsiveness of judicial and administrative processes to the needs of victims should be facilitated by:

(a) Informing victims of their role and the scope, timing and progress of the proceedings and of the disposition of their cases, especially where serious crimes are involved and where they have requested such information;
(b) Allowing the views and concerns of victims to be presented and considered at appropriate stages of the proceedings where their personal interests are affected, without prejudice to the accused and consistent with the relevant national criminal justice system;
(c) Providing proper assistance to victims throughout the legal process;
(d) Taking measures to minimise inconvenience to victims, protect their privacy, when necessary, and ensure their safety, as well as that of their families and witnesses on their behalf, from intimidation and retaliation;
(e) Avoiding unnecessary delay in the disposition of cases and the execution of orders or decrees granting awards to victims.

7. Informal mechanisms for the resolution of disputes, including mediation, arbitration and customary justice or of practices, should be utilised where appropriate, to facilitate conciliation and redress for victims.

Restitution

8. Offenders or third parties responsible for their behaviour should, where appropriate, make fair restitution to victims, their families or dependents. Such restitution Should include the return of property or payment for the harm or loss suffered, reimbursement of expenses incurred as a result of the victimisation, the provision of services and the restoration of rights.

9. Governments should review their practices, regulations and laws to consider restitution as an available sentencing option in criminal cases, in addition to other criminal sanctions.

10. In cases of substantial harm to the environment, restitution, if ordered, should include, as far as possible, restoration of the environment, reconstruction of the infrastructure, replacement of community facilities and reimbursement of the expenses of relocation, whenever such harm results in the dislocation of a community.

11. Where public officials or other agents acting in an official or quasi-official capacity have violated national criminal laws, the victims should receive restitution from the state whose officials or agents were responsible for the harm inflicted. In cases where the Government under whose authority the victimising act or omission occurred is no longer in existence, the state or Government successor in title should provide restitution to the victims.

Compensation

12. When compensation is not fully available from the offender or other sources, the states should endeavour to provide financial compensation to:

(a) Victims who have sustained significant bodily injury or impairment of physical or mental health as a result of serious crimes;
(b) The family, in particular dependents of persons who have died or become physically or mentally incapacitated as a result of such victimisation.

13. The establishment, strengthening and expansion of national funds for compensation to victims should be encouraged. Where appropriate, other funds may also be established for this purpose, including in those cases where the State of which the victim is a national is not in a position to compensate the victim for the harm.

Assistance

14. Victims should receive the necessary material, medical, psychological and social assistance through governmental, voluntary, community-based and indigenous means.

15. Victims should be informed of the availability of health and social services and other relevant assistance and be readily afforded access to them.

16. Police, justice, health, social service and other personnel concerned should receive training to sensitise them to the needs of victims, and guidelines to ensure proper and prompt aid.

17. In providing services and assistance to victims, attention should be given to those who have special needs because of the nature of the harm inflicted or because of factors such as those mentioned in paragraph 3 above.

B. Victims of Abuse of Power

18. "Victims" means persons who, individually or collectively, have suffered harm, including physical or mental injury, emotional suffering, economic loss or substantial impairment of their fundamental rights, through acts or omissions that do not yet constitute violations of national criminal laws but of internationally recognised norms relating to human rights.

19. States should consider incorporating into the national law norms prescribing abuses of power and providing remedies to victims of such abuses. In particular, such remedies should include restitution and/or compensation, and necessary material, medical, psychological and social assistance and support.

20. States should consider negotiating multilateral international treaties relating to victims, as defined in paragraph 18.

21. States should periodically review existing legislation and practices to ensure their responsiveness to changing circumstances, enact and enforce, if necessary, legislation prescribing acts that constitute serious abuses of political or economic power, as well as promoting policies and mechanisms for the prevention of such acts, and should develop and make readily available appropriate rights and remedies for victims of such acts.

5

National Human Rights Commission (NHRC) of India

Established under the Protection of Human Rights Act of 1993, the National Human Rights Commission functions from New Delhi with jurisdiction all over India. It consists of a Chairperson, four full time members and three ex-officio members.

Statutorily, the Commission shall perform all or any of the following functions, namely:

(a) inquire, *suo motu* or on a petition presented to it by a victim or any person on his behalf, into complaint of:

(i) violation of human rights or abetment thereof, or

(ii) negligence in the prevention of such violation, by a public servant;

(b) intervene in any proceeding involving any allegation of violation of human rights pending before a court with the approval of such court;

(c) visit, under intimation to the State Government, any jail or any other institution under the control of the State Government, where persons are detained or lodged for purposes of treatment, reformation or protection, to study the living conditions of the inmates and make recommendations thereon;

(d) review the safeguards provided by or under the Constitution or any law for the time being in force for the protection of human rights and recommend measures for their effective implementation;

(e) review the factors, including acts of terrorism, that inhibit the enjoyment of human rights and recommend appropriate remedial measures;

(f) study treaties and other international instruments on human rights and make recommendations for their effective implementation;

(g) undertake and promote research in the field of human rights;

(h) spread human rights literacy among various sections of society and promote awareness of the safeguards available for the protection of these rights through publications, the media, seminars and other available means;

(i) encourage the efforts of non-governmental organisations and institutions working in the field of human rights; and

(j) such other functions as it may consider necessary for the protection of Human Rights.

Powers of the Commission Relating to Inquiries-Investigation

The Commission shall, while inquiring into complaints, have all the powers of a civil court trying a suit under the Code of Civil Procedure, 1908, and in particular in respect of the following matters, namely:

(a) summoning and enforcing the attendance of witnesses and examining them on oath;

(b) discovery and production of any document;

(c) receiving evidence on affidavits;

(d) requisitioning any public record or copy thereof from any court or office;

(e) issuing commissions for the examination of witnesses or documents;

(f) any other matter which may be prescribed.

Investigations

The Commission may, for the purpose of conducting any investigation pertaining to the inquiry, utilise the services of any officer or investigation agency of the Central Government or any State Government with the concurrence of the Central Government or the State Government, as the case may be. *(Note: The Commission has its own investigative wing also)*

Procedure—Inquiry and Steps after Inquiry

The Commission while inquiring into the complaints of violations of human rights may—

(1) call for information or report from the Central Government or any State Government or any other authority or organisation subordinate thereto within such time as may be specified by it;

Provided that:

(a) if the information or report is not received within the time stipulated by the Commission, it may proceed to inquire into the complaint on its own;

(b) if, on receipt of information or report, the Commission is satisfied either that no further inquiry is required or that the required action has been initiated or taken by the concerned government or authority, it may not proceed with the complaint and inform the complainant accordingly;

(ii) without prejudice to anything contained in clause (i), if it considers necessary, having regard to the nature of the complaint, initiate an inquiry.

The Commission may take any of the following steps upon the completion of an inquiry, namely:

(1) Where the inquiry discloses the commission of violation of human rights or negligence in the prevention of violation

of human rights by a public servant, it may recommend to the concerned government or authority the initiation of proceedings for prosecution or such other action as the Commission may deem fit against the concerned person or persons;

(2) approach the Supreme Court or the High Court concerned for such direction, orders or writs as that Court may deem necessary;

(3) recommend to the concerned government or authority for the grant of such immediate interim relief to the victim or the members of his family as the Commission may consider necessary;

(4) subject to the provisions of clause (5) provide a copy of the inquiry report of the petitioner or his representative;

(5) the Commission shall send a copy of its inquiry report together with its recommendations to the concerned government or authority who shall, within a period of one month, or such further time as the Commission may allow, forward its comments on the report, including the action taken or proposed to be taken thereon, to the Commission;

(6) the Commission shall publish its inquiry report together with the comments of the concerned covernment authority, if any, and the action taken or proposed to be taken by the concerned government or authority on the recommendations of the Commission.

Procedure with Respect of Armed Forces

While dealing with complaints of violation of human rights by members of the armed forces, the Commission shall adopt the following procedure, namely:

(a) it may, either on its own motion or on receipt of a petition, seek a report from the Central Government;

(b) after the receipt of the report, it may, either not

proceed with the complaint or, as the case may be, makes its recommendations to that government.

(1) The Central Governmental shall inform the Commission of the action taken on the recommendations within three months or such further time as the Commission may allow.

(2) The Commission shall publish its report together with its recommendations made to the Central Government and the action taken by the government on such recommendations.

(3) The Commission shall provide a copy of the report published under sub-section (3) to the petitioner or his representative.

Role of N.H.R.C.

Under the dynamic chairmanship of Justice Ranganath Misra, the Commission has been playing a pivotal role in developing a cultural for Human Rights in the country. It has built an edifice of Human Rights accountability on the foundations of autonomy an transparency. While concentrating on immediate redressal and remedy of wrongs, it has taken up *suo motu* investigations and has established contacts with Central and State Governments and Human Rights organisations in India and abroad. It has also struck a fruitful collaboration and cooperation with non-governmental organisations both in India and abroad.

The N.H.R.C. has given priority to:

(a) Protection of Civil Liberties.

(b) Review of Legislations repugnant to Human Rights Principles. Its role in opposing TADA was commendable.

(c) Reforms in civil and police administration to usher in Human Rights culture.

(d) Reducing, with a view to ultimately eliminating, custodial violence and rapes.

(e) Redressal of Human Rights grievances of Scheduled Castes and Scheduled Tribes.

(f) Concentration on Human Rights of women and children.

NHRC, has right since its establishment believed that reforms in laws and treaties, rewards and punishment and even making structural and systems changes, were not themselves sufficient to promote and protect Human Rights. The nation requires vast programmes of social regeneration to deal with societal wrongs. Appropriate programmes to reorient the citizen, restrain the police and bureaucracy are the need of the hour.

Keeping the above in view, NHRC has taken positive to review draconian legislations. In respect of T.A.D.A., it addressed the Members of Parliament directly. It has initiated in depth studies in insurgency areas on the steps to be taken to safeguard Human Rights. It has initiated Human Rights Literacy drive in schools and colleges with the help of NCERT and U.G.C. It has enlisted media support to create Human Rights awareness, and participated and organised seminars and symposia. It has taken a lead in observing December 10 every year as Human Rights Day.

Under the direction of NHRC, data collection on Human Rights has been streamlined and all District Magistrates and District Superintendents of Police now report to NHRC directly on custodial deaths. During the period November, 1993-March 1994, NHRC received 496 complaints of Human Rights violation and during April 1994-March 1995, it received 6987 complaints. In 1994-95, of the 6987 cases reported, 5710 were taken up for consideration after scrutiny; 2483 were disposed off in limine; and 276 were disposed off with directions after enquiry.

Of the 1660 grave allegations dealt with by the NHRC, 111 pertained to death in police custody; 51 to death in judicial custody, 9 to deaths in the custody of armed forces etc.; 497 cases of custodial violence by police and 114 of illegal detentions. In respect of 36 cases of death in police custody, the police were exonerated. (Source: Second Annual Report of NHRC).

Establishment of National Human Rights Commission has brought about a qualitative change in the observance of Human Rights in the country. Now, for the first time, there is an independent organisation which looks into all complaints of violation and fixes accountability. There is now greater awareness to follow Human Rights principles among the Police, Army and Security Forces since all excesses will come to the attention and notice of NHRC and will be probed into thoroughly. 'Cover up' is no more possible.

Human Rights Courts

To deal expeditiously and effectively with proven cases of Human Rights violations, exclusive Human Rights Courts are being set up all over India. To associate public and N.G.Os. in the process of verifying allegations of violations, District Level Enquiry Committees are being set up.

NHRC is the first step to translate Human Rights rhetoric into tangible action. India has truly joined the advanced nations in implementing Human Rights in letter and spirit. In a country of continental dimensions with great diversity of language, traditions and practices, it will be unrealistic to expect overnight a change in attitudes congenial to the enjoyment of Human Rights. We have taken one small step in the right direction and it will lead us to a great leap to make our nation and society a more humane one.

For the benefit of readers, who may not have access to the Annual Reports of the National Human Rights Commission, we reproduce below extracts from the report for 1993-94, the full reports of 1994-95 and 1995-96.

EXTRACTS FROM ANNUAL REPORT OF NHRC FOR 1993-94

Conceptual Approach of the Commission

In the light of the extraordinary range of the functions assigned to the Commission and the scope of the powers conferred on it, it is evident that the Commission must act, and be seen to act at all times, with autonomy and transparency. Indeed, it is on these two conceptual pillars that its work must rest if the Commission is to sustain and enhance the trust reposed in it by the nation. Both of these attributes will therefore need to be scrupulously respected and nurtured. The autonomy of the Commission derives, inter alia, from the method of appointing its Members, their fixity of tenure, and statutory guarantees thereto, the status they have been accorded and the manner in which the staff responsible to the Commission—including its investigative agency—will be appointed and conduct themselves. The financial autonomy of the Commission, envisaged in Section 32 of the Act, will be a key factor in ensuring the independence and integrity of this Statutory body. In pursuance of this objective, the Commission has formulated an administrative structure for itself which envisages, among other things, a built-in financial advice system to ensure the needed autonomy in the financial management of the grants appropriated for the Commission by Parliament.

The transparency of the Commission rests both on its Stature and on the regulations which the Commission has subsequently framed to govern its procedures. The capacity to receive petitions, to provide petitioners with copies of its reports and decisions, and to place its reports before Parliament and the public are all central to the openness with which the Commission has functioned and proposes to function. Indeed, the Commission counts on the relationship that it will develop with non-governmental organisations, human rights activists, the media and public, to reinforce its message of transparency in the developing of a culture of human rights in the country.

The complexity and variety of human rights issues facing our nation has required another kind of discipline of the Commission in its effort to maximise the impact of its activities. While seeking to promote and protect all of the Fundamental Rights enshrined in the Constitution or covered by treaties to which India is a party, the Commission has nevertheless considered it essential to focus atleast initially on certain key human rights issues that are of the very highest concern to the people of this country. This has required the setting of priorities, particularly in respect of its *suo motu* activity even while recognising that all human rights are important and, indeed, indivisible.

It was with such considerations in mind that the Commission undertook, as its very first *suo motu* action, an examination of the Bijbehara incident in Jammu and Kashmir, involving the tragic death of civilians in a firing by the Border Security Force. And it was again with such considerations in mind that the Commission has focussed on other issues which go to the heart of civil liberties and the nature of society that we wish to create in India. Thus, the Commission has been particularly engaged, *suo motu* or on the basis of complaints, with instances of custodial death and rape, disappearance from custody, cruel, inhuman or degrading punishment and torture, gender related violence, atrocities against vulnerable sections of society—women, children and the disabled—often compounded when these vulnerable sections belong to the Scheduled Castes and Scheduled Tribes. It is for similar reasons that social evils such as dowry deaths and bonded and child labour are receiving the early attention of the Commission and that the Commission is engaged in seeing how best it can promote, through education and training in the broadest sense, a human rights culture worthy of the noble traditions of this country and its complex, pluralistic and multilayered society.

These matters are more fully commented upon in the sections of the report that follow. But the basic approach of this Commission, namely its determination to come to grips, as early as possible, with the gravest areas of human rights violations, will explain why in Section V below, dealing with Inquiry into Complaints, certain cases, rather than others, have been selected to highlight and illustrate the preoccupation of the Commission.

Inquiry into Complaints

During the relatively brief period covered by this report, the Commission had already registered 496 cases. Of the, 174 were admitted for further investigation/inquiry/report while 274 were dismissed. In respect of 48 cases the Commission disposed of complaints with observations to the effect that remedies were more appropriately available in other fora, and that the complainants should seek such remedies from them. In accordance with its Statute and regulations, the grounds for the dismissal of complaints were broadly that:

(i) The complaints did not fall within the purview of the Commission;

(ii) The matter was subjudice or pending before another Commission;

(iii) The event, which was the object of the complaint, had occurred more than one year before the making of the complaint;

(iv) The complaint was vague or frivolous and no specific case had been made out of a human rights violation.

A table indicating the number of complaints received, admitted, disposed of with observations or simply dismissed, may be seen at Annexure-II. A further statement of cases admitted for disposal is at Annexure-III.

In dealing with the increasing number of complaints, which are being received in the various languages of the country, the Commission has encountered certain difficulties resulting from the shortage of translators. Efforts are under way to remedy this situation, which should not be allowed to become an on-going problem, as the complaints being addressed to the Commission are likely to increase very substantially in the period ahead.

It is significant to note, in connection with the 496 cases registered, that 26 were the result of *suo motu* action by the Commission—many of the latter relating to allegations of custodial death or custodial rape. In consequence of the perception of the Commission that such grave violations of human rights must be boldly and swiftly dealt with, wherever they occur in the country, instructions were issued by the Commission to all State Governments and Union Territory Administrations, on 14 December 1993, asking for reports from District Magistrates/Superintendents of Police, within 24 hours of the occurrence of any such incidents. Failure to send reports, it was made clear, would give rise to a presumption by the Commission that an effort was being made to suppress knowledge of the incident. The communication of the Commission to all States/ Union Territories may be seen at Annexure-IV.

A further area of serious concern to the Commission results from the number of reports and complaints that it has received relating to the large number, and arbitrary nature, of detentions under the Terrorist and Disruptive Activities (Prevention) Act. While following up with inquiries on individual complaints, the Commission has also considered it essential to commence an in-depth study of this Act, its implementation and implications. The Commission has, accordingly, called for detailed information from the State Governments and Union Territory Administrations on the number of cases registered under this Act, the numbers arrested, the numbers on bail, the cases decided, and the convictions obtained. Data have begun to be received by the Commission, both directly from District Magistrates and from the Central and State Governments. The Law Commission is being associated with the study underway.

In the paragraphs that follow, resumes are provided of some of the more significant cases of which the Commission has been, or is, seized. These cases have been highlighted both to illustrate the variety and scope of the human rights issues being dealt with by the Commission and also the geographical spread of the complaints being addressed by it. Furthermore, these cases provide some idea of the diverse ways in which the Commission is handling cases, using to the full the various possibilities open to it under its Statute, in order to achieve the greater goal of promoting and protecting human rights countrywide.

Illustrative Cases

(i) Alleged Custodial Death of Shanskhem Kharasaiot in Cherrapunjee

The Commission took notice of an item broadcast over A.I.R. on 5 November 1993 that two persons had died as a result of police firing on a violent crowd gathered outside Sohra Police Station in Cherrapunjee in Meghalaya. It was reported that people had gathered outside the Police Station to protest against the alleged custodial death of Shamshkem Kharasaiot. The Commission immediately called for a report from the Chief Secretary, Meghalaya. On 19 November 1993, the State Government sent in interim report stating that in regard to the incident of alleged custodial death, Magisterial Inquiry had been ordered, and that in regard to the incident of police firing, a retired High Court Judge was being requested to investigate the matter. It was further reported that the next of kin of the deceased had been given Rs. 25,000 to meet funeral expenses etc.

Upon pursuing the interim report, the Commission called for a further report on the action taken and the State Government sent such a report on 15 January 1994. With regard to the custodial death, it stated that the Magisterial

Inquiry had prima facie indicted the Police Officer concerned. Criminal cases had been registered against him. It was further reported that ex-gratia àssistance of Rs. 50,000 had been given to the next kin of the deceased, and a near relative of the deceased had been given an appointment in government on compassionate grounds.

With regard to the deaths resulting from the police firing, it was reported that an inquiry by a retired High Court Judge was continuing.

On perusing the report, the Commission on 17 January, 1994, observed that in view of the several steps taken by the State Government, there appeared to be no necessity of the Commission pursuing the matter any further. The Commission placed on record its appreciation of the prompt responses by the State Government.

(ii) Alleged Custodial Death of Om Prakash in Delhi

A report appeared in newspaper dated 10 November, 1993, captioned "Youth dies in custody". It was stated that negligence on the part of the police led to the death of a 26 year old youth in lock-up in Sultanpuri Police Station of the North-West District. The Commission *suo motu* called for a report from the Chief Secretary of the National Capital Territory of Delhi. On 14 January, 1994, the Government of the National Capital Territory of Delhi informed the Commission that the Sub-Divisional Magistrate, who had conducted the inquest, had concluded that he died due to a fall while driving a two-wheeler under the influence of a alcohol. However, there appeared to be gross negligence on the part of officials who came in contact with Om Prakash shortly before his death. The government further indicated that departmental action had been ordered to be initiated against such officials as may be found to be negligent.

On 17 January, 1994, the Commission directed the government to furnish information regarding the result of departmental action. It was informed on 24 February, 1994, that a departmental inquiry had been ordered against five police officials for various procedural lapses, including delay in medical treatment of the deceased and a case u/s 304 A IPC has been registered. The Commission has since called for a further report on the conclusion of the departmental inquiry.

(iii) Alleged Custodial Death of Raja in Tamil Nadu

The Tamil Nadu State Legal Aid and Advice Board brought to the notice of the Commission a press report concerning the disappearance of Raja, aged 15 years, who had been taken into custody by Hosur Police in Dharmapuri district of Tamil Nadu. The alleged death of Raja in custody had generated widespread consternation. The Hosur Bar Association and Denkanikotti Bar Association had passed resolutions urging impartial inquiry. Newspapers had also given wide coverage to the incident. The Commission took cognisance of the incident and called for a report from the Government of Tamil Nadu.

The State Government informed the Commission on 22 February, 1994, that the three police officers concerned had been suspended and a Magisterial Inquiry into the incident had been ordered by the Collector. The Commission has since called for the report of the inquiry and government's response thereto.

(iv) Alleged Custodial Death of Chandrasekharan in Pondicherry

The Tamil Nadu State Legal Aid and Advice Board brought to the notice of the Commission that Chandrasekharan had died on 29 December 1993 allegedly in police custody. It was also pointed out that there was non-reporting by the Pondicherry Administration, in violation of the Commission's instructions dated 14 December 1993 requiring prompt reporting of custodial deaths. The Commission appointed K.R. Gururajan, retired Vice-Chairman of Railway Claims Tribunal, Madras, to investigate the matter under Section 14 of the Protection of Human Rights Act, 1993. While investigation by Gururajan was in progress, the Chief Secretary to the Government of Pondicherry reported that as a result of the Magisterial Inquiry which had been ordered by the Government of Pondicherry, the concerned policy officers had been suspended and cases had been registered against them under the relevant provisions of law. On perusing the report, the Commission directed that no further action by it was necessary. The investigation earlier ordered u/s 14 of the Act was accordingly dropped.

(v) Disappearance of two Journalists in Punjab

The Writers in Prison Committee of International P.E.N. in its report dated 31 January, 1994, had expressed concerned over the alleged disappearance of Ram Singh Biling and Avtar Singh Mander of Punjab.

Ram Singh Biling, Journalist for "Ajj di Awaj" and "Ajit", daily newspapers, published from Jallandhar, and District Secretary of Punjab Human Rights Organisation, was reportedly arrested near a police checkpoint in Bhogiwal village on 3 January, 1992. While being taken to the checkpoint, he is reported to have told a farmer that he feared his life was in danger. The family members, who saw him at the checkpoint on 4 January, were not allowed to speak to him. A farmers' delegation went to the police checkpoint on 6 January, 1992. They were told that Shri Biling had been detained temporarily, possibly on orders from security agencies. They promised an inquiry. Sources said that billing had died in police custody.

Avtar Singh Mander, Journalist, for daily "Ajit" newspaper, was reported to have been arrested on 23 September, 1992, at his house in Jallandhar. There are no details of any charges pressed against him.

The Commission has called for reports from the Government of Punjab in respect of the above cases, and these are awaited. The Commission proposes to pursue these cases.

(vi) Disappearance of Harjit Singh in Punjab

Amnesty International in its report dated 11 February, 1994, had expressed concern over the lack of progress in the legal proceedings initiated in October 1992 to clarify the whereabouts of Harjit Singh who had disappeared after his arrest in April 1992. This matter was also raised at a discussion which a visiting dignitary had with officials of the Commission.

According to the report, on 29 April, 1992, Harjit Singh, an employee of the Punjab State Electricity Board, was arrested by police officers. The police did note have an arrest warrant and subsequently denied the arrest. The police claimed that Harjit Singh and another man were captured on 11 May, 1992, after an armed encounter with them. The police said that they took both of them to recover hidden arms and that while doing so, they were attacked by armed militants, during which two men were killed. However, Harjit Singh was twice seen alive by his father in police custody after the police claimed that his son had been killed.

The Commission has taken cognisance of the incident and called for a report from the Government of Punjab which is awaited. This will be pursued by the Commission..

(vii) Alleged Rape by a Punjab Police Official

The Commission had received a complaint from a woman resident of Maharishi Balmiki Nagar, Ludhiana, that she was raped on 2 January, 1994, by Jagjit Singh, an employee of the Punjab Police. She stated that Jagjit Singh, who was known to her and her husband, took her to his house with an assurance that he would speak to her husband not to quarrel with her. Jagjit Singh raped her and threatened that if she narrated the incident to anybody, he would kill her and her husband. The next morning Jagjit Singh left the woman at her husband's house. After 8-10 days, Jagjit Singh came to the house again and asked the complainant to come to this house at night. He threatened her with dire consequences if she disobeyed him. The complainant thereafter narrated the incident to her elder sister who conveyed the same to the victim's husband, and later the victim made a complaint to the police, but no action was taken.

The Commission has called for a report from the Director-General of Police, Punjab, and this is awaited. The Commission proposes to pursue the case.

(viii) Atrocities against Women—Harijan Woman Paraded Naked

The Commission took cognisance of press reports dated 24 January, 1994, indicating that a Harijan woman had been paraded naked in Dauna village in Allahabad District in Uttar Pradesh. It was reported that the son of a Harijan woman, Shivpati, had stolen peas from the field of people belonging to the Kurmi community and that the son had abused the landowner on being reprimanded. This had occurred on 16 January, 1994. On 18 January the SHO of Ghoorpur police station was informed of tension in the village but he did not take any action. On 21 January, 1994, some Kurmi youth waylaid Shivpati, stripped her, beat her and forced her to walk the village streets.

Reports of the incident were widely published. Ms. Saroj Dubey, Member of Parliament, also addressed a letter to the Chairperson of the Commission, expressing deep concern over the incident and sought the intervention of the Commission.

The Commission called for a report from the Chief Secretary to the Government of U.P. The report is awaited. The Commission proposes to pursue the case.

(ix) Alleged Beating of a Harijan Girl by her Employer in Delhi

The Commission took cognisance of press reports appearing on 8 March, 1994, indicating that a 13-year old girl had been branded and beaten with iron rods. It was stated that Nirmala was branded with a hot hair dryer, and beaten with iron rods and a rolling pin, allegedly by a couple in Sarita Vihar, Delhi, who had employed Nirmala as a domestic help.

A report has been called for from the Government of National Capital Territory of Delhi which is awaited.

(x) Killing of an AASU Adviser and Four others by Army Personnel

The All Assam Students Union had sent a representation dated 4 March, 1994, to the Commission alleging that the adviser of their unit of Tinsukia District and 4 other persons were killed by Army personnel on 23 February, 1994. They were picked up from their homes during the period from 17 to 19 February, 1994. Their parents had approached the Tinsukia District Magistrate, local police stations and Army camps for their release. The District Magistrate assured them of safe release. When however the youths were not released, the parents filed a Writ Petition before the Guwahati High Court. According to the representation, the High Court directed that the apprehended persons be produced before the nearest Magistrate on 22 February, 1994. However, the Army personnel are alleged to have killed the five of them.

The All Assam Students Union complained that the State Government had failed to protect the innocent people of Assam both from "State terrorism and individual terrorism". They demanded that a high level inquiry be instituted and those found guilty be punished. They asked for intervention by the Commission.

The Commission, on 22 March 1994, called for a report from the Ministry of Defence. The report is awaited. The Commission proposes to pursue the case.

(xi) Beating of an Advocate by Police Sub-Inspector

Shri M. Udaya Bhanu, Advocate, Madras, had represented tot he Commission that on 20 January 1994, an advocate, Shri Luies was mercilessly beaten by Sub-Inspector of Police, Shri Devanesan. According to Shri Udaya Bhanu, Shri Luies had intervened when the Sub-Inspector was physically assaulting some beggers. The Sub-Inspector got violent and started beating Shri Luies. Shri Luies was admitted to hospital. Next morning, Inspector Shri Ranganathan forcibly took away Shri Luies to an unknown place.

On 21 January 1994, members of the Bar passed a resolution condemning the act of the Sub-Inspector and filed a petition before the Court for search of Shri Luies and his production before the Court.

The Commission has called for a report from the Chief Secretary, Government of Tamil Nadu. The Chief Secretary has informed the Commission that a Magisterial Inquiry into the incident has been ordered and that the Sub-Inspector, Shri Devanesan, has been placed under suspension. The matter remains under the consideration of the Commission.

(xii) Medical Ethics: Rights of the Disabled

The Commission, in its meeting held on 15 February, 1994, considered exports appearing in newspapers on the removal of uterus of mentally retarded women in Maharashtra. The reports indicated that the operations for the removal of uterus were carried out with the consent of the parents of these women. The reports also indicated the intervention of the Chief Minister, Maharashtra, to stop further operations being carried out.

Following a discussion on the matter, the Commission felt that the issue raised serious questions of medical ethics and the rights of persons suffering from disabilities and decided that, in the first instance, the views of the Medical Council of India should be obtained. The Medical Council has according been requested to give its considered views to the Commission, which intends to consider the matter further.

(xiii) Murder of a Newspaper Editor in Vadodara (Gujarat)

The Writers in Prison Committee of International P.E.N. had in February 1994 taken up with the Commission, inter alia, the case of Dinesh Pathak, a newspaper editor, who was stabbed to death reportedly by Shiv Sena activists on 22 May, 1993. The Commission took cognisance of the case and directed the authorities concerned to submit a report.

The Commission has since been informed that 19 Shiv Sena activists were involved in the crime and they have all been arrested. One of the arrested persons was killed when he tried to escape from police custody. Out of the accused who were arrested, 16 are still in judicial custody. The trial is likely to commence shortly.

Review of Existing Laws, Implementation of Treaties and other International Instruments on Human Rights

Subsections (d) and (f) of Section 12 of the Act respectively empower the Commission to review the safeguards provided by or under the Constitution or any law for the time being in force, and study treaties and other international instruments on human rights with a view to making recommendations for their effective implementation.

This is a vast and challenging undertaking which, in the four months since its establishment, the Commission has only begun to tackle but which it will increasingly need to come to grips with, as it develops its capacity for research and analysis.

In the short period since its inception, the Commission has directed its attention to starting an in-depth study of the Terrorist and Disruptive Activities (Prevention) Act (TADA), a task in which it has enlisted the assistance of the Law Commission. This is a matter of the highest importance to the Commission since it touches on three most sensitive areas: the Constitution, India's treaty obligations, and the determination of the nation to preserve and protect human rights despite the lethal impact of terrorism which, often fuelled and supported from beyond the borders of this country, is the mortal enemy of civil society and all the rights that the Indian polity holds sacred. The visits undertaken by the Commission to various States of the Republic, including those that have suffered the scourge of terrorism, will facilitate this study, by bringing to bear on it a first-hand awareness of the situation prevailing on the ground.

A second area of study for the Commission relates to the range of issues concerning the Rights of the Child including the vexed and cruel question of child labour. Here again, the Commission is establishing contact with the Law Commission, concerned non-Governmental organisations and the competent governmental and, indeed, international agencies. Visits planned to specific areas where child labour is particularly prevalent will, once again, provide insights to the Commission as it develops its views on how best to examine existing legislation and the implementation of international treaties and instruments on this matter. The Commission is engaged in a similar process in regard to bonded labour.

A third area of study of the Commission relates to legislation affecting the rights of women. The National Commission for Women, which is represented in the National Human Rights Commission through its Chairperson, has done considerable work in this area with the help of most eminent committee which it established for this purpose. The National Human Rights Commission intends to remain in close touch with us sister Commission on this matter, with a view to examining the issues on which it can best be of support and encouragement. This is a task which gains immediacy as, India is expected to submit her First Periodic

Report on implementation of the provisions of the Convention on the Elimination of All Forms of Discrimination Against Women (CEDAW) by August 1994.

Improving Jail Conditions

Section (12(c) of the Protection of Human Rights Act, 1993 empowers the Commission to visit, under intimation to the State Government, any jail or any other institution under the control of State Government, where persons are detained or lodged for purpose of treatment, reformation or protection to study the living conditions of the inmates and make recommendations thereon.

The Commission is deeply concerned about the appalling conditions of overcrowding lack of sanitation, poor medical facilities, inadequate diet and the like, in most of the jails in the country. These serious deficiencies are compounded by unconscionable delays in the disposal of cases for various reasons and mismanagement in the administration of jails, all of which need to be remedied.

The approach of the Commission has been twofold: first, to study the factors responsible for overcrowding in jails and the steps needed to reduce that overcrowding; second, to encourage such measures may be necessary to develop or improve the skills of inmates, with a view to enabling their re-orientation and facilitating their integration into society upon release from jail.

As an immediate undertaking, from which the experience gained may have valuable application elsewhere, the commission decided to commence its study of jail conditions in India by initiating a dialogue with the responsible authorities in the National Capital Territory of Delhi, specifically with regard to Tihar Jail.

The Commission is in touch with the competent judicial and executive authorities with a view to:

(i) expediting the trial of cases including those of some 3300 foreign nationals in various jails in the country;

(ii) convening meetings of the Sentence Revising Board for the release, whenever possible, of those serving life sentences who have already completed the maximum of 13½ years of their term; and

(iii) segregating juvenile prisoners sentenced for minor offences from those serving longer terms for heinous crimes.

The Commission proposes to support NGOs, and the State Legal Aid and Advice Boards, to intervene on behalf of convicts in suitable cause for securing parole by moving the appropriate courts.

The Commission intends to follow up vigorously on these matters, working closely with all others interested in bettering prison conditions.

Promotion of Human Rights Literacy

The promotion of human rights literacy in a society as complex and textured as ours is a task that is, at once, both daunting and crucially important. It is also a task that calls for great perseverance, for it requires a deep and lasting commitment. Indeed, there is no easy way to create a culture of human rights: all sections of society have a role to play, and an ideal to sustain, if the cause of human rights is to take root and flourish against the cruel odds of social injustice and inequality, the problems of poverty and the fanatical destructiveness of terrorism.

Soon after its establishment, the Commission decided—as a first series of steps—to concentrate on three key sectors of our society: first, the political parties, for ours is a nation profoundly devoted to multi-party democracy; second, the executive authority at all levels, for ours is a federal structure; and third, educationists and those responsible for curricula monitoring, for human rights literacy needs its teachers—and pupils if it is to take deep root in our soil.

The Commission accordingly addressed letters to the Presidents of political parties represented in the Lok Sabha, the Rajya Sabha or in the State Legislatures. The Commission observed the political parties, by their behaviour and the ideals that they propagate, can create the most powerful force for the promotion and protection of human rights of all of the citizens of our country. Should the example they set, however, be inimical to a decent respect for such rights, the consequences could be tragic for the nation. The Commission accordingly requested political parties to constitute Human Rights Cells at the Central, state and district levels, specific charged with the responsibility of promoting and protecting human rights and for encouraging or overseeing the conduct of their members. The cells would serve a dual purpose: to propagate and thus promote a climate conducive to human rights, and to provide a self-monitoring and self-regulatory mechanism to ensure that appropriate standards of conduct are observed by those engaged in the political process in our country. Further, it was suggested that the parties may each designate a senior leader who would remain in continuing touch with the Commission on all matters relating to the observance of human rights.

As regards the State Governments, it was suggested in letters to the Chief Ministers that Government servants serving in the States, in particular those serving in the police and allied cadres, be imparted appropriate training in human rights matters. It was further suggested that State Governments might consider establishing an Inter Departmental Task Force with the following purposes: (i) monitoring of departmental programmes to ensure that they are in consonance with human rights requirements; and (ii) monitoring the performance of officers to ensure that they are sensitive to human rights considerations.

Where there were complaints of official misbehaviour resulting from human rights violations, these should be speedily inquired into the exemplary action taken.

Insofar as the educational system is concerned, a number of steps have been taken. Meetings have been initiated with the Department of Education, Ministry of Human Resources Development, and the National Council for Educational Research and Training (NCERT), for evolving appropriately graded curricula for various levels of schooling. The Department of Education and the NCERT are in the process of preparing drafts for the imminent consideration of the Commission.

At the University level, the Commission has addressed communications to all Vice-Chancellors, proposing four measures:

(i) that the subject of human rights, in all of its dimensions, may find a clear place in the curriculum of the University;

(ii) that research, seminars and publications concerning human rights should be furthered;

(iii) that the Commission would encourage linkages between the academic community and non-governmental organisations so that the best academic minds can bring their talents to bear up on the practical work being done by such groups; and

(iv) that the Commission would welcome continuing contact with the Universities in these areas and that it would help, within its means and possibilities.

There have, by and large, been excellent responses from Vice-Chancellors and many Deans of Law Faculties. The Commission intends to give more concrete forms to these responses.

Other training institutions have also engaged the attention of the Commission. The most notable of these is the Sardar Vallabhbhai Patel National Police Academy in Hyderabad which has included the teaching of human rights in its courses at the instance of the Commission. At the State level, too, there are increasing instances of police training institutes focussing on this key aspect of professional training. Contacts have also been instituted with the Armed Forces, amongst whom there is a notable heightened appreciation of the necessity and value of imparting training in respect of human rights. Indeed, at the senior-most level of the Armed Forces, the Commission has recently noted an increasing sensitivity towards, and recognition of, the need to develop a culture of human rights. The Commission welcomes this development and wishes to see this trend maintained as a matter of high priority.

Non-Governmental Organisations

The exceptional role of non-governmental organisations (NGOs) in furthering human rights is given appropriate and special recognition in the Act. Section 12(i) expressly charges the Commission to "encourage the efforts of non-governmental organisations and institutions working in the field of human rights". This is a responsibility which the Commission readily assumes, for the cause has much to gain both from the practical help and from the constructive criticism that NGOs and the Commission can bring to bear in their mutual interaction and growing relationship.

There are three areas in which NGOs can be of particular assistance to the Commission. First, because of their grassroot contacts, they can most effectively identify human rights violations, articulate them and seek redress. The Commission sees a most positive role for NGOs in bringing complaints to its notice. Secondly, given the rapport that they have established with public at large, the assistance and cooperation of the NGOs can be of great value in the investigation of the more serious cases that come to be looked into by the Commission through its investigative staff—a group that will be put together with great care as to their sensitivity to human rights considerations. There can be instances when the Commission, in accordance with its Regulation No. 18, in addition to using its investigative staff, may choose to associate NGOs actively in investigation work. Thirdly, the high level of expertise of individual NGOs in specific areas of human rights work can be a source of great benefit to the Commission as it studies and makes recommendations on specific issues and problems. There would thus be a role for NGOs in the research and studies programme of the Commission as this develops.

The Commission has already had the benefit of interacting with a large number of NGOs, both Indian and foreign. Some of them have already brought complaints that are under consideration by the Commission, yet others have already helped the Commission by their reports and publications and by their vigilance in the defence of human rights.

In a country as large and as diverse as India, there is always the problem of being unaware, in Delhi, of the extent of talent and commitment amongst groups and individuals often far removed from the nation's capital but heroic in their devotion to principles and often in their accomplishments. The Commission is seeking to prepare an appropriate National Register of NGOs working in the field of human rights, both in order to develop practical links with them and between them, if they so choose. In undertaking this task, the Commission is seeking advice from prominent human rights activists and NGOs that have already established a reputation for probity and commitment.

Contacts with External Groups/Organisations

In a global climate of heightened awareness of human rights, it has come as no surprise to the Commission that its formation and activities should be the subject of considerable interest both at home and abroad.

The Commission welcomes this interest for its is convinced that a country like India, with its open and democratic society, its pluralism, its commitment to the Rule of Law, the Universal Declaration of Human Rights and its own Constitution, should be in the vanguard of the worldwide movement for human rights.

The Commission has therefore received a steady stream of eminent visitors, both from the diplomatic corps stationed in Delhi and from Governmental, Parliamentary, Judicial and Non-governmental bodies located abroad. The discussions thus far have, by and large, centered on the powers and functions of the Commission, its status, activities and procedures, and on certain issues that are central to the perception of the State of human rights in this country. The Commission has been gratified by the expressions of good wishes conveyed to it as it undertakes the responsibilities entrusted to it by Parliament. It looks forward to interacting continuously with external groups in the period ahead.

As part of its effort to serve the universal cause of human rights, the Commission has, within the terms of its Statute, been attentive to developments at the United Nations and related forums on matters concerning human rights. The Commission was thus represented at the recently concluded 50th session of the UN Human Rights Commission in Geneva when a statement was made on the 24 February 1994, on behalf of the Commission, expressly on the role of National Institutions. Likewise, the Commission was represented at the Second International Workshop of National Institutions held in Tunis, between 21-23 December, 1993. On the that occasion, a decision was taken to include this Commission in the ad-hoc Coordinating Committee of National Institutions, which most recently met in Geneva between 21-24 February of this year. The Commission is of the view that its participation in meetings of human rights groups and activists can be of great value to the country, to those who wish to learn of the situation in India, and indeed to all those engaged in furthering human rights worldwide.

State Commissions and Human Rights Courts

The Act was prescient in envisaging the need for State Human Rights Commissions and Human Rights Courts.

Under a federal system such as ours, it is evident that a concrete responsibility must rest with individual States both to promote and protect human rights and to redress grievances. The decentralisation of the complaint disposal mechanism thus becomes a necessity, not least so as to provide a redressal mechanism that is readily accessible and inexpensive in terms of time and cost.

The National Commission has therefore been advising State, both through letters to their Chief Ministers and through discussions with them, to set up State Commissions as envisaged in the Act. At the same time, for providing speedy trial of offences arising out of the violation of human rights, State Governments are also being encouraged, with the concurrence of the Chief Justices of the respective High Courts, to specify by notification Courts of Sessions to serve as Human Rights Courts.

These matters are, at present, under the consideration of State Governments and there are indications that some may act on them in the very near future.

Concluding Observations

The few months of activity covered by this report of the Commission, have seen the Commission establish its office, gather its nucleus staff, define its priorities and begin working in each of the areas of responsibility entrusted to it under its Statute.

The creation of the Commission has been considered a major development both at home and abroad signifying the earnestness of this country to promote and protect the human rights of all of its citizens. The responsibilities entrusted to the Commission are vast, the scope of its powers considerable by any reasonable standard of assessment, and while it can legitimately be argued that they should be enhanced in one or more directions, the Commission is of the view that the Statute provides a firm basis from which to launch its manifold activities, build its capabilities and begin to have a beneficial impact on the human rights situation in the country.

It has been observed elsewhere in this report that autonomy and transparency are the pillars on which the work of the Commission is and must be based. It is to remove ambiguities and impediments concerning its competence and autonomy, that the Commission is recommending, even at this stage and on the basis of its initial experience, certain amendments to its Statute. In essence they relate to Sections 2(1)(d) and 2(1)(f) on "definitions" which concern the "human rights" falling within the competence of the Commission; Sections 11(1)(b) and 11(2) which, together with Section 32, have a bearing on the administrative and financial autonomy of the Commission; Section 13(1)(f) concerning powers relating to inquiries; Section 18 concerned steps to be taken by the Commission on the completion of an inquiry; Section 30 concerning Human Rights Courts and Section 36 on the status of the National Commission vis-a-vis other Commissions, including State Commissions.

The Commission naturally reserves the right to return to the provisions of its Statute in the light of such experience as it may continue to gather in the period that lies ahead.

The commission is acutely aware that trust, in an area as sensitive as the protection of human rights, must be earned. This is a continuing process. The Commission is gratified that, already in the first months of its existence, its presence has drawn expressions of support and encouragement and that, in a practical expression of the faith reposed in it, increasing numbers of the citizens of this country are coming forward to inform the Commission of their difficulties and seeking its help in the redress of human rights grievances. The Commission is determined to be worthy of this trust.

The cause of human rights is not alien to this great and ancient country. It is inherent in the beliefs, both religious and secular, that constitute the spirit of India. Indeed, it was for the Fundamental Rights of Indians, civil and political, economic, social and cultural, that the struggle for independence was waged. And it was these rights that found pride of place in the Constitution adopted by our Republic. In the intervening years, much has occurred that has dimmed the promise of the Constitution, yet the belief of the people of India in their Fundamental Rights has never been diminished. It is in this context that the Protection of Human Rights Act, 1993, should be viewed. It provides the strongest reaffirmation by Parliament, since the framing of the Constitution, that respect for the rights of the people of India is central to the nation's well-being, progress and, indeed integrity.

The enactment of this Statute places on the Commission and all who strive to promote and protect human rights a most onerous responsibility. But it is a responsibility worthy of the standards that this nation has set for itself, standards which demand respect for the dignity and worth of each person who dwells in this Republic.

Sd/-
(Ranganath Misra)
Chairperson

Sd/-	Sd/-	Sd/-
(M. Fathima Beevi)	(S.S. Kang)	(Virendra Dayal)
Member	Member	Member

New Delhi, the
3rd June, 1994

6

NGOs and Human Rights

It is remarkable to note in the special context of India that the positive role that the non-governmental organisations (NGOs) can play in furthering the cause of human rights has been recognised both by the Protection of Human Rights Act, 1993 (PHR Act) and the National Commission on Human Rights (NHRC). PHR Act in Section 12(1) has enjoined upon the NHRC to encourage the efforts of the NGOs and institutions working in the field of human rights.

The NHRC on its part has, in its very first report clearly spelt out the three areas in which NGOs could be of direct assistance to it, in its mission. Firstly, because of their grassroots contacts, NGOs can most effectively identify human rights violations, articulate them and seek redress from the Commission. The Commission expects the NGOs to play an active and positive role in bringing violations and complaints to its notice. Secondly, because of the rapport the NGOs have with the public, they can be great assistance to the Commission by helping the Commission's investigating staff as well as undertake investigations of violations on behalf of the Commission. Thirdly, the NGOs can undertake research and serious studies on specific problems and issues in view of their specialised knowledge. The Commission had used NGOs in studying the problems of child labour and bonded labour.

The Commission also encourages and utilises the NGOs for organising seminars, training programmes and in spreading human rights awareness. To coordinate and canalise the efforts of NGOs working in the field of human rights and to make known their contribution to outside world, NHRC has compiled a National Register of NGOs working in human rights area. Presently, there are over 200 names in the register.

Due to historical reasons in India, human rights issues have been given emphasis by organisations owing allegiance to leftist political ideology. There have been many small and scattered social action groups raising the issues of oppression and exploitation trying to enlarge the scope of social legislation to improve the living conditions of the masses; women groups; environment groups; groups which extend support to the struggle for democracy and justice; legal fora and small political parties constituted to fight for group rights etc., form the broadbase of human rights groups. Human Rights violations by the State and its organs have been articulated by a 'specialist' group of NGOs known as Civil Liberties and Democratic Rights Groups.

Majority of these specialist groups have and are suffering from 'institutional instability'. They become very vocal and active in pursuing a specific agenda and go into hibernation thereafter. Many of them have suffered splits and strayed into different fields. Most of these organisations are reluctant to share information about their organisation, membership, funds etc.

1. **Andhra Pradesh Civil Liberties Committee (APCLC)**
   Contact Person: K.G. Kannabiran, 10-3-29/2, East Marredpalli, Secunderabad-500 030
   Journal: *SWECHHA (Telugu);* Frequency: *monthly*

2. **Association for the Protection of Democratic Rights (APDR)**
   Contact Person: Sujata Bhadro, 18, Madan Baral Lane, Calcutta-700 012
   Journal: *ADHIKAR (Bengali);* Frequency: *occasional*

3. **Committee for the Protection of Democratic Rights (CPDR), Mumbai**

   Contact Person: Jyoti Punwani, C/o Super Book House, Colaba Causeway, Mumbai-400 005

   Journal: *ADHIKAR RAKSHA (English);* Frequency: *bimonthly*

4. **Lok Adhikar Sangh, Gujarat**

   Contact Person: Girish C. Patel, M-4/70/539, Shastri Nagar, Near Vijay Nagar, Ahmedabad-380 073

5. **Citizens' Committee for Civil Liberties and Democratic Rights, Goa**

   Contact Person: Roland Martins/Hugo D'Souza, The Book Shop, Near Civil Court, Altinho, Mapusa, Goa-403 507

6. **People's Union for Democratic Rights (PUDR), Delhi**

   Contact Person: Nandita Haksar, 56, Munirka Enclave, New Delhi-110 067

7. **Citizens for Democracy (CFD)**

   Contact Person: V.M. Tarkunde, B-17, Maharani Bagh, New Delhi-110 065

8. **Karnataka Civil Liberties Committee (KCLC)**

   Contact Person: Prof. Hasan Mansur, 9 Bathing Ghat lane, Chickpet, Bangalore-560 053

9. **Organising Committee for Democratic Rights (OCDR)**

   Contact Person: Bhaktavatsalam/Ramanujan, 7 Krishnaji Road, Tirupattur, North Arcot-635 601

10. **People's Union for Civil Liberties (PUCL), National**

    Contact Person: Dr. Y.P. Chhibbar, A-11, Pushpanjali, Delhi-110 092

Journal: *PUCL BULLETIN (English, Hindi);* Frequency: *monthly* The PUCL is a national body with branches in many cities of the country. Names of contact persons and addresses can be requested from the PUCL office.

11. All India Federation of Organisation for Democratic Rights (ALFOFDR)

Contact Address: C/o Lokshahi Hakk Sanghatana

Journal: *IN DEFECNCE OF DEMOCRATIC RIGHTS (English)*; Frequency: *bimonthly*

A federation organisation set up in 1982, the ALFOFDR Currently has the following organisations as its constituents.

(a) **Association for Democratic Rights, Punjab**

Contact Person: Jagmohan Singh, BXX-838, Krishna Nagar, Opp. R.P. Theatre, Ludhiana, Punjab.

Journal: *JAMHURI ADHIKAR (Punjabi);* Frequency: *occasional*

(b) **Ganatantrik Adhikar Suraksha Sanghatana (Orissa)**

Contact Person: Shushil Rai, C/o Rameshchandra Sharma, Patra Sahi, Station Bazar, Cuttack-753 003

(c) **Janadhipathya Avakasa Samarakshna Samiti (Kerala)**

Contact Person: V.V. Sarathi, Advocate, Palghat

(d) **Janatantrik Adhikar Suraksha Sanghatana, Rajasthan**

Contact Person: Ugrasen Rao, Nirala Printers, 1, Sambhavanath Marg, Lokhasa Chowk, Udaipur-313 001

(e) **Lokshahi Hakk Sanghatana**

Contact Person: Rajini X Desai, 8D, 'B' Building, Harbour Heights, Off. Victoria Bunder Road, Colaba, Mumbai-400 005

Journal: *LOK HAKK (Marathi);* Frequency: occasional

(f) **Organisation for the Protection of Democratic Rights (OPDR)**

Contact Person: Bhaskar Rao, 4, College New Quarters, Nagaram, Tenali, Andhra Pradesh-552 268

12. **Indian People's Human Rights Commission**

Contact Person: P.A. Sebastian, 104, Central Y.M.C.A., 12, N. Parikh Marg, Colaba, Mumbai-400 039

Andhra Pradesh Civil Liberties Committee

The Andhra Pradesh Civil Liberties Committee (APCLC) took birth in 1973 with P. Venkateswarlu, a High Court lawyer, as its first General Secretary. Soon after its formation, the APCLC was immobilised following the proclamation of national emergency (June 1975). From the time of its first annual conference in 1978, APCLC has been functioning regularly. K.G. Kannabhiran was elected President in the first annual conference in 1978 and he continued as President of APCLC till 1993, when Shri M.T. Khan replaced him.

The APCLC has been advocating the cause of revolutionary movements, particularly those of CPI (ML)-PWG, the most violent left extremist group in Andhra Pradesh. Its activities are directed mainly on opposing what it perceives to be forms of state repression on revolutionary movements viz., unlawful arrests, torture and encounter death of revolutionaries and draconian laws like NSA and TADA.

The APCLC advocates that any movement or mass struggle originates from social, political, cultural and economic factors and as such it is not correct to view these mass movements as mere law and order problems.

The APCLC tries to achieve its objectives mostly by taking up campaigns through meetings and protest actions like rallies, dharnas etc. It strive to bring awareness among the people and mobilise their opinion against government's alleged undemocratic actions. The APCLC also file cases in courts of law for redressal of the grievances of the victims of state repression and other undemocratic methods. Discerning observes do not fail to notice that though the APCLC promptly condemns any state repression or violence it seldom condemns PWG's violence.

In December 1993 the 8th State Conference of APCLC was held in which K.G. Kannabhiran was replaced by M.T. Khan as President of APCLC. The present office bearers of APCLC are:

President

M.T. Khan

Vice-Presidents

(1) Prof. Hara Gopal—Central University, Hyderabad
(2) Prof. Ilaiah—Osmania University, Hyderabad
(3) Prof. Abdul Basha—Nagarjuna University, Guntur

Genl. Secretary

Dr. K. Bala Gopal

Joint Secretaries

(1) Madhava Rao—Nizamabad
(2) Prof. Seshaiah—S.K.D. University, Anantapur
(3) S.S.C. Bose—Vijayawada
(4) Burra Ramulu—Warangal
(5) A. Purushotham—Mahabubnagar

Treasurer

Dr. Madhusudhan Raj—Osmania University, Hyderabad

All India Peoples Resistance Forum

The All India Peoples Resistance Forum (AIPRF) was founded in 1992 jointly by the CPML-PWG of Andhra Pradesh and Maoist Communit Centre (MCC) and the CPML-Party Unit of Bihar, as a platform to build up public opinion against the alleged state repression on the left extremists by mobilising leftist intellectuals and Human Rights activists. During its formative years, the AIPRF organised a few seminars at New Delhi and Calcutta where 'wanton repression' unleashed on the weaker sections particularly in Bihar in the name of counter extremist measures, was condemned. These seminars however, did not create much impact as the agenda had a limited appeal. In order to widen its influence among masses, the AIPRF decided to step up its mass activities on populist issues.

In the first All India Conference of AIPRF held at Kolkata in March 1994, Goru Madhava Rao of Andhra Pradesh and Vijay Kumar Arya of Bihar were elected as President and General Secretary respectively.

The first AP State Conference of AIPRF was held at Visakhapatnam in February 1995. The conference elected D. Sudhakar Rao of CPML Party Unit as President and G.N. Saibaba (Pro-PWG) as General Secretary.

Now in the year, 2005 the NGOs boom is still at swing. No doubt, some NGOs are sincere and honest in activities, however many NGOs are seen aiming a publicity and money. As envisages if different forums are vocal they may prove instrumental in raising issues of human rights.

7

Positive Action for a Humane Society

Most basically 'Human Rights' recognise the inherent dignity and fundamental freedoms of all members of human family and are the foundations for all basic freedoms, justice and peace in the world. Peace and progress in a society will be possible only when the State—the Government—and the people are conscious of the needs to ensure that everyone enjoys Human Rights. Mere assertion of the principles of Human Rights in the Constitution and various laws will not ensure this. Positive steps need be taken to make the rhetoric of Human Rights into attainable realities. This calls for a massive campaign of Human Rights consciousness.

Human Rights movement in India has suffered so far, due to the activists adopting a negative attitude to highlight the violations only and demanding punitive action. So much so, the term Human Rights has become synonymous with punitive action. This has resulted in taking evasive action by the concerned to prevent violations coming to light than making efforts to implement human rights. This has to change and a positive content should be injected into the movement.

In India, keeping in tune with the social philosophy of the Constitution, the fundamental rights and the directive principles, hundreds of pieces of social legislation have been enacted, which cover the entire gamut of Human Rights. Unless the bureaucracy in the field, who are to implement these social legislations, are aware of their import, their enforcement would lack fervour and substance.

Therefore, it is imperative that 'Human Rights' teaching should be made part of the pre-induction and post-induction training programmes at all levels of bureaucracy. Field workers, particularly those involved in developmental activities are to be sensitised and made aware of the significance of their role in ensuring human dignity.

Criminal Justice System functionaries, viz., the Police, Judiciary and the Correctional Administration undertake many coercive functions for the State. Unless they are aware of the basic tenets of Human Rights, violations of the same will take place and people will be deprived of their basic freedoms and rights. The need of the hour therefore is to educate them about the proper ways of carrying out their functions keeping in view the requirements of Human Rights. Sensitisation of these three groups to the need to take care of the dignity and freedoms of the citizens would call for a well organised programme to teach Human Rights at all the pre-induction and post-induction training. It is necessary to show to these functionaries that they can efficiently perform their tasks without violating Human Rights. Modification of procedures, practices and operational skills which are repugnant to human rights would become necessary.

Human Rights, as a subject of study, should be included in the curricula and syllabi of schools, colleges and universities. Mere reiteration of Human Rights standards will not make them understand their importance. They should be taught how, in their day-to-day life, observance of Human Rights would enhance the quality of life in the society.

People's representatives—the Members of Legislatures (MLA's) and Parliament (MP's) are the policy-makers in the country. Special programmes to acquaint them with the basic tenets of Human Rights are to be conceived and implemented.

The media, popularly known as fourth estate in

democratic system has an important role to play in moulding the public opinion. They can give a positive orientation and direction to the Human Rights movement. Representatives of the media are to be made aware of the basic need to observe Human Rights and requested to propagate the same. Similarly, film makers and T.V. producers are to be sensitised and requested not to highlight the violations of Human Rights in their works. In a developing country, voluntary workers, the non-governmental organisations have a crucial role to play. There are many dedicated and sincere workers. One can imagine their anger and frustration, when they come across blatant violations of Human Rights in the field. All of them should eschew agitational approach for the implementation of Human Rights and instead concentrate on cooperation and collaboration. Since they are close to the grassroots, their moral influence will bring about a sea-change in the attitude of the bureaucracy. Confrontation and antagonism will only perpetuate the violations and only a change of heart can herald observance. Therefore, it is necessary that the NGO's should approach this issue from a positive angle.

In principle, Human Rights are the ideals under which liberal democracies flourish. A positive approach to make everyone of these lofty ideals will ensure enhancement of the quality of life in the society. Unless and until people are convinced about the need to observe them in all their activities, these will remain utopian dreams. Infact, a man worth name cannot damage for human rights. If you have means for subsistence and can help yourself only then there is scope for human rights. This is the real position.

APPENDIX—I

UNIVERSAL DECLARATION OF HUMAN RIGHTS

Adopted and proclaimed by General Assembly resolution 217 A (III) of 10 December 1948

Preamble

Whereas recognition of the inherent dignity and of the equal and inalienable rights of all members of the human family is the foundation of freedom, justice and peace in the world,

Whereas disregard and contempt for human rights have resulted in barbarous acts which have outraged the conscience of mankind, and the advent of a world in which human beings shall enjoy freedom of speech and belief and freedom from fear and want has been proclaimed as the highest aspiration of the common people,

Whereas it is essential, if man is not to be compelled to have recourse, as a last resort, to rebellion against tyranny and oppression, that human rights should be protected by the rule of law,

Whereas it is essential to promote the development of friendly relations between nations,

Whereas the peoples of the United Nations have in the Charter reaffirmed their faith in fundamental human rights, in the dignity and worth of the human person and in the equal rights of men and women and have determined to promote social progress and better standards of life in larger freedom,

Whereas Member-States have pledged themselves to achieve, in cooperation with the United Nations, the promotion of universal respect for and observance of human rights and fundamental freedoms,

Whereas a common understanding of these rights and freedoms is of the greatest importance for the full realisation of this pledge,

Now, therefore,

The General Assembly,

Proclaim as this Universal Declaration of Human Rights as a common standard of achievement for all peoples and all nations, to the end that every individual and every organ of society, keeping this Declaration constantly in mind, shall strive by teaching and education to promote respect for these rights and freedoms and by progressive measures, national and international, to secure their universal and effective recognition and observance, both among the peoples of Member-States themselves and among the peoples of territories and their jurisdiction.

Article 1

All human beings are born free and equal in dignity and rights. They are endowed with reason and conscience and should act towards one another in a spirit of brotherhood.

Article 2

Everyone is entitled to all the rights and freedoms set forth in this Declaration, without distinction of any kind such as race, colour, sex, language, religion, political or other opinion, national or social origin, property, birth or other status.

Furthermore, no distinction shall be made on the basis of the political, jurisdictional or international status of the country or territory to which a person belongs, whether it be independent, trust, non-self-governing or under any other limitations of sovereignty.

Article 3

Everyone has the right to life, liberty and security of person.

Article 4

No one shall be held in slavery or servitude; slavery and the slave trade shall be prohibited in all their forms.

Article 5

No one shall be subjected to torture or to cruel, inhuman or degrading treatment or punishment.

Article 6

Everyone has the right to recognition everywhere as a person before the law.

Article 7

All are equal before the law and are entitled without any discrimination to equal protection of the law. All are entitled to equal protection against any discrimination in violation of this Declaration and against any incitement to such discrimination.

Article 8

Everyone has the right to an effective remedy by the competent national tribunals for acts violating the fundamental rights granted him by the constitution or by law.

Article 9

No one shall be subjected to arbitrary arrest, detention or exile.

Article 10

Everyone is entitled in full equality to a fair and public hearing by an independent and impartial tribunal, in the determination of his rights and obligations and of any criminal charge against him.

Article 11

1. Everyone charged with a penal offence has the right to be presumed innocent until proved guilty according to

law in a public trial at which he has had all the guarantees necessary for his defence.

2. No one shall be held guilty of any penal offence on account of any act or omission which did not constitute a penal offence, under national or international law, at the time when it was committed. Nor shall a heavier penalty be imposed than the one that was applicable at the time the penal offence was committed.

Article 12

No one shall be subjected to arbitrary interference with his privacy, family, home or correspondence, nor to attacks upon his honour and reputation. Everyone has the right to the protection of the law against such interference or attacks.

Article 13

1. Everyone has the right to freedom of movement and residence within the borders of each State.

2. Everyone has the right to leave any country, including his own, and to return to his country.

Article 14

1. Everyone has the right to seek and to enjoy in other countries asylum from persecution.

2. This right may not be invoked in the case of prosecutions gnuinely arising from non-political crimes or from acts contrary to the purposes and principles of the United Nations.

Article 15

1. Everyone has the right to a nationality.

2. No one shall be arbitrarily deprived of his nationality nor denied the right to change his nationality.

Article 16

1. Men and women of full age, without any limitation due to race, nationality or religion, have the right to marry and to found a family. They are entitled to equal rights as to marriage, during marriage and at its dissolution.

2. Marriage shall be entered into only with the free and full consent of the intending spouses.

3. The family is the natural and fundamental group unit of society and is entitled to protection by society and the State.

Article 17

1. Everyone has the right to own property as well as in association with others.

2. No one shall be arbitrarily deprived of his property.

Article 18

Everyone has the right to freedom of thought, conscience and religion; this right includes freedom to change his religion or belief, and freedom, either alone or in community with others and in public or private, to manifest his religion or belief in teaching, practice, worship and observance.

Article 19

Everyone has the right to freedom of opinion and expression; this right includes freedom to hold opinions without interference and to seek, receive and impart information and ideas through any media and regardless of frontiers.

Article 20

1. Everyone has the right to freedom of peaceful assembly and association.

2. No one may be compelled to belong to an association.

Article 21

1. Everyone has the right to take part in the government of his country, directly or through freely chosen representatives.

2. Everyone has the right to equal access to public service in his country.

3. The will of the people shall be the basis of the authority of government; this will shall be expressed in periodic and genuine elections which shall be by universal and equal suffrage and shall be held by secret vote or by equivalent free voting procedures.

Article 22

Everyone, as a member of society, has the right to social security and is entitled to realisation, through national effort and international cooperation and in accordance with the organisation and resources of each State, of the economic, social and cultural rights indispensable for his dignity and the free development of his personality.

Article 23

1. Everyone has the right to work, to free choice of employment, to just and favourable conditions of work and to protection against unemployment.

2. Everyone, without any discrimination, has the right to equal pay for equal work.

3. Everyone who works has the right to just and favourable remuneration ensuring for himself and his family an existence worthy of human dignity, and supplemented, if necessary, by other means of social protection.

4. Everyone has the right to form and join trade unions for the protection of his interests.

Article 24

Everyone has the right to rest and leisure, including reasonable limitation of working hours and periodic holidays with pay.

Article 25

1. Everyone has the right to a standard of living adequate for the health and well-being of himself and of his family, including food, clothing, housing and medical care and necessary social services, and the right to security in the event of unemployment, sickness, disability, widowhood, old age or other lack of livelihood in circumstances beyond his control.

2. Motherhood and childhood are entitled to special care and assistance. All children, whether born in or out of wedlock, shall enjoy the same social protection.

Article 26

1. Everyone has the right to education. Education shall be free at least in the elementary and fundamental stages. Elementary education shall be compulsory. Technical and professional education shall be made generally available and higher education shall be equally accessible to all on the basis of merit.

2. Education shall be directed to the full development of the human personality and to the strengthening of respect for human rights and fundamental freedoms. It shall promote understanding, tolerance and friendship among all nations, racial or religious groups, and shall further the activities of the United Nations for the maintenance of peace.

3. Parents have a prior right to choose the kind of education that shall be given to their children.

Article 27

1. Everyone has the right freely to participate in the cultural life of the community, to enjoy the arts, to share in scientific advancement and its benefits.

2. Everyone has the right to the protection of the moral and material interests resulting from any scientific, literary or artistic production of which he is the author.

Article 28

Everyone is entitled to a social and international order in which the rights and freedom set forth in this Declaration can be fully realised.

Article 29

1. Everyone has duties to the community in which alone the free and full development of his personality is possible.

2. In the exercise of his rights and freedoms, everyone shall be subject only to such limitations as are determined by law solely for the purpose of securing due recognition and respect for the rights and freedoms of others and of meeting the just requirements of morality, public order and the general welfare in a democratic society.

3. These rights and freedoms may in no case be exercised contrary to the purposes and principles of the United Nations.

Article 30

Nothing in this Declaration may be interpreted as implying for any State, group or person any right to engage in any activity or to perform any act aimed at the destruction of any of the rights and freedoms set forth herein.

APPENDIX—II

INTERNATIONAL HUMAN RIGHTS INSTRUMENTS

Standards under other International Instruments to which India is a State Party

Some of the other international instruments that India is a state party to are the:

1. International Convention on the Elimination of All Forms of Racial Discrimination, 1965, (CERD).
2. Convention on the Elimination of All forms of Discrimination against Women, 1979, (CEDAW).

Some of the rights guaranteed by these instruments that may be relevant to refugees are listed below :

RIGHT	CERD	CEDAW
Protecting interests of the child Nationality	5(d)(ix)	9
Expression/thought, conscience, religion	5(d)(vii), 5(d)(vii)	
Association/Peaceful Assembly	5(d)(ix)	
Privacy		
Protection of the Refugee Child		12
Medical care		6
Against sexual exploitation		
Education	5(e)(iv)	10
Religion		
Legal assistance/access to courts		
Enter/depart from country	5(d)(ii)	
Movement/residence	5(d)(i)	
Employment	5(d)(i)	11
Social Security	5(e)(iv)	

INDIA

Date of Admission to UN: 30 October 1945

TREATIES: RATIFICATIONS AND RESERVATIONS

Land and People: India has not provided a core document for use by the treaty bodies.

Economic, Social and Cultural Rights

Acceded: 10 April 1979.

India's second periodic report was due 30 June 1991; the third periodic report was due 30 June 1996.

Reservations and Declarations: Articles 1, 4, 7(c) and 8.

Civil and Political Rights

Acceded: 10 April 1979.

India's fourth periodic report is due 31 December 2001.

Reservations and Declarations: Articles 1, 9, and 13.

Racial Discrimination

Signed: 2 March 1967; ratified: 3 December 1968.

India's 15th periodic report was due 4 January 1998

Reservations and Declarations: Article 22.

Discrimination against Women

Signed: 30 July 1980; ratified: 9 July 1993.

India's initial report (CEDAW/C/IND/1) was submitted and is scheduled for consideration by the Committee at its January 2000 session; the second periodic report was due 8 August 1998.

Reservations and Declarations: Articles 5(a), 16(1), 16(2) and 29(1).

Torture

Signed: 14 October 1997.

Rights of the Child

Acceded: 11 December 1992.

India's initial report (CRC/C/28/Add.10) is scheduled for consideration by the Committee at its January 2000 session; the second periodic report is due 10 January 2000.

Reservations and Declarations: Article 32.

LIST OF HUMAN RIGHTS COVENANTS, CONVENTIONS AND TREATIES TO WHICH INDIA IS A PARTY

1. *Convention on the prevention and punishment of the Crime of Genocide:* Adopted by the General Assembly of the United Nations on 9 December 1948 by Resolution 260 (III). Entered into force on 12 January 1951. (India signed if on 29 November 1949 and ratified on 27 August 1959).
2. *International Convention on the Elimination of all forms of racial discrimination:* Adopted by the General Assembly of the United Nations in Resolution 2166 (XX) on 21 December 1965. Entered into force on 4 January 1969. (India signed it on 2 March 1967 and ratified on 3rd December 1968).
3. *International Covenant on Economic, Social and Cultural Rights:* Adopted by the General Assembly of the United Nations in Resolution 2200 (XXI) of 16 December 1966. (India's accession deposited on 10 April 1979).
4. *International Covenant on Civil and Political Rights:* Adopted by the General Assembly of the United Nations in Resolution 2200 (XXI) of 16 December 1966. Entered into force on *23* March 1976. (India's accession deposited on 10 April 1979).
5. *Convention on the Non-Applicability of statutory limitations to war crimes and crimes against humanity:* Adopted by the General Assembly of the United Nations on Resolution 2391 (XXII) of 26 November 1968. Entered into force on 11 November 1970. (India's acceded to it on 12 January 1971, with effect from 17 August 1977).
6. *International Convention on the Superssion and punishment of the crime of Apartheid:* Adopted by the General Assembly of the United Nations in Resolution 4068 (XXVIII) of 30 November 1973.

Entered into force on 18 July 1976. (India's accession dated 22 September 1977).

7. *Slavery Convention, 1926:* Entered into force on 9 March 1927. (India's ratified it on 18 June 1927).
8. *Supplementary Convention on the abolition of slavery, the slave trade, and institutions and practices similar to slavery, 1956:* Entered into force on 30 April 1957. (India signed it on 7 September 1956 and ratified on 25 June 1960).
9. *Convention for the suppression of the traffic in persons and of the exploitation of the — prostitution of others:* Approved by the General Assembly of the United Nations in Resolution 317 (IV) of 2 December 1949. Entered into force on 25 June 1951. (India signed it on 9 May 1950 and ratified on 9 Janaury 1953).
10. *Final Protocol to the Convention for the suppression of the traffic in person and of the Exploitation of the prostitution of others of 21 March 1950:* Entered into force on 25 July 1951. (India signed it on 9 May 1950 and ratified on 9 January 1953).
11. *Convention on the political rights of women:* Adopted by the General Assembly of United Nations in Resolution 640 (VII) of 20 December 1952. Entered into force on 7 July 1954. (India signed it on 29 April 1953 and ratified on 1 November 1961).
12. *Convention on the Nationality of Married women:* Done at New York on 26 February 1957. Entered into force on 11 August 1958. (India signed it on 15 May 1957).
13. International Convention Against Apartheid in Sports.
14. Convention on the Right of the Child.
15. Convention on the Political Rights of Women.
16. 1953 Protocol Amending the 1926 Slavery Convention.

17. Slavery Convention of 1926 as amended.

Convention on the Prevention and Punishment of the Crime of Genocide

Approved and proposed for signature and ratification or accession by General Assembly resolution 160 A (III) of 9 December 1948

Entry into force: **12 January 1951, in accordance with** article XIII

The Contracting Parties,

Having considered the declaration made by the General Assembly of the United Nations in its resolution 96 (I) dated 11 December 1946 that genocide is a crime under international law, contrary to the spirit and aims of the United Nations and condemned by the civilised world,

Recognising that at all periods of history genocide has inflicted great losses on humanity, and

Being convinced that, in order to liberate mankind from such an odious scourge, international co-operation is required,

Hereby agree as hereinafter provided:

Article I

The Contracting Parties confirm that genocide, whether committed in lime of peace or in time of war, is a crime under international law which they undertake to prevent and to punish.

Article II

In the present Convention, genocide means any of the following acts committed with intent to destroy, in whole or in part, a national, ethnical, racial or religious group, as such:

(a) Killing members of the group;
(b) Causing serious bodily or mental harm to members of the group;
(c) Deliberately inflicting on the group conditions of life calculated to bring about its physical destruction in whole or in part;
(d) Imposing measures intended to prevent births within the group;
(e) Forcibly transferring children of the group to another group.

Article III

The following acts shall be punishable:

(a) Genocide;
(b) Conspiracy to commit gneocide;
(c) Direct and public incitement to commit genocide;
(d) Attempt to commit genocide;
(e) Complicity in genocide.

Article IV

Persons committing genocide or any of the other acts enumerated in article III shall be punished, whether they are constitutionally responsible rulers, public officials or private individuals.

Article V

The Contracting Parties undertake to enact, in accordance with their respective Constitutions, the necessary legislation to give effect to the provisions of the present Convention, and, in particular, to provide effective penalties for persons guilty of genocide or any of the other acts enumerated in article III.

Article VI

Persons charged with genocide or any of the other acts

enumerated in article III shall be tried by a competent tribunal of the State in the territory of which the act was committed, or by such international penal tribunal as may have jurisdiction with respect to those Contracting Parties which shall have accepted its jurisdiction.

Article VII

Genocide and the other acts enumerated in article III shall not be considered as political crimes for the purpose of extradition.

The Contracting Parties pledge themselves in such cases to grant extradition in accordance with their laws and treaties in force.

Article VIII

Any Contracting Party may call upon the competent organs of the United Nations to take such action under the Charter of the United Nations as they consider appropriate for the prevention and suppression of acts of genocide or any of the other acts enumerated in article III.

Article IX

Disputes between the Contracting Parties relating to the interpretation, application or fulfilment of the present Convention, including those relating to the responsibility of a State for genocide or for any of the other acts enumerated in article III, shall be submitted to the International Court of Justice at the request of any of the parties to the dispute.

Article X

The present Convention, of which the Chinese, English, French, Russian and Spanish texts are equally authentic, shall bear the date of 9 December 1948.

Article XI

The present Convention shall be open until 31 December 1949 for signature on behalf of any Member of the United

Nations and of any non-member State to which an invitation to sign has been addressed by the General Assembly.

The present Convention shall be ratified, and the instruments of ratification shall be deposited with the Secretary-General of the United Nations.

After 1 January 1950, the present Convention may be acceded to on behalf of any Member of the United Nations and of any non-member State which has received an invitation as aforesaid.

Instruments of accession shall be deposited with the Secretary-General of the United Nations.

Article XII

Any Contracting Party may at any time, by notification addressed to the Secretary-General of the United Nations, extend the application of the present Convention to all or any of the territories for the conduct of whose foreign relations that Contracting Party is responsible.

Article XIII

On the day when the first twenty instruments of ratification or accession have been deposited, the Secretary-General shall draw up a *proces-verbal and* transmit a copy thereof to each Member of the United Nations and to each of the non-member States contemplated in article XI.

The present Convention shall come into force on the ninetieth day following the date of deposit of the twentieth instrument of ratification or accession.

Any ratification or accession effected, subsequent to the latter date shall become effective on the ninetieth day following the deposit of the instrument of ratification or accession.

Article XIV

The present Convention shall remain in effect for a

period often years as from the date of its coming into force.

It shall thereafter remain in force for successive periods of five years for such Contracting Parties as have not denounced it at least six months before the expiration of the current period.

Denunciation shall be effected by a written notification addressed to the Secretary-General of the United Nations.

Article XV

If, as a result of denunciations, the number of Parties to the present Convention should become less than sixteen the Convention shall cease to be in force as from the date on which the last of these denunciations shall become effective.

Article XVI

A request for the revision of the present Convention may be made at any time by any Contracting Party by means of a notification in writing addressed to the Secretary-General.

The General Assembly shall decide upon the steps, if any, to be taken in respect of such request.

Article XVII

The Secretary-General of the United Nations shall notify all Members of the United Nations and the non-member States contemplated in article XI of the following:

(a) Signatures, ratifications and accessions received in accordance with article XI;

(b) Notifications received in accordance with article XII;

(c) The date upon which the present Convention comes into force in accordance with article XIII;

(d) Denunciations received in accordance with article XIV;

(e) The abrogation of the Convention in accordance with article XV;

(f) Notifications received in accordance with article XVI.

Article XVIII

The original of the present Convention shall be deposited in the archives of the United Nations.

A certified copy of the Convention shall be transmitted to each Member of the United Nations and to each of the non-member States contemplated in article XI.

Article XIX

The present Convention shall be registered by the Secretary-General of the United Nations on the date of its coming into force.

International Convention on the Elimination of All Forms of Racial Discrimination

Adopted and opened for signature and ratification by General Assembly resolution 2106 A (XX) of 21 December 1965

Entry into force: 4 January 1969, in accordance with article 19

The States Parties to this Convention,

Considering that the Charter of the United Nations is based on the principles of the dignity and equality inherent in all human beings, and that all Member States have pledged themselves to take joint and separate action, in co-operation with the Organisation, for the achievement of one of the purposes of the United Nations which is to promote and encourage universal respect for and observance of human rights and fundamental freedoms for all, without distinction as to race, sex, language or religion,

Considering that the Universal Declaration of Human Rights proclaims that all human beings are born free and equal in dignity and rights and that everyone is entitled to all the rights and freedoms set out therein, without distinction of any kind, in particular as to race, colour or national origin,

Considering that all human beings are equal before the law and are entitled to equal protection of the law against any discrimination and against any incitement to discrimination,

Considering that the United Nations has condemned colonialism and all practices of segregation and discrimination associated therewith, in whatever form and wherever they exist, and that the Declaration on the Granting of Independence to Colonial Countries and Peoples of 14 December 1960 (General Assembly resolution 1514 (XV)) has affirmed and solemnly proclaimed the necessity of bringing them to a speedy and unconditional end,

Considering that the United Nations Declaration on the Elimination of All Forms of Racial Discrimination of 20 November 1963 (General Assembly resolution 1904 (XVIII)) solemnly affirms the necessity of speedily eliminating racial discrimination throughout the world in all its forms and manifestations and of securing understanding of and respect for the dignity of the human person,

Convinced that any doctrine of superiority based on racial differentiation is scientifically false, morally condemnable, socially unjust and dangerous, and that there is no justification for racial discrimination, in theory or in practice, anywhere,

Reaffirming that discrimination between human beings on the grounds of race, colour or ethnic origin is an obstacle to friendly and peaceful relations among nations and is capable of disturbing peace and security among peoples and the harmony of persons living side by side even within one and the same State,

Convinced that the existence of racial barriers is repugnant to the ideals of any human society,

Alarmed by manifestations of racial discrimination still in evidence in some areas of the world and by governmental policies based on racial superiority or hatred, such as policies of *apartheid,* segregation or separation,

Resolved to adopt all necessary measures for speedily eliminating racial discrimination in all its forms and manifestations, and to prevent and combat racist doctrines and practices in order to promote understanding between races and to build an international community free from all forms of racial segregation and racial discrimination,

Bearing in mind the Convention concerning Discrimination in respect of Employment and Occupation adopted by the International Labour Organisation in 1958, and the Convention against Discrimination in Education adopted by the United Nations Educational, Scientific and Cultural Organisation in 1960,

Desiring to implement the principles embodied in the United Nations Declaration on the Elimination of All Forms of Racial Discrimination and to secure the earliest adoption of practical measures to that end.

Have agreed as follows:

PART I

Article 1

1. In this Convention, the term "racial discrimination" shall mean any distinction, exclusion, restriction or preference based on race, colour, descent, or national or ethnic origin which has the purpose or effect of nullifying or impairing the recognition, enjoyment or exercise, on an equal footing, of human rights and fundamental freedoms in the political, economic, social, cultural or any other field of public life.

2. This Convention shall not apply to distinctions, exclusions, restrictions or preferences made by a State Party to this Convention between citizens and non-citizens.

3. Nothing in this Convention may be interpreted as affecting in any way the legal provisions of States Parties concerning nationality, citizenship or naturalisation, provided that such provisions do not discriminate against any particular nationality.

4. Special measures taken for the sole purpose of securing adequate advancement of certain racial or ethnic groups or individuals requiring such protection as may be necessary in order to ensure such groups or individuals equal enjoyment or exercise of human rights and fundamental freedoms shall not be deemed racial discrimination, provided, however, that such measures do not, as a consequence, lead to the maintenance of separate rights for different racial groups and that they shall not be continued after the objectives for which they were taken have been achieved.

Article 2

1. States Parties condemn racial discrimination and undertake to pursue by all appropriate means and without delay a policy of eliminating racial discrimination in all its forms and promoting understanding among all races, and, to this end:

(a) Each State Party undertakes to engage in no act or practice of racial discrimination against persons, groups of persons or institutions and to ensure that all public authorities and public institutions, national and local, shall act in conformity with this obligation;

(b) Each State Party undertakes not to sponsor, defend or support racial discrimination by any persons or organisations;

(c) Each State Party shall take effective measures to

review governmental, national and local policies, and to amend, rescind or nullify any laws and regulations which have the effect of creating or perpetuating racial discrimination wherever it exists;

(d) Each State Party shall prohibit and bring to an end, by all appropriate means, including legislation as required by circumstances, racial discrimination by any persons, group or organisation;

(e) Each State Party undertakes to encourage, where appropriate, inte-grationist multiracial organisations and movements and other means of eliminating barriers between races, and to discourage anything which tends to strengthen racial division.

2. States Parties shall, when the circumstances so warrant, take, in the social, economic, cultural and other fields, special and concrete measures to ensure the adequate development and protection of certain racial groups or individuals belonging to them, for the purpose of guaranteeing them the full and equal enjoyment of human rights and fundamental freedoms. These measures shall in no case entail as a consequence the maintenance of unequal or separate rights for different racial groups after the objectives for which they were taken have been achieved.

Article 3

States Parties particularly condemn racial segregation and apartheid and undertake to prevent, prohibit and eradicate all practices of this nature in territories under their jurisdiction.

Article 4

States Parties condemn all propaganda and all organisations which are based on ideas or theories of superiority of one race or group of persons of one colour or ethnic origin, or which attempt to justify or promote racial hatred and discrimination in any form, and undertake to adopt immediate and positive measures designed to eradicate all incitement to, or acts of, such discrimination and, to this end, with due regard to the principles embodied in the Universal Declaration of Human Rights and the rights expressly set forth in article 5 of this Convention, *inter alia:*

(a) Shall declare an offence punishable by law all dissemination of ideas based on racial superiority or hatred, incitement to racial discrimination, as well as all acts of violence or incitement to such acts against any race or group of persons of another colour or ethnic origin, and also the provision of any assistance to racist activities, including the financing thereof;

(b) Shall declare illegal and prohibit organisations, and also organised and all other propaganda activities, which promote and incite racial discrimination, and shall recognise participation in such organisations or activities as an offence punishable by law;

(c) Shall not permit public authorities or public institutions, national or local, to promote or incite racial discrimination.

Article 5

In compliance with the fundamental obligations laid down in article 2 of this Convention, States Parties undertake to prohibit and to eliminate racial discrimination in all its forms and to guarantee the right of everyone, without distinction as to race, colour, or national or ethnic origin, to equality before the law, notably in the enjoyment of the following rights:

(a) The right to equal treatment before the tribunals and all other organs administering justice;

(b) The right to security of person and protection by the State against violence or bodily harm, whether inflicted by government officials or by any individual group or institution;

(c) Political rights, in particular the rights to participate in elections—to vote and to stand for election—on the basis of universal and equal suffrage, to take part in the Government as well as in the conduct of public affairs at any level and to have equal access to public service;

(d) Other civil rights, in particular:

  (i) The right to freedom of movement and residence within the border of the State;
  (ii) The right to leave any country, including one's own, and to return to one's country;
  (iii) The right to nationality;
  (iv) The right to marriage and choice of spouse;
  (v) The right to own property alone as well as in association with others;
  (vi) The right to inherit;
  (vii) The right to freedom of throught, conscience and religion;
  (viii) The right to freedom of opinion and expression;
  (ix) The right to freedom of peaceful assembly and association;

(e) Economic, social and cultural rights, in particular:

  (i) The rights to work, to free choice of employment, to just and favourable conditions of work, to protection against unemployment, to equal pay for equal work, to just and favourable remuneration;
  (ii) The right to form and join trade unions;
  (iii) The right to housing;
  (iv) The right to public health, medical care, social security and social services;

(v) The right to education and training;

(vi) The right to equal participation in cultural activities;

(f) The right of access to any place or service intended for use by the general public, such as transport, hotels, restaurants, cafes, theatres and parks.

Article 6

States Parties shall assure to everyone within their jurisdiction effective protection and remedies, through the competent national tribunals and other State institutions, against any acts of racial discrimination which violate his human rights and fundamental freedoms contrary to this Convention, as well as the right to seek from such tribunals just and adequate reparation or satisfaction for any damage suffered as a result of such discrimination.

Article 7

States Parties undertake to adopt immediate and effective measures, particularly in the fields of teaching, education, culture and information, with a view to combating prejudices which lead to racial discrimination and to promoting understanding, tolerance and friendship among nations and racial or ethnical groups, as well as to propagating the purposes and principles of the Charter of the United Nations, the Universal Declaration of Human Rights, the United Nations Declaration on the Elimination of All Forms of Racial Discrimination, and this Convention.

PART II

Article 8

1. There shall be established a Committee on the Elimination of Racial Discrimination (hereinafter referred to as the Committee) consisting of eighteen experts of high moral standing and acknowledged impartiality elected by States Parties from among their nationals, who shall serve

in their personal capacity, consideration being given to equitable geographical distribution and to the representation of the different forms of civilisation as well as of the principal legal systems.

2. The members of the Committee shall be elected by secret ballot from a list of persons nominated by the States Parties. Each State Party may nominate one person from among its own nationals.

3. The initial election shall be held six months after the date of the entry into force of this Convention. At least three months before the date of each election the Secretary-General of the United Nations shall address a letter to the States Parties inviting them to submit their nominations within two months. The Secretary-General shall prepare a list in alphabetical order of all persons thus nominated, indicating the States Parties which have nominated them, and shall submit it to the States Parties.

4. Elections of the members of the Committee shall be held at a meeting of States Parties convened by the Secretary-General at United Nations Headquarters. At that meeting, for which two thirds of the States Parties shall constitute a quorum, the persons elected to the Committee shall be nominees who obtain the largest number of votes and an absolute majority of the votes of the representatives of States Parties present and voting.

5. (a) The members of the Committee shall be elected for a term of four years. However, the terms of nine of the members elected at the first election shall expire at the end of two years; immediately after the first election the names of these nine members shall be chosen by lot by the Chairman of the Committee;

(b) For the filling of casual vacancies, the State Party whose expert has ceased to function as a member of the Committee shall appoint another expert from among its nationals, subject to the approval of the Committee.

6. States Parties shall be responsible for the expenses of the members of the Committee while they are in performance of Committee duties.

Article 9

1. States Parties undertake to submit to the Secretary-General of the United Nations, for consideration by the Committee, a report on the legislative, judicial, administrative or other measures which they have adopted and which give effect to the provisions of this Convention: *(a)* within one year after the entry into force of the Convention for the State concerned; and *(b)* thereafter every two years and whenever the Committee so requests. The Committee may request further information from the States Parties.

2. The Committee shall report annually, through the Secretary-General, to the General Assembly of the United Nations on its activities and may make suggestions and general recommendations based on the examination of the reports and information received from the States Parties. Such suggestions and general recommendations shall be reported to the General Assembly together with comments, if any, from States Parties.

Article 10

1. The Committee shall adopt its own rules of procedure.
2. The Committee shall elect its officers for a term of two years.
3. The secretariat of the Committee shall be provided by the Secretary-General of the United Nations.
4. The meetings of the Committee shall normally be held at United Nations Headquarters.

Article 11

1. If a State Party considers that another State Party is not giving effect to the provisions of this Convention, it may bring the matter to the attention of the Committee. The Committee shall then transmit the communication to

the State Party concerned. Within three months, the receiving State shall submit to the Committee written explanations or statements clarifying the matter and the remedy, if any, that may have been taken by that State.

2. If the matter is not adjusted to the satisfaction of both parties, either by bilateral negotiations or by any other procedure open to them, within six months after the receipt by the receiving State of the initial communication, either State shall have the right to refer, the matter, again to the Committee by notifying the Committee and also the other State.

3. The Committee shall deal with a matter referred to it in accordance with paragraph 2 of this article after it has ascertained that all available domestic remedies have been invoked and exhausted in the case, in conformity with the generally recognised principles of international law. This shall not be the rule where the application of the remedies is unreasonably prolonged.

4. In any matter referred to it, the Committee may call upon the States Parties concerned to supply any other relevant information.

5. When any matter arising out of this article is being considered by the Committee, the States Parties concerned shall be entitled to send a representative to take part in the proceedings of the Committee, without voting rights, while the matter is under consideration.

Article 12

1. (a) After the Committee has obtained and collated all the information it deems necessary, the Chairman shall apppoint an *ad hoc* Conciliation Commission (hereinafter referred to as the Commission) comprising five persons who may or may not be members of the Committee. The members of the Commission shall be appointed with the unanimous consent of the parties to the dispute, and its good offices shall be made available to the States concerned

with a view to an amicable solution of the matter on the basis of respect for this Convention;

(b) If the States parties to the dispute fail to reach agreement within three months on all or part of the composition of the Commission, the members of the Commission not agreed upon by the States parties to the dispute shall be elected by secret ballot by a two-thirds majority vote of the Committee from among its own members.

2. The members of the Commission shall serve in their personal capacity. They shall not be nationals of the States parties to the dispute or of a State not Party to this Convention.

3. The Commission shall elect its own Chairman and adopt its own rules of procedure.

4. The meetings of the Commission shall normally be held at United Nations Headquarters or at any other convenient place as determined by the Commission.

5. The secretariat provided in accordance with article 10, paragraph 3, of this Convention shall also service the Commission whenever a dispute among States Parties brings the Commission into being.

6. The States parties to the dispute shall share equally all the expenses of the members of the Commission in accordance with estimates to be provided by the Secretary-General of the United Nations.

7. The Secretary-General shall be empowered to pay the expenses of the members of the Commission, if necessary, before reimbursement by the States parties to the dispute in accordance with paragraph 6 of this article.

8. The information obtained and collated by the Committee shall be made available to the Commission, and the Commission may call upon the States concerned to supply any other relevant information.

Article 13

1. When the Commission has fully considered the matter, it shall prepare and submit to the Chairman of the Committee a report embodying its findings on all questions of fact relevant to the issue between the parties and containing such recommendations as it may think proper for the amicable solution of the dispute.

2. The Chairman of the Committee shall communicate the report of the Commission to each of the States parties to the dispute. These States shall, within three months, inform the Chairman of the Committee whether or not they accept the recommendations contained in the report of the Commission.

3. After the period provided for in paragraph 2 of this article, the Chairman of the Committee shall communicate the report of the Commission and the declarations of the States Parties concerned to the other States Parties to this Convention.

Article 14

1. A State Party may at any time declare that it recognises the competence of the Committee to receive and consider communications from individuals or groups of individuals within its jurisdiction claiming to be victims of a violation by that State Party of any of the rights set forth in this Convention. No communication shall be received by the Committee if it concerns a State Party which has not made such a declaration.

2. Any State Party which makes a declaration as provided for in paragraph 1 of this article may establish or indicate a body within its national legal order which shall be competent to receive and consider petitions from individuals and groups of individuals within its jurisdiction who claim to be victims of a violation of any of the rights set forth in this Convention and who have exhausted other available local remedies.

3. A declaration made in accordance with paragraph 1 of this article and the name of any body established or indicated in accordance with paragraph 2 of this article shall be deposited by the State Party concerned with the Secretary-General of the United Nations, who shall transmit copies thereof to the other States Parties. A declaration may be withdrawn at any time by notification to the Secretary-General, but such a withdrawal shall not affect communications pending before the Committee.

4. A register of petitions shall be kept by the body established or indicated in accordance with paragraph 2 of this article, and certified copies of the register shall be filed annually through appropriate channels with the Secretary-General on the understanding that the contents shall not be publicly disclosed.

5. In the event of failure to obtain satisfaction from the body established or indicated in accordance with paragraph 2 of this article, the petitioner shall have the right to communicate the matter to the Committee within six months.

6. (a) The Committee shall confidentially bring any communication referred to it to the attention of the State Party alleged to be violating any provision of this Convention, but the identity of the individual or groups of individuals concerned shall not be revealed without his or their express consent. The Committee shall not receive anonymous communications;

(b) Within three months, the receiving State shall submit to the Committee written explanations or statements clarifying the matter and the remedy, if any, that may have been taken by that State.

7. (a) The Committee shall consider communications in the light of all information made available to it by the State Party concerned and by the petitioner. The Committee shall not consider any communication from a petitioner unless it has ascertained that the petitioner has exhausted

all available domestic remedies. However, this shall not be the rule where the application of the remedies is unreasonably prolonged;

(b) The Committee shall forward its suggestions and recommendations, if any, to the State Party concerned and to the petitioner.

8. The Committee shall include in its annual report a summary of such communications and, where appropriate summary of the explanations and statements of the States. Parties concerned and of its own suggestions and recommendations.

9. The Committee shall be competent to exercise the functions provided for in this article only when at least ten States Parties to this Convention are bound by declarations in accordance with paragraph 1 of this article.

Article 15

1. Pending the achievement of the objectives of the Declaration on the Granting of Independence to Colonial Countries and Peoples, contained in General Assembly resolution 1514 (XV) of 14 December 1960, the provisions of this Convention shall in no way limit the right of petition granted; to these peoples by other international instruments or by the United Nations and its specialised agencies.

2. (a) The Committee established under article 8, paragraph 1, of this Convention shall receive copies of the petitions from, and submit expressions of opinion and recommendations on these petitions to, the bodies of the United Nations which deal with matters directly related to the principles and objectives of this Convention in their consideration of petitions from the inhabitants of Trust and Non-Self-Governing Territories and all other territories to which General Assembly resolution 1514 (XV) applies, relating to matters covered by this Convention which are before these bodies;

(b) The Committee shall receive from the competent bodies of the United Nations copies of the reports concerning the legislative, judicial, administrative or other measures directly related to the principles and objectives of this Convention applied by the administering Powers within the Territories mentioned in subparagraph (a) of this paragraph, and shall express opinions and make recommendations to these bodies.

3. The Committee shall include in its report to the General Assembly a summary of the petitions and reports it has received from United Nations bodies, and the expressions of opinion and recommendations of the Committee relating to the said petitions and reports.

4. The Committee shall request from the Secretary-General of the United Nations all information relevant to the objectives of this Convention and available to him regarding the Territories mentioned in paragraph 2 *(a)* of this article.

Article 16

The provisions of this Convention concerning the settlement disputes or complaints shall be applied without prejudice to other procedures for settling disputes or complaints in the field of discrimination laid down in the constituent instruments of, or conventions adopted by, the United Nations and its specialised agencies, and shall not prevent the States Parties from having recourse to other procedures for settling a dispute in accordance with general or special international agreements in force between them.

PART III

Article 17

1. This Convention is open for signature by any State Member of the United Nations or member of any of its specialised agencies, by any State Party to the Statute of the International Court of Justice, and by any other State

which has been invited by the General Assembly of the United Nations to become a Party to this Convention.

2. This Convention is subject to ratification. Instruments of ratification shall be deposited with the Secretary-General of the United Nations.

Article 18

1. This Convention shall be open to accession by any State referred to in article 17, paragraph 1, of the Convention.

2. Accession shall be effected by the deposit of an instrument of accession with the Secretary-General of the United Nations.

Article 19

1. This Convention shall enter into force on the thirtieth day after the date of the deposit with the Secretary-General of the United Nations of the twenty-seventh instrument of ratification or instrument of accession.

2. For each State ratifying this Convention or acceding to it after the deposit of the twenty-seventh instrument of ratification or instrument of accession, the Convention shall enter into force on the thirtieth day after the date of the deposit of its own instrument of ratification or instrument of accession.

Article 20

1. The Secretary-General of the United Nations shall receive and circulate to all States which are or may become Parties to this Convention reservations made by States at the time of ratification or accession. Any State which objects to the reservation shall, within a period of ninety days from the date of the said communication, notify the Secretary-General that it does not accept it.

2. A reservation incompatible with the object and purpose of this Convention shall not be permitted, nor shall a

reservation the effect of which would inhibit the operation of any of the bodies established by this Convention be allowed. A reservation shall be considered incompatible or inhibitive if at least two thirds of the States Parties to this Convention object to it.

3. Reservations may be withdrawn at any time by notification to this effect addressed to the Secretary-General. Such notification shall take effect on the date on which it is received.

Article 21

A State Party may denounce this Convention by written notification to the Secretary-General of the United Nations. Denunciation shall take effect one year after the date of receipt of the notification by the Secretary-General.

Article 22

Any dispute between two or more States Parties with respect to the interpretation or application of this Convention, which is not settled by negotiation or by the procedures expressly provided for in this Convention, shall, at the request of any of the parties to the dispute, be referred to the International Court of Justice for decision, unless the disputants agree to another mode of settlement.

Article 23

1. A request for the revision of this Convention may be made at any time by any State Party by means of a notification in writing addressed to the Secretary-General of the United Nations.

2. The General Assembly of the United Nations shall decide upon the steps, if any, to be taken in respect of such a request.

Article 24

The Secretary-General of the United Nations shall inform

all States referred to in article 17, paragraph 1, of this Convention of the following particulars:

(a) Signatures, ratifications and accessions under articles 17 and 18;

(b) The date of entry into force of this Convention under article 19;

(c) Communications and declarations received under articles 14, 20 and 23;

(d) Denunciations under article 21.

Article 25

1. This Convention, of which the Chinese, English, French, Russian and Spanish texts are equally authentic, shall be deposited in the archives of the United Nations.

2. The Secretary-General of the United Nations shall transmit certified copies of this Convention to all States belonging to any of the categories mentioned in article 17, paragraph 1, of the Convention.

ADOPTED BY THE GENERAL ASSEMBLY OF THE UN IN RES. 2200 (XXI) OF 16 DEC. 1966

Preamble

The State parties to present Covenant considering that, in accordance with the Principles proclaimed in the Charter of the United Nations, recognition of the inherent dignity and of the equal and inalienable rights of all the members of the human family is the foundation of freedom, justice and peace in the world,

Recognising that these rights derive from the inherent dignity of the human person,

Recognising that, in accordance with the Universal Declaration of Human Rights, the ideal of free human beings enjoying freedom from fear and want can only be achieved if conditions are created whereby everyone may enjoy his economic, social and cultural rights, as well as his civil and political rights,

Considering the obligation of states under the charter of the United Nations to promote universal respect for, and observance of, human rights and freedoms,

Realising that the individual, having duties to other individuals and to the community to which he belongs, is under a responsibility to strive for the promotion and observance of the rights recognised in the present Covenant,

Agree upon the following Articles:

PART I

Article 1

1. All peoples have the right of self-determination. By virtue of that right they freely determine their political status and freely pursue their economic, social and cultural development.
2. All peoples may, for their own ends, freely dispose of their natural wealth and resources without prejudice to any obligations arising out of international economic cooperation, based upon the principle of mutual benefit, and international law. In no case may a people be deprived of its own means of subsistence.
3. The State Parties to the present Covenant, including those having responsibility for the administration of Non-Self-Governing and Trust Territories, shall promote the realisation of the right of self-determination, and shall respect that right, in conformity with the provisions of the Charter of the United Nations.

PART II

Article 2

1. Each State Party to the present Covenant undertakes to take steps, individually and through international assistance and co-operation, especially economic and technical, to the maximum of its available resources, with a view to achieving progressively the full realisation of the rights recognised in the present covenant by all appropriate means, including particularly the adoption of legislative measures.
2. The State parties to the present Covenant undertake to guarantee that the rights enunciated in the present Covenant will be exercised without discrimination of any kind as to race, colour, sex, language, religion, political or other opinion, national or social origin, property, birth or other status.
3. Developing countries, with due regard to human rights and their national economic, may determine to what extent they would guarantee the economic rights recognised in the present Covenant to non-nationals.

Article 3

The state parties to the present Covenant undertake to ensure the equal right of men and women to the enjoyment of all economic, social and cultural rights set forth in the present covenant.

Article 4

The State Parties to the present Covenant recognise that, in the enjoyment of those rights provided by the State in conformity with the present Covenant, the State may subject such rights only to such limitations as are determined by law only in so far as this rights and solely for the purpose of promoting the general welfare in a democratic society.

Article 5

1. Nothing in the present Covenant may be interpreted as implying for any State, group or person any right to engage in any activity or to perform any act aimed at the destruction of any of the rights or freedoms recognised herein, or at their limitation to a greater extent than is provided for in the present Covenant.
2. No restriction upon or derogation from any of the fundamental human rights recognised or existing in any country in virtue of law, conventions, regulations or custom shall be admitted on the pretext that the present Covenant does not recognise such rights or that it recognises them to a lesser extent.

PART III

Article 6

1. The State Parties to the present Covenant recognise the right to work, which includes the rights of everyone to the opportunity to gain his living by work which he freely chooses or accepts, and will take appropriate steps to safeguard this right.
2. The steps to be taken by a State Party to the present Covenant to achieve the full realisation of this right shall include technical and vocational guidance and training programs, policies and techniques to achieve steady economic, social and cultural development under conditions safeguarding fundamental political and economic freedoms to the individual.

Article 7

The State Parties to the present Covenant recognise the rights of everyone to the enjoyment of just and favourable conditions of work which ensure, in particular:

(a) Remuneration which provides all workers, as a minimum, with:

   (i) Fair wages and equal remuneration for work of equal value without distinction of any kind, in particular women being guaranteed conditions of work not inferior to those enjoyed by men, with equal pay for equal work;

   (ii) A decent living for themselves and their families in accordance with the provisions of the present Covenant;

(b) Safe and healthy working conditions;

(c) Equal opportunity for everyone to be promoted in his employment to an appropriate higher level, subject to no considerations other than those of seniority and competence;

(d) Rest, leisure and reasonable limitation of working hours and periodic holidays with pay, as well as remuneration for public holidays.

Article 8

1. The State Parties to the present Covenant undertake to ensure:

   (a) The right of everyone to form trade unions and join the trade union of his choice, subject only to the rules of the organisation concerned, for the promotion and protection of his economic and social interests. No restrictions may be placed on the exercise of this right other than those prescribed by law and which are necessary in a democratic society in the interests of national security or public order or for the protection of the rights and freedoms of others;

   (b) The right of trade unions to establish national federations or confederations and the right of the latter to form or join international trade-union organisations;

(c) The right of trade unions to function freely subject to no limitations other than those prescribed by law and which are necessary in a democratic society in the interests of national security of public order or for the protection of the, rights and freedoms of others;

(d) The right to strike, provided that it is exercised in conformity with the laws of the particular country.

2. This Article shall not prevent the imposition of lawful restrictions on the exercise of these rights by members of the armed forces or of the police or of the administration of the state.
3. Nothing in this Article shall authorise State Parties to the International Labour Organisation Convention of 1948 concerning freedom of association and protection of the freedom of association and protection of the right to organise legislative measures which would prejudice, or apply the law in such a manner as would prejudice, the guarantees provided for in that Convention.

Article 9

The State Parties to the present Covenant recognise the right of everyone to social security, including social insurance.

Article 10

The State Parties to the present Covenant recognise that:

1. The widest possible protection and assistance should be accorded to the family, which is the natural and fundamental group unit of society, particularly for

its establishment and while it is responsible for the care and education of dependent children, marriage must be entered into with the free consent of the intending spouses.

2. Special protection should be accorded to mothers during a reasonable period before and after childbirth. During such period working mothers should be accorded paid leave or leave with adequate social security benefits.
3. Special measures of protection and assistance should be taken on behalf of all children and young persons without any discrimination for reasons of parentage or other conditions. Children and young persons should be protected from economic and social exploitation. Their employment in work harmful to their morals or health or dangerous to life or likely to hamper their normal development should be punishable by law. States should also set age limits below which the paid employment of child labour should be prohibited and punishable by law.

Article 11

1. The State Parties to the present Covenant recognise the right of everyone to an adequate standard of living for himself and his family, including adequate food, clothing and housing and to the continuous improvement of living conditions. The state parties will take appropriate steps to ensure the realisation of this right, recognising to this effect the essential importance of international co-operation based on free consent.
2. The State Parties to the present Covenant, recognising the fundamental rights of everyone to be free from hunger, shall take, individually and through international cooperation, the measures, including specific programs, which are needed:

(a) To improve methods of production, conservation and distribution of food by making full use of technical and scientific knowledge, by disseminating knowledge of the principles of nutrition and by developing or reforming agrarian systems in such a way as to achieve the most efficient development and utilisation of natural resources;

(b) Taking into account the problems of both food-importing and food-exporting countries, to ensure an equitable distribution of world food supplies in relation to need.

Article 12

1. The State Parties to the present covenant recognise the right of everyone to the enjoyment of the highest attainable standard of physical and mental health.
2. The steps to be taken by the State parties to the present covenant to achieve the full realisation of this right shall include those necessary for;
   (a) The provision for the reduction of the stillbirth-rate and of infant mortality and for the healthy development of the child;
   (b) The improvement of all aspects of environmental and industrial hygiene;
   (c) The prevention treatment and control of epidemic, endemic, occupational and other diseases;
   (d) The creation of conditions which would assure to all medical service and medical attention in the event of sickness.

Article 13

1. The State Parties to the present Covenant recognise the right of everyone to education. They agree that

education shall be directed to the full development of the human personality and the sense of its dignity, and shall strengthen the respect for human rights and fundamental freedoms. They further agree that education shall enable all persons to participate effectively in a free society, promote understanding, tolerance and friendship among all nations and all racial, ethnic or religious groups, and further the activities of the United Nations for the maintenance of peace.

2. The State Parties to the present Covenant recognise that, with a view to achieving the full realisation of this right;
   (a) Primary education shall be compulsory and available free to all;
   (b) Secondary education in its different forms, including technical and vocational secondary education, shall be made generally available and accessible to all by every appropriate means, and in particular by the progressive introduction of free educations;
   (c) Higher education shall be make equally accessible to all, on the basis of capacity, by every appropriate means, and in particular by the progressive introduction of free educations;
   (d) Fundamental education shall be encouraged or intensified as far as possible for those persons who have not received or completed the whole period of their primary education;
   (e) The development of a system of schools at all levels shall be actively pursued, an adequate fellowship system shall be established, and the material conditions of teaching staff shall be continuously improved.
3. The State parties to the present Covenant undertake

to have respect for the liberty of parents and, when applicable, legal guardians to choose for their children schools, other than those established by the public authorities, which conform to such minimum educational standards as may be laid down or approved by the state and to ensure the religious and moral education of their children in conformity with their own convictions.

4. No part of this Article shall be construed so as to interfere with the liberty of individuals and bodies to establish and direct educational institutions, subject always to the observance of the principles set forth in paragraph 1 of this Article and to the requirement that the education given in such institutions shall conform to such minimum standards as may be laid down by the State.

Article 14

Each State Party to the present Covenant which, at the time of becoming a Party, has not been able to secure in its metropolitan territory or other territories under its jurisdiction compulsory primary education, free of charge, undertakes, within two years, to work out and adopt a detailed plan of action for the progressive implementation, within a reasonable number of years, to be fixed in the plan, of the principles of compulsory education free of charge for all.

Article 15

1. The State Parties to the present Covenant recognise the right of everyone:
    (a) To take part in cultural life.
    (b) To enjoy the benefits of scientific progress and its application;
    (c) To benefit from the protection of the moral and material interests resulting from any

scientific, literary or artistic production of which he is the author.

2. The steps to be taken by the State Parties to the present Covenant to achieve the full realisation of this right shall include those necessary for the conservation, the development and the diffusion of science and culture.
3. The State Parties to the present Covenant recognise the benefits to be derived from the encouragement and development of international contacts and co-operation in the scientific and cultural fields.
4. The State Parties to the present covenant recognise the benefits to be derived from the encouragement and development of international contacts and co-operation in the scientific and cultural fields.

PART IV

Article 16

1. The State Parties to the present Covenant undertake to submit in conformity with this part of the Covenant reports on the measures which they have adopted and the progress made in achieving the observance of the rights recognised herein.
2. (a) All reports shall be submitted to the Secretary-General of the United Nations, who shall transmit copies to the Economic and Social Council for consideration in accordance with the provisions of the present Covenant;

   (b) The Secretary-General of the United Nations shall also transmit to the specialised agencies copies of the reports, or any relevant parts therefrom, from State Parties to the present Covenant which are also members of these specialised agencies in so far as there reports, or parts therefrom, relate to any matters which fall within the responsibilities of the said agencies in accordance with their constitutional instruments.

Article 17

1. The State Parties to the present Covenant shall furnish their reports in stages, in accordance with a program to be established by the Economic and Social Council within one year of the entry into force of the present Covenant after consultation with the State Parties and the specialised agencies concerned.
2. Reports may indicate factors and difficulties affecting the degree of fulfilment of obligations under the present Covenant.
3. Where relevant information has previously been furnished to the United Nations or to any specialised agency by any state party to the present Covenant, it will not be necessary to reproduce that information so furnished will suffice.

Article 18

Pursuant to its responsibilities under the Charter of the United Nations in the field of human rights and fundamental freedoms, the Economic and Social Council may make arrangements with the specialised agencies in respect of their reporting to it on the progress made in achieving the observance of the provisions of the present Covenant falling within the scope of their activities. These reports may include particulars of decisions and recommendations on such implementation adopted by their competent organs,

Article 19

The Economic and Social Council may transmit to the Commission on Human Rights for study and and general recommendations or, as appropriate, for information the reports concerning human rights submitted by States in accordance with Articles 16 and 17, and those concerning human rights submitted by the specialised agencies in accordance with Article 18.

Article 20

The State Parties to the present Covenant and the specialised agencies concerned may submit comments to the Economic and Social Council on any general recommendation under Article 19 or reference to such general recommendation in any report of the Commission on Human Rights or any documentation referred to therein.

Article 21

The Economic and Social Council may submit from time to time to the General Assembly reports with recommendations of a general nature and a summary of the information received from the State Parties to the present Covenant and the specialised agencies on the measures taken and the progress made in achieving general observance of the recognised in the present Covenant.

Article 22

The Economic and Social Council may bring to the attention of other organs of the United Nations, their subsidiary organs and specialised agencies concerned with furnishing technical assistance any matters arising out of the reports referred to in this part of the present Covenant which may assist such bodies in deciding, each within its field of competence, on the advisability of international measures likely to contribute to the effective progressive implementation of the present Covenant.

Article 23

The State Parties to the present Covenant agree that international action for the achievement of the rights recognised in the present Covenant includes such methods as the conclusion of conventions, the adoption of recommendations, the furnishing of technical assistance and the holding of regional meetings and technical meetings for the purpose of consultation and study organised in conjunction with the Governments concerned.

Article 24

Nothing in the present Covenant shall be interpreted as impairing the provisions of the Charter of the United Nations and of the constitutions of the specialised agencies which define the respective responsibilities of the various organs of the United Nations, and of the specialised agencies in regard to the matters dealt with in the present Covenant.

Article 25

Nothing in the present Covenant shall be interpreted as impairing the inherent right of all peoples to enjoy and utilise fully and freely their natural wealth and resources.

PART V

Article 26

1. The present Covenant is open for signature by any state member of the United Nations or member of any of its specialised agencies, by any State party to the Statute of the International Court of Justice, and by any other State which has been invited by the General Assembly of the United Nations to become a party to the present covenant.
2. The present Covenant is subject to ratification. Instruments of ratification shall be deposited with the Secretary-General of the United Nations.
3. The present covenant shall be open to accession by any State referred to in paragraph 1 of this Article.
4. Accession shall be effected by the deposit of an instrument of accession with the Secretary-General of the United Nations.

5. The Secretary-General of the United Nations shall inform all states which have signed the present covenant or acceded to it of the deposit of each instrument of ratification or accession.

Article 27

1. The present Covenant shall enter into face three months after the date of the deposit with the Secretary General of the United Nations of the thirty-fifth instrument of ratification or instrument of accession.
2. For each State ratifying the present Covenant or acceding to it after the deposit of the thirty-fifth instrument of ratification or instrument of accession, the present Covenant shall enter into force three months after the date of the deposit of its own instrument of ratification or instrument or accession.

Article 28

The provisions of the present Covenant shall extend to all parts of federal States without any limitations or exceptions.

Article 29

1. Any State Party to the present Covenant may propose an amendment and file it with the Secretary-General of the United Nations. The Secretary-General shall thereupon communicate any proposed amendments to the State Parties to the present Covenant with a request that they notify him whether they favour a conference of State Parties for the purpose of considering and voting upon the proposals. In me event that at least one-third of the State Parties favors such a conference, the Secretary-General shall convene the conference under the auspices of the United Nations. Any amendment adopted by a majority of the State Parties present and voting at

the conference shall be submitted to the General Assembly of the United Nations for approval.

2. Amendments shall come into force when they have been approved by the General Assembly of the United Nations and accepted by a two-thirds majority of the State Parties to the present Covenant in accordance with their respective constitutional processes.
3. When amendments come into force they shall be binding on those State Parties which have accepted them, other State Parties still being bound by the provisions of the present Covenant and any earlier amendment which they have accepted.

Article 30

Irrespective of the notifications made under Article 26, paragraph 5. the Secretary-General of the United Nations shall inform all states referred to in paragraph 1 of the same Article of the following particulars:

(a) Signatures, ratifications and accessions under Article 26;

(b) The date of the entry into force of the present Covenant under Article 27 and the date of the entry into force of any amendments under Article 29.

Article 31

1. The present Covenant, of which the Chinese, English, French, Russian and Spanish texts are equally authentic, shall be deposited in the archives of the United Nations.
2. The Secretary-General of the United Nations shall transmit certified copies of the present Covenant to all States referred to in Article 26.

INTERNATIONAL COVENANT ON CIVIL AND POLITICAL RIGHTS

Adopted by the General Assembly of the Un in Res. 2200 (XXI) of 16 Dec, 1966 Entered into Force on 23 March 1976

Preamble

The States Parties to the Present Covenant,

Considering that, in accordance with the principles proclaimed in the Charter of the United Nations, recognition of the inherent dignity and of the equal and inalienable rights of all members of the human family is the foundation of freedom, justice and peace in the world;

Recognising that, these rights are derived from the inherent dignity of the human person;

Recognising that, in accordance with the Universal Declaration of Human Rights, the ideal of free human being, enjoying civil and political freedom and freedom from fear and want can only be achieved if conditions are created whereby, everyone may enjoy his civil and political rights, as well as his economic, social and cultural rights;

Considering the obligation of States under the Charter of the United Nations to promote universal respect for, and observance of, human rights and freedoms;

Realising that the individual, having duties to other individuals and to the community to which he belongs, is under a responsibility to strive for the promotion and observance of the rights recognised in the present Covenant;

Agree upon the following articles:

PART I

Article 1

1. All peoples have the right of self-determination. By virtue of that right they freely determine their political status and freely pursue their economic, social and cultural development.

2) All peoples may, for their own ends, freely dispose of their natural wealth and resources without prejudice to any obligations arising out of international economic co-operation, based upon the principle of mutual benefit, and international law. In no case may a people be deprived of its own means of subsistence.

3) The States Parties to the present Covenant, including those having responsibility for the administration of Non-Self-Governing and Trust Territories, shall promote the realisation of the right of self-determination, and shall respect that right, in conformity with the provisions of the Charter of the United Nations.

PART II

Article 2

1. Each State Party to the present Covenant undertakes to respect and to ensure to all individuals within its territory and subject to its jurisdiction the rights recognised in the present Covenant, without distinction of any kind, such as race, colour, sex, language, religion, political or other opinion, national or social origin, property, birth or other status.

2. Where, not already provided for by existing legislative or other measures, State Party to the present Covenant undertakes to take the necessary steps, in accordance with its constitutional processes and with the provisions of the present Covenant, to adopt such legislative or other measures as may be necessary to give effect to the rights recognised in the present Covenant.

3. Each State Party to the present Covenant undertakes:

(a) To ensure that any person whose rights or freedoms as herein recognised are violated shall have an effective remedy, notwithstanding, that the violation has been committed by persons acting in an official capacity;

(b) To ensure that any person claiming such a remedy shall have his right thereto determined by competent judicial, administrative or legislative authorities, or by any other competent authority provided for by the legal system of the State, and to develop the possibilities of judicial remedy;

(c) To ensure that the competent authorities shall enforce such remedies when granted.

Article 3

The States Parties to the present Covenant undertake to ensure the equal right of men and women to the enjoyment of all civil and political rights set forth in the present Covenant.

Article 4

1. In time of public emergency which threatens the life of the nation and the existence of which is officially proclaimed, the States Parties to the present Covenant may take measures derogating from their obligations under the present Covenant to the extent strictly required by the exigencies of the situation, provided that, such measures are not inconsistent with their other obligations under international law and do not involve discrimination solely on the ground of race, colour, sex, language, religion or social origin.

2. No derogation from articles 6, 7, 8 (paragraphs 1 and 2), 11, 15, 16 and 18 may be made under this provision.

3. Any State Party to the present Covenant availing itself of the right of derogation shall immediately inform the other States Parties to the present Covenant, through the intermediary of the Secretary-General of the United Nations, of the provisions from which it has derogated and of the reasons by which it was actuated. A further communication shall be made, through the same intermediary, on the date on which it terminates such derogation.

Article 5

1. Nothing in the present Covenant may be interpreted as implying, for any State, group or person any right to engage in any activity or perform any act aimed at the destruction of any of the rights and freedoms recognised herein or at their limitation to a greater extent than as provided for in the present Covenant.

2. There shall be no restriction upon or derogation from any of the fundamental human rights recognised or existing in any State Party to the present Covenant pursuant to law, conventions, regulations or custom on the pretext that the present Covenant does not recognise such rights or that it recognises them to a lesser extent.

PART III

Article 6

1. Every human being has the inherent right to life. The right shall be protected by law. No one shall be arbitrarily deprived of his life.

2. In countries which have not abolished the death penalty, sentence of death may be imposed only for the most serious crimes in accordance with the law in force at the time of the commission of the crime and not contrary to the provisions of the present Covenant and to the Convention on the Prevention and Punishment of the Crime of Genocide. This penalty can only be carried out pursuant to a final judgement rendered by a competent court.

3. When deprivation of life constitutes the crime of genocide, it is understood that nothing in this article shall authorise any State Party to the present Covenanted derogate in any way from any obligation assumed under the provisions of the Convention on the Prevention and Punishment of the Crime of Genocide.

4. Anyone sentenced to death shall have the right to seek pardon or commutation of the sentence. Amnesty,

pardon or commutation of the sentence of death may be granted in all cases.

5. Sentence of death shall not be imposed for crimes committed by persons below eighteen years of age and shall not be carried out on pregnant women.

6. Nothing in this article shall be invoked to delay or to prevent the abolition of capital punishment by any State Party to the present Covenant.

Article 7

No one shall be subjected to torture or to cruel, inhuman or degrading treatment or punishment. In particular, no one shall be subjected without his free consent to medical or scientific experimentation.

Article 8

1. No one shall be held in slavery; slavery and the slave-trade in all their forms shall be prohibited.

2. No one shall be held in servitude.

3. (a) No one shall be required to perform forced or compulsory labour;

(b) Paragraph 3 (a) shall not be held to preclude, in countries where imprisonment with hard labour may be imposed as a punishment for a crime, the performance of hard labour in pursuance of a sentence to such punishment by a competent court;

)c) For the purpose of this paragraph the term "forced or compulsory labour" shall not include:

(i) Any work or service, not referred to in sub-paragraph (b), normally required of a person who is under detention in consequence of a lawful order of a court, or of a person during conditional release from such detention;

(ii) Any service of a military character and, in countries where conscientious objection is recognised, any national service required by law of conscientious objectors;

(iii) Any service exacted in cases of emergency or calamity, threatening the life or well-being of the community;

(iv) Any work or service which forms part of normal civil obligations.

Article 9

1. Everyone has the right to liberty and security of person. No one shall be subjected to arbitrary arrest or detention. No one shall be deprived of his liberty except on such grounds and in accordance with such procedure as are established by law.

2. Anyone who is arrested shall be informed, at the time of arrest, of the reasons for his arrest and shall be promptly informed of the charges against him.

3. Anyone arrested or detained on a criminal charge shall be brought promptly before a judge or any other officer authorised by law to exercise judicial power and shall be entitled to trial within a reasonable time or to release. It shall not be a general rule that persons awaiting trial shall be detained in custody, but release may be subject to guarantees to appear for trial, at any stage of the judicial proceedings, and, should occasion arise, for execution of the judgement.

4. Anyone who is deprived of his liberty by arrest or detention shall be entitled to take proceedings before a court, in order that, the court may decide without delay on the lawfulness of his detention and order his release if the detention is not lawful.

5. Anyone who has been the victim of unlawful arrest or detention shall have an enforceable right to compensation.

Article 10

1. All persons deprived of their liberty shall be treated with humanity and with respect for the inherent dignity of the human person.

2. (a) Accused persons shall, save in exceptional circumstances, be segregated from convicted persons and shall be subject to separate treatment appropriate to their status as unconvicted persons;

(b) Accused juvenile persons shall be separated from adults and brought as speedily as possible for adjudication.

3. The penitentiary system shall comprise treatment of prisoners the essential aim of which shall be their reformation and social rehabilitation. Juvenile offenders shall be segregated from adults and be accorded treatment appropriate to their age and legal status.

Article 11

No one shall be imprisoned merely on the ground of inability to fulfil a contractual obligation.

Article 12

1. Everyone lawfully within the territory of a State shall, within that territory, have the right to liberty of movement and freedom to choose his residence.

2. Everyone shall be free to leave any country, including his own.

3. The above-mentioned rights shall not be subject to any restrictions except those which are provided by law, are necessary to protect national security, public order (*ordre* public), public health or morals or the rights and freedoms of others, and are consistent with the other rights recognised in the present Covenant.

4. No one shall be arbitrarily deprived of the right to enter his own country.

Article 13

An alien in the territory of a State Party to the present Covenant may be lawfully expelled therefrom only in pursuance of a decision reached in accordance with law and shall, except where compelling reasons of national security otherwise: require, be allowed to submit the reasons against his expulsion and to have his case reviewed by, and be represented for the purpose before, the competent authority or a person or persons especially designated by the competent authority.

Article 14

1. All persons shall be equal before the courts and tribunals. In the determination of any criminal charge against him or of his rights and obligations in a suit of law, everyone shall be entitled to a fair public hearing by a competent, independent and impartial tribunal established by law. The Press and the public may be excluded from all or part of a trial for reasons of morals, public order *(ordre* public) or national security in a democratic society, or, when the interest of the private lives of the parties so requires, or to the extent strictly necessary in the opinion of the court in special circumstances where publicity would prejudice the interests of a justice; but any judgement rendered in a criminal case or in a suit at law shall be made public except where the interest of juvenile persons otherwise requires or the proceedings concern matrimonial disputes or the guardianship of children.

2. Everyone charged with a criminal offence shall have the right to be presumed innocent until proved guilty according to law.

3. In the determination of any criminal charge against him, everyone shall be entitled to the following minimum guarantees, in full equality:

(a) To be informed promptly and in detail in a language

which he understands of the nature and cause of the charge against him;

(b) To have adequate time and facilities for the preparation of his defence and to communicate with a counsel of his own choosing;

(c) To be tried without undue delay;

(d) To be tried in his presence, and to defend himself in person or through legal assistance of his own choosing; to be informed, if he does not have legal assistance, of this right; and to have legal assistance assigned to him, in any case where the interests of justice so require, and without payment by him in any such case if he does not have sufficient means to pay for it;

(e) To examine, or have examined, the witnesses against him and to obtain the attendance and examination of witnesses on his behalf under the same conditions as witnesses against him;

(f) To have the free assistance of an interpreter, if he cannot understand or speak the language used in court;

(g) Not to be compelled to testify against himself or to confess guilt.

4. In the case of juvenile persons, the procedure shall be such as will take account of their age and the desirability of promoting their rehabilitation.

5. Everyone convicted of a crime shall have the right to his conviction and sentence being reviewed by a higher tribunal according to law.

6. When a person has by a final decision been convicted of a criminal offence and when subsequently his conviction has been reversed or he has been pardoned on the ground that a new or newly discovered fact shows conclusively that there has been a miscarriage of justice, the person who has

suffered punishment as a result of such conviction shall be compensated according to law, unless it is proved that the non-disclosure of the known fact in time is wholly or partly attributable to him.

7. No one shall be liable to be tried or punished again for an offence for which he has already been finally convicted or acquitted in accordance with the law and penal procedure of each country.

Article 15

1. No one shall be held guilty of any criminal offence on account of any act or omission which did not constitute a criminal offence, under national or international law, at the time when it was committed. Nor shall a heavier penalty be imposed than the one that was applicable at the time when the criminal offence was committed. If, subsequent to the commission of the offence, provision is made by law for the imposition of a lighter penalty, the offender shall benefit thereby.

2. Nothing in this article shall prejudice the trial and punishment of any person for any act or omission which, at the time when it was committed, was criminal according to the general principles of law recognised by the community of nations.

Article 16

Everyone shall have the right to recognition everywhere as a person before the law.

Article 17

1. No one shall be subjected to arbitrary or unlawful interference with his privacy, family, home or correspondence nor to unlawful attacks on his honour and reputation.

2. Everyone has the right to the protection of the jaw against such interference or attacks.

Article 18

1. Everyone shall have the right to freedom of thought, conscience and religion. This right shall include freedom to have or to adopt a religion or belief of his choice, and freedom, either individually or in community with others and in public or private, to manifest his religion or belief in worship, observance, practice and teaching.

2. No one shall be subject to coercion which would impair his freedom to have or to adopt a religion or belief of his choice.

3. Freedom to manifest one's religion or beliefs may be subject only to such limitations, as are prescribed by law, and are necessary to protect public safety, order, health or morals or the fundamental rights and freedoms of others.

4. The States Parties to the present Covenant undertake to have respect for the liberty of parents and, when applicable, legal guardians to ensure the religious and moral education of their children in conformity with their own convictions.

Article 19

1. Everyone shall have the right to hold opinions without interference.

2. Everyone shall have the right to freedom of expression; this right shall include freedom to seek, receive and impart information and ideas of all kinds, regardless of frontiers, either orally, in writing or in print, in the form of art, or through any other media of his choice.

3. The exercise of the rights provided for in paragraph 2 of this article carries with it special duties and responsibilities. It may therefore be subject to certain restrictions, but these shall only be such as are provided by law and are necessary:

(a) For respect of the rights or reputations of others;

(b) For the protection of national security or of public order (*ordre* public), or of public health or morals.

Article 20

1. Any propaganda for war shall be prohibited by law.

2. Any advocacy of national, racial or religious hatred that constitutes incitement to discrimination, hostility or violence shall be prohibited by law.

Article 21

The right of peaceful assembly shall be recognised. No restrictions may be placed on the exercise of this right other than those imposed in conformity with the law and, which are necessary in a democratic society in the interests of national security or public safety, public order *(ordre* public), the protection of public health or morals or the protection of rights and freedoms of others.

Article 22

1. Everyone shall have the right to freedom of association with others, including the right to form and join trade unions for the protection of his interests.

2. No restrictions may be placed on the exercise of this right other than those which are prescribed by law and which are necessary in a democratic society in the interests of national security or public safety, public order *(ordre* public), the protection of public health or morals or the protection of the rights and freedoms of others. This article shall not prevent the imposition of lawful restrictions on members of the armed forces and of the police in their exercise of this right.

3. Nothing in this article shall authorise States Parties to the International Labour Organisation Convention of 1948 concerning Freedom of Association and Protection of the Right to Organise to take legislative measure which

would prejudice, or apply the law in such a manner as to prejudice, the guarantees provided for in that Convention.

Article 23

1. The family is the natural and fundamental group-unit of society and is entitled to protection by society and the State.

2. The right of men and women of marriageable age to marry and to found a family shall be recognised.

3. No marriage shall be entered into, without the free and full consent of the intending spouses.

4. States Parties to the present Covenant shall take appropriate steps to ensure equality of rights and responsibilities of spouses as to marriage, during marriage and at its dissolution. In the case of dissolution, provision shall be made for the necessary protection of the children.

Article 24

1. Every child shall have, without any discrimination of race, colour, sex, language, religion, national or social origin, property or birth, the right to such measures of protection as are required by his status as a minor, on the part of his family, society and the State.

2. Every child shall be registered immediately after birth and shall have a name.

3. Every child has the right to acquire a nationality.

Article 25

Every citizen shall have the right and the opportunity, without any of the distinctions mentioned in article 2 and without unreasonable restrictions:

(a) To take part in the conduct of public affairs, directly or through freely chosen representatives;

(b) To vote and to be elected at genuine periodic elections which shall be by universal and equal suffrage and shall be held by secret ballot, guaranteeing the free expression of the will of the electors;

(c) To have access, on general terms of equality, to public service in his country.

Article 26

All persons are equal before the law and are entitled without any discrimination to the equal protection of the law. In this respect, the law shall prohibit any discrimination and, guarantee to all persons equal and effective protection against discrimination on any ground such as race, colour, sex, language, religion, political or other opinion, national or social origin, property, birth or other status.

Article 27

In those States in which ethnic, religious or linguistic minorities exist, persons belonging to such minorities shall not be denied the right, in community with the other members of their group, to enjoy their own culture, to profess and practice their own religion, or to use their own language.

PART IV

Article 28

1. There shall be established a Human Rights Committee (hereafter referred to in the present Covenant as the Committee). It shall consist of eighteen members and shall carry out the functions provided for hereinafter.

2. The Committee shall be composed of nationals of the States Parties to the present Covenant who shall be persons of high moral character and recognised competence in the field of human rights, consideration being given to the usefulness of the participation of some persons having legal experience.

3. The members of the Committee shall be elected and shall serve in their personal capacity.

Article 29

1. The members of the Committee shall be elected by secret ballot from a list of persons possessing the qualifications prescribed in article 28 and nominated for the purpose by the States Parties to the present Covenant.

2. Each State Party to the present Covenant may nominate not more than two persons. These persons shall be nationals of the nominating State.

3. A person shall be eligible for renomination.

Article 30

1. The initial election shall be held not later than six months after the date of the entry into force of the present Covenant.

2. At least four months before the date of each election to the Committee, other than an election to fill a vacancy declared in accordance with article 34, the Secretary-General of the United Nations shall address a written invitation to the States Parties to the present Covenant to submit their nominations for membership of the Committee within three months.

3. The Secretary-General of the United Nations shall prepare a list in alphabetical order of all the persons thus nominated with an indication of the States Parties which have nominated, them, and shall submit it to the States Parties to the present Covenant no later than one month before the date of each election.

4. Elections of the members of the Committee shall be held at a meeting of the States Parties to the present Covenant convened by the Secretary-General of the United Nations at the Headquarters of the United Nations. At that

meeting, for which two-third of the States Parties to the present Covenant shall constitute a quorum, the persons elected to the Committee shall be those nominees who obtain the largest number of votes and an absolute majority of the votes of the representatives of States Parties present and voting.

Article 31

1. The Committees may not include more than one national of the same State.

2. In the election of the Committee, consideration shall be given to equitable geographical distribution of membership and to the representation of the different forms of civilisation and of the principal legal systems.

Article 32

1. The members of the Committee shall be elected for a terra of four years. They shall be eligible for re-election if renominated. However, the terms of nine of the members elected at the first election shall expire at the end of two years; immediately after the first election, the names of these nine members shall be chosen by lot by the Chairman of the meeting referred to in article 30, paragraph 4.

2. Elections at the expiry of office shall be held in accordance with the preceding articles of this part of the present Covenant.

Article 33

1. If, in the unanimous opinion of the other members, a member of the Committee has ceased to carry out his functions for any cause other than absence of a temporary character, the Chairman of the Committee shall notify the Secretary-General of the United Nations, who shall then declare the seat of that member to be vacant.

2. In the event of the death or the resignation of a member of the Committee, the Chairman shall immediately

notify the Secretary-General of the United Nations, who shall declare the seat vacant from the date of death or the date on which the resignation takes effect.

Article 34

1. When a vacancy is declared in accordance with article 33 and if the term of office of the member to be replaced does not expire within six months of the declaration of the vacancy, the Secretary-General of the United Nations shall notify each of the States Parties to the present Covenant, which may within two months submit nominations in accordance with article 29 for the purpose of filling the vacancy.

2. The Secretary-General of the United Nations shall prepare a list in alphabetical order of the persons thus nominated and shall submit it to the States Parties to the present Covenant. The election to fill the vacancy shall then take place in accordance with the relevant provisions of this part of the present Covenant.

3. A member of the Committee elected to fill a vacancy declared in accordance with article 33 shall hold office for the remainder of the term of the member who vacated the seat on the Committee under the provisions of that article.

Article 35

The members of the Committee shall, with the approval of the General Assembly of the United Nations, receive emoluments from United Nations resources on such terms and conditions as the General Assembly may decide, having regard to the importance of the Committee's responsibilities.

Article 36

The Secretary-General of the United Nations shall provide the necessary staff and facilities for the effective performance, of the functions of the Committee under the present Covenant.

Article 37

1. The Secretary-General of the United Nations shall convene the initial meeting of the Committee at the Headquarters of the United Nations.

2. After its initial meeting, the Committee shall meet at such times as shall be provided in its rules of procedure.

3. The Committee shall normally meet at the Headquarters of the United Nations or at the United Nations office at Geneva.

Article 38

Every member of the Committee shall, before taking up his duties, make a solemn declaration in an open committee that he will perform his functions impartially and conscientiously.

Article 39

1. The Committee shall elect its officers for a term of two years. They may be re-elected.

2. The Committee shall establish its own rules of procedure, but these rule shall provide, inter alia, that:

(a) Twelve members shall constitute a quorum;
(b) Decisions of the Committee shall be made by a majority vote of the members present.

Article 40

1. The States Parties to the present Covenant undertake to submit reports on the measures they have adopted which give effect to the rights recognised herein and on the progress made in the enjoyment of those rights:

(a) Within one year of the entry into force of the present Covenant for the States Parties concerned;
(b) Thereafter, whenever the Committee so requests.

2. All reports shall be submitted to the Secretary-

General of United Nations, who shall transmit them to the Committee for consideration. Reports shall indicate the factors and difficulties, if any, affecting the implementation of the present Covenant.

3. The Secretary-General of the United Nations may, after consultation with the Committee, transmit to the specialised agencies concerned, copies of such parts of the reports as may fall within their field of competence.

4. The Committee shall study the reports submitted by the States Parties to the present Covenant. It shall transmit its reports, and such general comments as it may consider appropriate, to the States Parties. The Committee may also transmit to the Economic and Social Council these comments along with the copies of the reports it has received from States Parties to the present Covenant.

5. The States Parties to the present Covenant may submit to the Committee observations on any comments that may be made in accordance with paragraph 4 of this article.

Article 41

1. A State Party to the present Covenant may at anytime declare under this article that it recognises the competence of the Committee to receive and consider communications to the effect that a State Party claims that another State Party is not fulfilling its obligations under the present Covenant. Communications under this article may be received and considered only if submitted by a State Party which has made a declaration recognising in regard to itself the competence of the Committee. No communication shall be received by the Committee if it concerns a State Party which has not made such a declaration. Communications received under this article shall be dealt with in accordance with the following procedure:

(a) If a State Party to the present Covenant considers

that, another State Party is not giving effect to the provisions of the present Covenant, it may, by written communication, bring the matter to the attention of that State Party. Within three months after the receipt of the communication, the receiving State shall afford the State which sent the communication an explanation or any other statement in writing, clarifying the matter, which should include, to the extent possible and pertinent, reference to domestic procedures and remedies taken, pending, or available in the matter;

(b) If the matter is not adjusted to the satisfaction of both States Parties concerned within six months after the receipt by the receiving State of the initial communication, either State shall have the right to refer the matter to the Committee, by notice given to the Committee and the other State;

(c) The Committee shall deal with a matter referred to it only after it has ascertained that all available domestic remedies have been invoked and exhausted in the matter, in conformity with the generally recognised principles of international law. This shall not be the rule where the application of the remedies is unreasonably prolonged;

(d) The Committee shall hold closed meetings when examining communications under the article;

(e) Subject to the provisions of sub-paragraph (c), the Committee shall make available its good offices to the States Parties concerned with a view to a friendly solution of the matter on the basis of respect for human rights and fundamental freedoms as recognised in the present Covenant;

(f) In any matter referred to it, the Committee may call upon the States Parties concerned, referred to in sub-paragraph (b), to supply any relevant information;

(g) The States Parties concerned, referred to in sub-paragraph (b) shall have the right to be represented when the matter is being considered in the Committee and to make submissions orally and/or in writing;

(h) The Committee shall, within twelve months after the date of receipt of notice under sub-paragraph (b), submit a report:

(i) If a solution within the terms of sub-paragraph (e) is reached, the Committee shall confine its report to a brief statement of the facts and of the solution reached;

(ii) If a solution within the terms of sub-paragraph (e) is not reached, the Committee shall confine its report to a brief statement of the facts; the written submissions and record of the oral submissions made by the States Parties concerned shall be attached to the report. In every matter, the report shall be communicated to the States Parties concerned.

2. The provisions of this article shall come into force when ten States Parties to the present Covenant have made declarations under paragraph 1 of this article. Such declarations shall be deposited by the States Parties with the Secretary-General of the United Nations, who shall transmit copies thereof to the other States Parties. A declaration may be withdrawn at any time by notification to the Secretary-General. Such a withdrawal shall not prejudice the consideration of any matter which is the subject of a communication already transmitted under this article; no further communication by any State Party shall be received after the notification of withdrawal of the declaration has been received by the Secretary-General, unless the State Party concerned has made a new declaration.

Article 42

1. (a) If a matter referred to the Committee in accordance with article 41 is not resolved to the satisfaction of the States Parties concerned, the Committee may, with the prior consent of the States Parties concerned, appoint an ad hoc Conciliation Commission (hereinafter referred to as the Commission). The good offices of the Commission shall be made available to the States Parties concerned with a view to an amicable solution of the matter on the basis of respect for the present Covenant;

(b) The Commission shall consist of five persons, acceptable to the States Parties concerned. If the States Parties concerned fail to reach agreement within three months on all or part of the composition of the Commission, the member of the Commission concerning whom no agreement has been reached shall be elected by secret ballot by a two-thirds majority vote of the Committee from among its members.

2. The members of the Commission shall serve in their personal capacity. They shall not be nationals of the States Parties concerned, or of a State, not party to the present Covenant, or of State Party which has not made a declaration under article 41.

3. The Commission shall elect its own Chairman and adopt its own rules of procedure.

4. The meetings of the Commission shall normally be held at the Headquarters of the United Nations or at the United Nations Office at Geneva. However, they may be held at such other convenient places as the Commission may determine in consultation with the Secretary-General of the United Nations and the States Parties concerned.

5. The secretariat provided in accordance with article 36 shall also service the Commissions appointed under this article.

6. The information received and collated by the Committee shall be made available to the Commission and the Commission may call upon the States Parties concerned to supply any other relevant information.

7. When the Commission has fully considered the matter, but in any event not later than twelve months after having been seized of the matter, it shall submit to the Chairman of the Committee a report for communication to the States Parties concerned:

(a) If the Commission is unable to complete its consideration of the matter within twelve months, it shall confine its report to a brief statement of the status of its consideration of the matter;

(b) If an amicable solution to the matter on the basis of respect for human rights as recognised in the present Covenant is reached, the Commission shall confine its report to a brief statement of the facts and of the solution reached;

(c) If a solution within the terms of sub-paragraph (b) is not reached, the Commission's report shall embody its findings on all questions of fact relevant to the issues between the States Parties concerned, and its views on the possibilities of an amicable solution of the matter. This report shall also contain the written submissions and a record of the oral submissions made by the States Parties concerned;

(d) If the Commission's report is submitted under sub-paragraph (c), the State Parties concerned shall, within three months of the receipt of the report, notify the Chairman of the Committee whether or not they accept the contents of the report of the Commission.

8. The provisions of this article are without prejudice to the responsibilities of the Committee under article 41.

9. The States Parties concerned shall share equally all the expenses of the members of the Commission in accordance with estimates to be provided by the Secretary-General of the United Nations.

10. The Secretary-General of the United Nations shall be empowered to pay the expenses of the members of the Commission, if necessary, before reimbursement by the States Parties concerned, in accordance with paragraph 9 of this article.

Article 43

The members of the Committee, and of the ad hoc Conciliation Commissions which may be appointed under article 42, shall be entitled to the facilities, privileges and immunities of experts on mission for the United Nations as laid down in the relevant sections of the Convention on the Privileges and Immunities of the United Nations.

Article 44

The provisions for the implementation of the present Covenant shall apply without prejudice to the procedures prescribed in the field of human rights by, or under the constituent instruments and the conventions of the United Nations and of the specialised agencies, and shall not prevent the States Parties to the present Covenant from having recourse to other procedures for settling a dispute, in accordance with general or special international agreements in force between them.

Article 45

The Committee shall submit to the General Assembly of the United Nations, through the Economic and Social Council, an annual report on its activities.

PART V

Article 46

Nothing in the present Covenant shall be interpreted as impairing the provisions of the Charter of the United Nations and of the constitutions of the specialised agencies which define the respective responsibilities of the various organs of the United Nations and of the specialised agencies in regard to the matters dealt within the present Covenant.

Article 47

Nothing in the present Covenant shall be interpreted as impairing the inherent right of all peoples to enjoy and utilise fully and freely their natural wealth and resources.

PART VI

Article 48

1. The present Covenant is open for signature by any State Member of the United Nations or member of any of its specialised agencies, by any State Party to the Statute of the International Court of Justice, and, by any other State which has been invited by the General Assembly of the United Nations to become a party to the present Covenant.

2. The present Covenant is subject to ratification. Instruments of ratification shall be deposited with the Secretary-General of the United Nations.

3. The present Covenant shall be open to accession by any State referred to in paragraph 1 of this article.

4. Accession shall be effected by the deposit of an instrument of accession with the Secretary-General of the United Nations.

5. The Secretary-General of the United Nations shall inform all States which have signed this Covenant or acceded to it, of the deposit of each instrument of ratification or accession.

Article 49

1. The present Covenant shall enter into force three months after the date of the deposit with the Secretary-General of the United Nations of the thirty-fifth instrument of ratification or instrument of accession.

2. For each State ratifying the present Covenant or acceding to it after the deposit of the thirty-fifth instrument of ratification or instrument of accession, the present Covenant shall enter into force three months after the date of the deposit of its own instrument of ratification or instrument of accession.

Article 50

The provisions of the present Covenant shall extend to all parts of Federal States without any limitations or exceptions.

Article 51

1. Any State Party to the present Covenant may propose an amendment and file it with the Secretary-General of the United Nations. The Secretary-General of the United Nations shall thereupon communicate any proposed amendments to the States Parties to the present Covenant with a request that they notify him whether they favour a conference of States Parties for the purpose of considering and voting upon the proposals. In the event that at least one-third of the States Parties favours such a conference, the Secretary-General shall convene the conference under the auspices of the United Nations. Any amendment adopted by a majority of the States Parties present and voting at the conference shall be submitted to the General Assembly of the United Nations for approval.

2. Amendments shall come into force when they have been approved by the General Assembly of the United Nations and accepted by a two-thirds majority of the States Parties to the present Covenant in accordance with their respective constitutional processes.

3. When amendments come into force, they shall be binding on those States Parties which have accepted them, other States Parties still being bound by the provisions of the present Covenant and any earlier amendment which they have accepted.

Article 52

Irrespective of the notifications made under article 48 paragraph 5, the Secretary-General of the United Nations shall inform all States referred to in paragraph 1 of the same article of the following particulars:

(a) Signature, ratifications and accessions under article 48;

(b) The date of the entry into force of the present Cover under article 49 and the date of the entry into force of a, amendments under article 51.

Article 53

1. The present Covenant, of which the Chinese, English, French, Russian and Spanish texts are equally authentic, shall be deposited in the archives of the United Nations.

2. The Secretary-General of the United Nations shall transmit certified copies of the present Covenant to all States referred to in article 48.

CONVENTION ON THE NON-APPLICABILITY OF STATUTORY LIMITATIONS TO WAR CRIMES AND CRIMES AGAINST HUMANITY

Adapted and Opened for Signature, Ratification and Accession by General Assembly resolution 2391 (XXIII) of 26 November 1968

Entry Into Force: 11 November 1970, in Accordance with Article VIII

PREAMBLE

States Parties to the Present Convention

Recalling resolutions of the General Assembly of the United Nations 3 (I) of 13 February 1946 and 170 (II) of 31 October 1947 on the extradition and punishment of war criminals, resolution 95 (I) of 11 December 1946 affirming the principles of international law recognised by the Charter of the International Military Tribunal, Nurnberg, and the judgement of the Tribunal, and resolutions 2184 (XXI) of 12 December 1966 and 2202 (XXI) of 16 December 1966 which expressly condemned as crimes against humanity the violation of the economic and political rights of the indigenous population on the one hand and the policies of *apartheid* on the other,

Recalling resolutions of the Economic and Social Council of the United Nations 1074 D (XXXIX) of 28 July 1965 and 1158 (XLI) of 5 August 1966 on the punishment of war criminals and of persons who have committed crimes against humanity,

Noting that none of the solemn declarations, instruments or conventions relating to the prosecution and punishment of war crimes and crimes against humanity made provision for a period of limitation,

Considering that war crimes and crimes against humanity are among the gravest crimes in international law,

Convinced that the effective punishment of war crimes and crimes against humanity is an important element in the prevention of such crimes, the protection of human rights and fundamental freedoms, the encouragement of confidence, the furtherance of co-operation among peoples and the promotion of international peace and security,

Noting that the application to war crimes and crimes against humanity of the rules of municipal law relating to the period of limitation for ordinary crimes is a matter of serious concern to world public opinion, since it prevents the prosecution and punishment of persons responsible fc those crimes,

Recognising that it is necessary and timely to affirm in international law, through this Convention, the principle that there is no period of limitation for war crimes and crimes against humanity, and to secure its universal application,

Have agreed as follows:

Article I

No statutory limitation shall apply to the following crimes, irrespective of the date of their commission:

(a) War crimes as they are defined in the Charter of the International Military Tribunal, Nurnberg, of 8 August 1945 and confirmed by resolutions 3 (I) of 13 February 1946 and 95 (I) of 11 December 1946 of the General Assembly of the United Nations, particularly the "grave breaches" enumerated in the Geneva Conventions of 12 August 1949 for the protection of war victims;

(b) Crimes against humanity whether committed in time of war or in time of peace as they are defined in the Charter of the International Military Tribunal, Nurnberg, of 8 August 1945 and confirmed by resolutions 3 (I) of 13 February 1946 and 95 (I) of

11 December 1946 of the General Assembly of the United Nations, eviction by armed attack or occupation and inhuman acts resulting from the policy of *apartheid,* and the crime of genocide as defined in the 1948 Convention on the Prevention and Punishment of the Crime of Genocide, even if such acts do not constitute a violation of the domestic law of the country in which they were committed.

Article II

If any of the crimes mentioned in article I is committed, the provisions of this Convention shall apply to representatives of the State authority and private individuals who, as principals or accomplices, participate in or who directly incite others to the commission of any of those crimes, or who conspire to commit them, irrespective of the degree of completion, and to representatives of the State authority who tolerate their commission.

Article III

The States Parties to the present Convention undertake to adopt all necessary domestic measures, legislative or otherwise, with a view to making possible the extradition, in accordance with international law, of the persons referred to in article II of this Convention.

Article IV

The States Parties to the present Convention undertake to adopt, in accordance with their respective constitutional processes, any legislative or other measures necessary to ensure that statutory or other limitations shall not apply to the prosecution and punishment of the crimes referred to in articles I and II of this Convention and that, where they exist, such limitations shall be abolished.

Article V

This Convention shall, until 31 December 1969, be open for signature by any State Member of the United

Nations or member of any of its specialised agencies or of the International Atomic Energy Agency, by any State Party to the Statute of the International Court of Justice, and by any other State which has been invited by the General Assembly of the United Nations to become a Party to this Convention.

Article VI

This Convention is subject to ratification. Instruments of ratification shall be deposited with the Secretary-General of the United Nations.

Article VII

This Convention shall be open to accession by any State referred to in article V. Instruments of accession shall be deposited with the Secretary-General of the United Nations.

Article VIII

1. This Convention shall enter into force on the ninetieth day after the date of the deposit with the Secretary-General of the United Nations of the tenth instrument of ratification or accession.

2. For each State ratifying this Convention or acceding to it after the deposit of the tenth instrument of ratification or accession, the Convention shall enter into force on the ninetieth day after the date of the deposit of its own instrument of ratification or accession.

Article IX

1. After the expiry of a period of ten years from the date on which this Convention enters into force, a request for the revision of the Convention may be made at any time by any Contracting Party by means of a notification in writing addressed to the Secretary-General of the United Nations.

2. The General Assembly of the United Nations shall

decide upon the steps, if any, to be taken in respect of such a request.

Article X

1. This Convention shall be deposited with the Secretary-General of the United Nations.

2. The Secretary-General of the United Nations shall transmit certified copies of this Convention to all States referred to in article V.

3. The Secretary-General of the United Nations shall inform all States referred to in article V of the following particulars:

(a) Signatures of this Convention, and instruments of ratification and accession deposited under articles V, VI and VII;
(b) The date of entry into force of this Convention in accordance with article VIII;
(c) Communications received under article IX.

Article XI

This Convention, of which the Chinese, English, French, Russian and Spanish texts are equally authentic, shall bear the date of 26 November 1968.

In Witness Whereof the undersigned, being duly authorised for that purpose, have signed this Convention.

INTERNATIONAL CONVENTION ON THE SUPPRESSION AND PUNISHMENT OF THE CRIME OF APARTHEID

Adopted and Opened for Signature and Ratification by General Assembly resolution 3068 (XXVIII) of 30 November 1973

Entry Into Force: 18 July 1976, in Accordance with Article XV

The States Parties to the Present Convention

Recalling the provisions of the Charter of the United Nations, in which all Members pledged themselves to take joint and separate action in cooperation with the Organisation for the achievement of universal respect for, and observance of, human rights and fundamental freedoms for all without distinction as to race, sex, language or religion,

Considering the Universal Declaration of Human Rights, which states that all human beings are born free and equal in dignity and rights and that everyone is entitled to all the rights and freedoms set forth in the Declaration, without distinction of any kind, such as race, colour or national origin,

Considering the Declaration on the Granting of Independence to Colonial Countries and Peoples, in which the General Assembly stated that the process of liberation is irresistible and irreversible and that, in the interests of human dignity, progress and justice, an end must be put to colonialism and all practices of segregation and discrimination associated therewith,

Observing that, in accordance with the International Convention on the Elimination of All Forms of Racial Discrimination, States particularly condemn racial segregation and *apartheid* and undertake to prevent, prohibit and eradicate all practices of this nature in territories under their jurisdiction,

Observing that, in the Convention on the Prevention and Punishment of the Crime of Genocide, certain acts which may also be qualified as acts of *apartheid* constitute a crime under international law,

Observing that, in the Convention on the Non-Applicability of Statutory Limitations to War Crimes and Crimes against Humanity, "inhuman acts resulting from the policy of *apartheid*" are qualified as crimes against humanity,

Observing that the General Assembly of the United Nations has adopted a number of resolutions in which the policies and practices of *apartheid* are condemned as a crime against humanity,

Observing that the Security Council has emphasised that *apartheid* and its continued intensification and expansion seriously disturb and threaten international peace and security,

Convinced that an International Convention on the Suppression and Punishment of the Crime of *apartheid* would make it possible to take more effective measures at the international and national levels with a view to the suppression and punishment of the crime of *apartheid,*

Have agreed as follows:

Article I

1. The States Parties to the present Convention declare that *apartheid is* a crime against humanity and that inhuman acts resulting from the policies and practices of *apartheid* and similar policies and practices of racial segregation and discrimination, as defined in article II of the Convention, are crimes violating the principles of international law, in particular the purposes and principles of the Charter of the United Nations, and constituting a serious threat to international peace and security.

2. The States Parties to the present Convention declare criminal those organisations, institutions and individuals committing the crime of *apartheid.*

Article II

For the purpose of the present Convention, the term "the crime of *apartheid*", which shall include similar policies and practices of racial segregation and discrimination as practised in southern Africa, shall apply to the following inhuman acts committed for the purpose of establishing and maintaining domination by one racial group of persons over any other racial group of persons and systematically oppressing them:

(a) Denial to a member or members of a racial group or groups of the right to life and liberty of person:

(i) By murder of members of a racial group or groups;

(ii) By the infliction upon the members of a racial group or groups of serious bodily or mental harm, by the infringement of their freedom or dignity, or by subjecting them to torture or to cruel, inhuman or degrading treatment or punishment;

(iii) By arbitrary arrest and illegal imprisonment of the members of a racial group or groups;

(b) Deliberate imposition on a racial group or groups of living conditions calculated to cause its or their physical destruction in whole or in part;

(c) Any legislative measures and other measures calculated to prevent a racial group or groups from participation in the political, social, economic and cultural life of the country and the deliberate creation of conditions preventing the full development of such a group or groups, in particular by denying to members of a racial group or groups basic human rights and freedoms, including the right to work, the right to form recognised trade unions, the right to education, the right to leave and to return to their country, the right to a nationality, the right to freedom of movement and residence, the right to freedom of opinion and expression, and the right to freedom of peaceful assembly and association;

(d) Any measures, including legislative measures, designed to divide the population along racial lines by the creation of separate reserves and ghettos for the members of a racial group or groups, the prohibition of mixed marriages among members of various racial groups, the expropriation of landed property belonging to a racial group or groups or to members thereof;

(e) Exploitation of the labour of the members of a racial group or groups, in particular by submitting them to forced labour;

(f) Persecution of organisations and persons, by depriving them of fundamental rights and freedoms, because they oppose *apartheid.*

Article III

International criminal responsibility shall apply, irrespective of the motive involved, to individuals, members of organisations and institutions and representatives of the State, whether residing in the territory of the State in which the acts are perpetrated or in some other State, whenever they:

(a) Commit, participate in, directly incite or conspire in the commission of the acts mentioned in article II of the present Convention;

(b) Directly abet, encourage or co-operate in the commission of the crime of *apartheid.*

Article IV

The States Parties to the present Convention undertake:

(a) To adopt any legislative or other measures necessary

to suppress as well as to prevent any encouragement of the crime of *apartheid* and similar segregationist policies or their manifestations and to punish persons guilty of that crime;

(b) To adopt legislative, judicial and administrative measures to prosecute, bring to trial and punish in accordance with their jurisdiction persons responsible for, or accused of, the acts defined in article II of the present Convention, whether or not such persons reside in the territory of the State in which the acts are committed or are nationals of that State or of some other State or are stateless persons.

Article V

Persons charged with the acts enumerated in article II of the present Convention may be tried by a competent tribunal of any State Party to the Convention which may acquire jurisdiction over the person of the accused or by an international penal tribunal having jurisdiction with respect to those States Parties which shall have accepted its jurisdiction.

Article VI

The States Parties to the present Convention undertake to accept and carry out in accordance with the Charter of the United Nations the decisions taken by the Security Council aimed at the prevention, suppression and punishment of the crime of *apartheid,* and to co-operate in the implementation of decisions adopted by other competent organs of the United Nations with a view to achieving the purposes of the Convention.

Article VII

1. The States Parties to the present Convention undertake to submit periodic reports to the group established under article IX on the legislative, judicial, administrative or other measures that they have adopted and that give effect to the provisions of the Convention.

2. Copies of the reports shall be transmitted through the Secretary-General of the United Nations to the Special Committee on *apartheid.*

Article VIII

Any State Party to the present Convention may call upon any competent organ of the United Nations to take such action under the Charter of the United Nations as it considers appropriate for the prevention and suppression of the crime of *apartheid.*

Article IX

1. The Chairman of the Commission on Human Rights shall appoint a group consisting of three members of the Commission on Human Rights, who are also representatives of States Parties to the present Convention, to consider reports submitted by States Parties in accordance with article VII.

2. If, among the members of the Commission on Human Rights, there are no representatives of States Parties to the present Convention or if there are fewer than three such representatives, the Secretary-General of the United Nations shall, after consulting all States Parties to the Convention, designate a representative of the State Party or representatives of the States Parties which are not members of the Commission on Human Rights to take part in the work of the group established in accordance with paragraph 1 of this article, until such time as representatives of the States Parties to the Convention are elected to the Commission on Human Rights.

3. The group may meet for a period of not more than five days, either before the opening or after the closing of the session of the Commission on Human Rights, to consider the reports submitted in accordance with article VII.

Article X

1. The States Parties to the present Convention empower

the Commission on Human Rights:

(a) To request United Nations organs, when transmitting copies of petitions under article 15 of the International Convention on the Elimination of All Forms of Racial Discrimination, to draw its attention to complaints concerning acts which are enumerated in article II of the present Convention;

(b) To prepare, on the basis of reports from competent organs of the United Nations and periodic reports from States Parties to the present Convention, a list of individuals, organisations, institutions and representatives of States which are alleged to be responsible for the crimes enumerated in article II of the Convention, as well as those against whom legal proceedings have been undertaken by States Parties to the Convention;

(c) To request information from the competent United Nations organs concerning measures taken by the authorities responsible for the administration of Trust and Non-Self-Governing Territories, and all other Territories to which General Assembly resolution 1514 (XV) of 14 December 1960 applies, with regard to such individuals alleged to be responsible for crimes under article II of the Convention who are believed to be under their territorial and administrative jurisdiction.

2. Pending the achievement of the objectives of the Declaration on the Granting of Independence to Colonial Countries and Peoples, contained in General Assembly resolution 1514 (XV), the provisions of the present Convention shall in no way limit the right of petition granted to those peoples by other international instruments or by the United Nations and its specialised agencies.

Article XI

1. Acts enumerated in article II of the present Convention

shall not be considered political crimes for the purpose of extradition.

2. The States Parties to the present Convention undertake in such cases to grant extradition in accordance with their legislation and with the treaties in force.

Article XII

Disputes between States Parties arising out of the interpretation, application or implementation of the present Convention which have not been settled by negotiation shall, at the request of the States parties to the dispute, be brought before the International Court of Justice, save where the parties to the dispute have agreed on some other form of settlement.

Article XIII

The present Convention is open for signature by all States. Any State which does not sign the Convention before its entry into force may accede to it.

Article XIV

1. The present Convention is subject to ratification. Instruments of ratification shall be deposited with the Secretary-General of the United Nations.

2. Accession shall be effected by the deposit of an instrument of accession with the Secretary-General of the United Nations.

Article XV

1. The present Convention shall enter into force on the thirtieth day after the date of the deposit with the Secretary-General of the United Nations of the twentieth instrument of ratification or accession.

2. For each State ratifying the present Convention or acceding to it after the deposit of the twentieth instrument of ratification or instrument of accession, the Convention

shall enter into force on the thirtieth day after the date of the deposit of its own instrument of ratification or instrument of accession.

Article XVI

A State Party may denounce the present Convention by written notification to the Secretary-General of the United Nations. Denunciation shall take effect one year after the date of receipt of the notification by the Secretary-General.

Article XVII

1. A request for the revision of the present Convention may be made at any time by any State Party by means of a notification in writing addressed to the Secretary-General of the United Nations.

2. The General Assembly of the United Nations shall decide upon the steps, if any, to be taken in respect of such request.

Article XVIII

The Secretary-General of the United Nations shall inform all States of the following particulars:

(a) Signatures, ratifications and accessions under articles XIII and XIV;

(b) The date of entry into force of the present Convention under article XV;

(c) Denunciations under article XVI;

(d) Notifications under article XVII.

Article XIX

1. The present Convention, of which the Chinese, English, French, Russian and Spanish texts are equally authentic, shall be deposited in the archives of the United Nations.

2. The Secretary-General of the United Nations shall transmit certified copies of the present Convention to all States.

SLAVERY CONVENTION

Signed at Geneva on 25 September 1926

Entry into force: 9 March 1927, in accordance with article 12. The Convention was amended by the Protocol done at the Headquarters of the United Nations, New York, on 7 December 1953; the amended Convention entered into force on 7 July 1955, the date on which the amendments, set forth in the annex to the Protocol of 7 December 1953, entered into force in accordance with article III of the Protocol.

Whereas the signatories of the General Act of the Brussels Conference of 1889-90 declared that they were equally animated by the firm intention of putting an end to the traffic in African slaves,

Whereas the signatories of the Convention of Saint-Germain-en-Laye of 1919, to revise the General Act of Berlin of 1885 and the General Act and Declaration of Brussels of 1890, affirmed their intention of securing the complete suppression of slavery in all its forms and of the slave trade by land and sea,

Taking into consideration the report of the Temporary Slavery Commission appointed by the Council of the League of Nations on June 12th, 1924,

Desiring to complete and extend the work accomplished under the Brussels Act and to find a means of giving practical effect throughout the world to such intentions as were expressed in regard to slave trade and slavery by the signatories of the Convention of Saint-Germain-en-Laye, and recognising that it is necessary to conclude to that end more detailed arrangements than are contained in that Convention,

Considering, moreover, that it is necessary to prevent forced labour from developing into conditions analogous to slavery,

Have decided to conclude a Convention and have accordingly appointed as their Plenipotentiaries [*names omitted*]

... *have agreed* as follows:

Article 1

For the purpose of the present Convention, the following definitions are agreed upon:

(1) Slavery is the status or condition of a person over whom any or all of the powers attaching to the right of ownership are exercised.

(2) The slave trade includes all acts involved in the capture, acquisition or disposal of a person with intent to reduce him to slavery; all acts involved in the acquisition of a slave with a view to selling or exchanging him; all acts of disposal by sale or exchange of a slave acquired with a view to being sold or exchanged, and, in general, every act of trade or transport in slaves.

Article 2

The High Contracting Parties undertake, each in respect of the territories placed under its sovereignty, jurisdiction, protection, suzerainty or tutelage, so far as they have not already taken the necessary steps:

(a) To prevent and suppress the slave trade;

(b) To bring about, progressively and as soon as possible, the complete abolition of slavery in all its forms.

Article 3

The High Contracting Parties undertake to adopt all appropriate measures with a view to preventing and suppressing the embarkation, disembarkation and transport of slaves in their territorial waters and upon all vessels flying their respective flags.

The High Contracting Parties undertake to negotiate as soon as possible a general Convention with regard to the slave trade which will give them rights and impose upon them duties of the same nature as those provided for in the Convention of June 17th, 1925, relative to the International Trade in Anns (Articles 12, 20, 21, 22, 23, 24 and paragraphs 3, 4 and 5 of Section II of Annex II), with the necessary adaptations, it being understood that this general Convention will not place the ships (even of small tonnage) of any High Contracting Parties in a position different from that of the other High Contracting Parties.

It is also understood that, before or after the coming into force of this general Convention, the High Contracting Parties are entirely free to conclude between themselves, without, however, derogating from the principles laid down in the preceding paragraph, such special agreements as, by reason of their peculiar situation, might appear to be suitable in order to bring about as soon as possible the complete disappearance of the slave trade.

Article 4

The High Contracting Parties shall give to one another every assistance with the object of securing the abolition of slavery and the slave trade.

Article 5

The High Contracting Parties recognise that recourse to compulsory or forced labour may have grave consequences and undertake, each in respect of the territories placed under its sovereignty, jurisdiction, protection, suzerainty or tutelage, to take all necessary measures to prevent compulsory or forced labour from developing into conditions analogous to slavery.

It is agreed that:

(1) Subject to the transitional provisions laid down in

paragraph (2) below, compulsory or forced labour may only be exacted for public purposes.

(2) In territories in which compulsory or forced labour for other than public purposes still survives, the High Contracting Parties shall endeavour progressively and as soon as possible to put an end to the practice. So long as such forced or compulsory labour exists, this labour shall invariably be of an exceptional character, shall always receive adequate remuneration, and shall not involve the removal of the labourers from their usual place of residence.

(3) In all cases, the responsibility for any recourse to compulsory or forced labour shall rest with the competent central authorities of the territory concerned.

Article 6

Those of the High Contracting Parties whose laws do not at present make adequate provision for the punishment of infractions of laws and regulations enacted with a view to giving effect to the purposes of the present Convention undertake to adopt the necessary measures in order that severe penalties may be imposed in respect of such infractions.

Article 7

The High Contracting Parties undertake to communicate to each other and to the Secretary-General of the League of Nations any laws and regulations which they may enact with a view to the application of the provisions of the present Convention.

Article 8

The High Contracting Parties agree that disputes arising between them relating to the interpretation or application of this Convention shall, if they cannot be settled by direct negotiation, be referred for decision to the Permanent Court of International Justice. In case either or both of the States Parties to such a dispute should not be Parties to the Protocol of December 16th, 1920, relating to the Permanent Court of International Justice, the dispute shall be referred, at the choice of the Parties and in accordance with the constitutional procedure of each State, either to the Permanent Court of International Justice or to a court of arbitration constituted in accordance with the Convention of October 18th, 1907, for the Pacific Settlement of International Disputes, or to some other court of arbitration.

Article 9

At the time of signature or of ratification or of accession, any High Contracting Party may declare that its acceptance of the present Convention does not bind some or all of the territories placed under its sovereignty, jurisdiction, protection, suzerainty or tutelage in respect of all or any provisions of the Convention; it may subsequently accede separately on behalf of any one of them or in respect of any provision to which any one of them is not a Party.

Article 10

In the event of a High Contracting Party wishing to denounce the present Convention, the denunciation shall be notified in writing to the Secretary-General of the League of Nations, who will at once communicate a certified true copy of the notification to all the other High Contracting Parties, informing them of the date on which it was received.

The denunciation shall only have effect in regard to the notifying State, and one year after the notification has reached the Secretary-General of the League of Nations.

Denunciation may, also be made separately in respect of any territory placed under its sovereignty, jurisdiction, protection, suzerainty or tutelage.

Article 11

The present Convention, which will bear this day's date and of which the French and English texts are both authentic, will remain open for signature by the States Members of the League of Nations until April 1st, 1927.

The Secretary-General of the League of Nations will subsequently bring the present Convention to the notice of States which have not signed it, including States which are not Members of the League of Nations, and invite them to accede thereto. A State desiring to accede to the Convention shall notify its intention in writing to the Secretary-General of the League of Nations and transmit to him the instrument of accession, which shall be deposited in the archives of the League.

The Secretary-General shall immediately transmit to all the other High Contracting Parties a certified true copy of the notification and of the instrument of accession, informing them of the date on which he received them.

Article 12

The present Convention will be ratified and the instruments of ratification shall be deposited in the office of the Secretary-General of the League of Nations. The Secretary-General will inform all the High Contracting Parties of such deposit.

The Convention will come into operation for each State on the date of the deposit of its ratification or of its accession.

In Faith Whereof the Plenipotentiaries signed the present Convention.

Done at Geneva the twenty-fifth day of September, one thousand nine hundred and twenty-six, in one copy, which will be deposited in the archives of the League of Nations. A certified copy shall be forwarded to each signatory State.

SUPPLEMENTARY CONVENTION ON THE ABOLITION OF SLAVERY, THE SLAVE TRADE, AND INSTITUTIONS AND PRACTICES SIMILAR TO SLAVERY

Adopted by a Conference of Plenipotentiaries convened by Economic and Social Council resolution 608 (XXI) of 30 April 1956 and done at Genera on 7 September 1956

Entry Into Force: 30 April 1957, in Accordance with Article 13

Preamble

The States Parties to the Present Convention,

Considering that freedom is the birthright of every human being,

Mindful that the peoples of the United Nations reaffirmed in the Charter their faith in the dignity and worth of the human person,

Considering that the Universal Declaration of Human Rights, proclaimed by the General Assembly of the United Nations as a common standard of achievement for all peoples and all nations, states that no one shall be held in slavery or servitude and that slavery and the slave trade shall be prohibited in all their forms,

Recognising that, since the conclusion of the Slavery Convention signed at Geneva on 25 September 1926, which was designed to secure the abolition of slavery and of the slave trade, further progress has been made towards this end,

Having regard to the Forced Labour Convention of 1930 and to subsequent action by the International Labour Organisation in regard to forced or compulsory labour,

Being aware, however, that slavery, the slave trade

and institutions and practices similar to slavery have not yet been eliminated in all parts of the world,

Having decided, therefore, that the Convention of 1926, which remains operative, should now be augmented by the conclusion of a supplementary convention designed to intensify national as well as international efforts towards the abolition of slavery, the slave trade and institutions and practices similar to slavery,

Have agreed as follows:

SECTION I. - INSTITUTIONS AND PRACTICES SIMILAR TO SLAVERY

Article 1

Each of the States Parties to this Convention shall take all practicable and necessary legislative and other measures to bring about progressively and as soon as possible the complete abolition or abandonment of the following institutions and practices, where they still exist and whether or not they are covered by the definition of slavery contained in article 1 of the Slavery Convention signed at Geneva on 25 September 1926:

(a) Debt bondage, that is to say, the status or condition arising from a pledge by a debtor of his personal services or of those of a person under his control as security for a debt, if the value of those services as reasonably assessed is not applied towards the liquidation of the debt or the length and nature of those services are not respectively limited and defined;

(b) Serfdom, that is to say, the condition or status of a tenant who is by law, custom or agreement bound to live and labour on land belonging to another person and to render some determinate service to such other person, whether for reward or not, and is not free to change his status;

(c) Any institution or practice whereby:

(i) A woman, without the right to refuse, is promised or given in marriage on payment of a consideration in money or in kind to her parents, guardian, family or any other person or group; or

(ii) The husband of a woman, his family, or his clan, has the right to transfer her to another person for value received or otherwise; or

(iii) A woman on the death of her husband is liable to be inherited by another person;

(d) Any institution or practice whereby a child or young person under the age of 18 years, is delivered by either or both of his natural parents or by his guardian to another person, whether for reward or hot, with a view to the exploitation of the child or young person or of his labour.

Article 2

With a view to bringing to an end the institutions and practices mentioned in article 1 (c) of this Convention, the States Parties undertake to prescribe, where appropriate, suitable minimum ages of marriage, to encourage the use of facilities whereby the consent of both parties to a marriage may be freely expressed in the presence of a competent civil or religious authority, and to encourage the registration of marriages.

SECTION II. - THE SLAVE TRADE

Article 3

1. The act of conveying or attempting to convey slaves from one country to another by whatever means of transport, or of being accessory thereto, shall be a criminal offence under the laws of the States Parties to this Convention and persons convicted thereof shall be liable to very severe penalties.

2. (a) The States Parties shall take all effective measures to prevent ships and aircraft authorised to fly their flags from conveying slaves and to punish persons guilty of such acts or of using national flags for that purpose.

(b) The States Parties shall take all effective measures to ensure that their ports, airfields and coasts are not used for the conveyance of slaves.

3. The States Parties to this Convention shall exchange information in order to ensure the practical co-ordination of the measures taken by them in combating the slave trade and shall inform each other of every case of the slave trade, and of every attempt to commit this criminal offence, which comes to their notice.

Article 4

Any slave who takes refuge on board any vessel of a State Party to this Convention shall ipso facto be free.

SECTION III. - SLAVERY AND INSTITUTIONS AND PRACTICES SIMILAR TO SLAVERY

Article 5

In a country where the abolition or abandonment of slavery, or of the institutions or practices mentioned in article 1 of this Convention, is not yet complete, the act of mutilating, branding or otherwise marking a slave or a person of servile status in order to indicate his status, or as a punishment, or for any other reason, or of being accessory thereto, shall be a criminal offence under the laws of the States Parties to this Convention and persons convicted thereof shall be liable to punishment.

Article 6

1. The act of enslaving another person or of inducing another person to give himself or a person dependent upon him into slavery, or of attempting these acts, or being

accessory thereto, or being a party to a conspiracy to accomplish any such acts, shall be a criminal offence under the laws of the States Parties to this Convention and persons convicted thereof shall be liable to punishment.

2. Subject to the provisions of the introductory paragraph of article 1 of this Convention, the provisions of paragraph 1 of the present article shall also apply to the act of inducing another person to place himself or a person dependent upon him into the servile status resulting from any of the institutions or practices mentioned in article 1, to any attempt to perform such acts, to being accessory thereto, and to being a party to a conspiracy to accomplish any such acts.

SECTION IV. - DEFINITIONS

Article 7

For the purposes of the present Convention:

(a) "Slavery" means, as defined in the Slavery Convention of 1926, the status or condition of a person over whom any or all of the powers attaching to the right of ownership are exercised, and "slave" means a person in such condition or status;

(b) "A person of servile status" means a person in the condition or status resulting from any of the institutions or practices mentioned in article 1 of this Convention;

(c) "Slave trade" means and includes all acts involved in the capture, acquisition or disposal of a person with intent to reduce him to slavery; all acts involved in the acquisition of a slave with a view to selling or exchanging him; all acts of disposal by sale or exchange of a person acquired with a view to being sold or exchanged; and, in general, every act of trade or transport in slaves by whatever means of conveyance.

SECTION V. - CO-OPERATION BETWEEN STATES PARTIES AND COMMUNICATION OF INFORMATION

Article 8

1. The States Parties to this Convention undertake to co-operate with each other and with the United Nations to give effect to the foregoing provisions.

2. The Parties undertake to communicate to the Secretary-General of the United Nations copies of any laws, regulations and administrative measures enacted or put into effect to implement the provisions of this Convention.

3. The Secretary-General shall communicate the information received under paragraph 2 of this article to the other Parties and to the Economic and Social Council as part of the documentation for any discussion which the Council might undertake with a view to making further recommendations for the abolition of slavery, the slave trade or the institutions and practices which are the subject of this Convention.

SECTION VI. - FINAL CLAUSES

Article 9

No reservations may be made to this Convention.

Article 10

Any dispute between States Parties to this Convention relating to its interpretation or application, which is not settled by negotiation, shall be referred to the International Court of Justice at the request of any one of the parties to the dispute, unless the parties concerned agree on another mode of settlement.

Article 11

1. This Convention shall be open until 1 July 1957 for signature by any State Member of the United Nations or of

a specialised agency. It shall be subject to ratification by the signatory States, and the instruments of ratification shall be deposited with the Secretary-General of the United Nations, who shall inform each signatory and acceding State.

2. After 1 July 1957 this Convention shall be open for accession by any State Member of the United Nations or of a specialised agency, or by any other State to which an invitation to accede has been addressed by the General Assembly of the United Nations. Accession shall be effected by the deposit of a formal instrument with the Secretary-General of the United Nations, who shall inform each signatory and acceding State.

Article 12

1. This Convention shall apply to all non-self-governing trust, colonial and other non-metropolitan territories for the international relations of which any State Party is responsible; the Party concerned shall, subject to the provisions of paragraph 2 of this article, at the time of signature, ratification or accession declare the non-metropolitan territory or territories to which the Convention shall apply *ipso facto* as a result of such signature, ratification or accession.

2. In any case in which the previous consent of a non-metropolitan territory is required by the constitutional laws or practices of the Party or of the non-metropolitan territory, the Party concerned shall endeavour to secure the needed consent of the non-metropolitan territory within the period of twelve months from the date of signature of the Convention by the metropolitan State, and when such consent has been obtained the Party shall notify the Secretary-General. This Convention shall apply to the territory or territories named in such notification from the date of its receipt by the Secretary-General.

3. After the expiry of the twelve-month period mentioned in the preceding paragraph, the States Parties concerned shall inform the Secretary-General of the results of the consultations with those non-metropolitan territories for whose international relations they are responsible and whose consent to the application of this Convention may have been withheld.

Article 13

1. This Convention shall enter into force on the date on which two States have become Parties thereto.

2. It shall thereafter enter into force with respect to each State and territory on the date of deposit of the instrument of ratification or accession of that State or notification of application to that territory.

Article 14

1. The application of this Convention shall be divided into successive periods of three years, of which the first shall begin on the date of entry into force of the Convention in accordance with paragraph 1 of article 13.

2. Any State Party may denounce this Convention by a notice addressed by that State to the Secretary-General not less than six months before the expiration of the current three-year period. The Secretary-General shall notify all other Parties of each such notice and the date of the receipt thereof.

3. Denunciations shall take effect at the expiration of the current three-year period,

4. In cases where, in accordance with the provisions of article 12, this Convention has become applicable to a non-metropolitan territory of a Party, that Party may at any time thereafter, with the consent of the territory concerned, give notice to the Secretary-General of the United Nations denouncing this Convention separately in respect of that

territory. The denunciation shall take effect one year after the date of the receipt of such notice by the Secretary-General, who shall notify all other Parties of such notice and the date of the receipt thereof.

Article 15

This Convention, of which the Chinese, English, French, Russian and Spanish texts are equally authentic, shall be deposited in the archives of the United Nations Secretariat. The Secretary-General shall prepare a certified copy thereof for communication to States Parties to this Convention, as well as to all other States Members of the United Nations and of the specialised agencies.

In Witness Whereof the undersigned, being duly authorised thereto by their respective Governments, have signed this Convention on the date appearing opposite their respective signatures.

Done at the European Office of the United Nations at Geneva, this seventh day of September one thousand nine hundred and fifty-six.

CONVENTION FOR THE SUPPRESSION OF THE TRAFFIC IN PERSONS AND OF THE EXPLOITATION OF THE PROSTITUTION OF OTHERS

Approved by General Assembly resolution 317 (IV) of 2 December 1949

Entry Into Force: 25 July 1951, in Accordance with Article 24

Preamble

Whereas prostitution and the accompanying evil of the traffic in persons for the purpose of prostitution are incompatible with the dignity and worth of the human person and endanger the welfare of the individual, the family and the community,

Whereas, with respect to the suppression of the traffic in women and children, the following international instruments are in force:

(1) International Agreement of 18 May 1904 for the Suppression of the White Slave Traffic, as amended by the Protocol approved by the General Assembly of the United Nations on 3 December 1948,

(2) International Convention of 4 May 1910 for the Suppression of the White Slave Traffic, as amended by the above-mentioned Protocol,

(3) International Convention of 30 September 1921 for the Suppression of the Traffic in Women and Children, as amended by the Protocol approved by the General Assembly of the United Nations on 20 October 1947,

(4) International Convention of 11 October 1933 for the Suppression of the Traffic in Women of Full Age, as amended by the aforesaid Protocol,

Whereas the League of Nations in 1937 prepared a draft Convention extending the scope of the above-mentioned instruments, and

Whereas developments since 1937 make feasible the conclusion of a convention consolidating the above-mentioned instruments and embodying the substance of the 1937 draft Convention as well as desirable alterations therein:

Now therefore
The Contracting parties
Hereby agree as hereinafter provided:

Article 1

The Parties to the present Convention agree to punish any person who, to gratify the passions of another:

(1) Procures, entices or leads away, for purposes of prostitution, another person, even with the consent of that person;

(2) Exploits the prostitution of another person, even with the consent of that person.

Article 2

The Parties to the present Convention further agree to punish any person who:

(1) Keeps or manages, or knowingly finances or takes part in the financing of a brothel;

(2) Knowingly lets or rents a building or other place or any part thereof for the purpose of the prostitution of others.

Article 3

To the extent permitted by domestic law, attempts to commit any of the offences referred to in articles 1 and 2, and acts preparatory to the commission thereof, shall also be punished.

Article 4

To the extent permitted by domestic law, intentional participation in the acts referred to in articles 1 and 2 above shall also be punishable.

To the extent permitted by domestic law, acts of participation shall be treated as separate offences whenever this is necessary to prevent impunity.

Article 5

In cases where injured persons are entitled under domestic law to be parties to proceedings in respect of any of the offences referred to in the present Convention, aliens shall be so entitled upon the same terms as nationals.

Article 6

Each Party to the present Convention agrees to take all the necessary measures to repeal or abolish any existing law, regulation or administrative provision by virtue of which persons who engage in or are suspected of engaging in prostitution are subject either to special registration or to the possession of a special document or to any exceptional requirements for supervision or notification.

Article 7

Previous convictions pronounced in foreign States for offences referred to in the present Convention shall, to the extent permitted by domestic law, be taken into account for the purpose of:

(1) Establishing recidivism;

(2) Disqualifying the offender from the exercise of civil rights.

Article 8

The offences referred to in articles 1 and 2 of the present Convention shall be regarded as extraditable offences in any extradition treaty which has been or may hereafter be concluded between any of the Parties to this Convention.

The Parties to the present Convention which do not make extradition conditional on the existence of a treaty shall henceforward recognise the offences referred to in articles 1 and 2 of the present Convention as cases for extradition between themselves.

Extradition shall be granted in accordance with the law of the State to which the request is made.

Article 9

In States where the extradition of nationals is not permitted by law, nationals who have returned to their own State after the commission abroad of any of the offences referred to in articles 1 and 2 of the present Convention shall be prosecuted in and punished by the courts of their own State,

This provision shall not apply if, in a similar case

between the Parties to the present Convention, the extradition of an alien cannot be granted.

Article 10

The provisions of article 9 shall not apply when the person charged with the offence has been tried in a foreign State and, if convicted, has served his sentence or had it remitted or reduced in conformity with the laws of that foreign State.

Article 11

Nothing in the present Convention shall be interpreted as determining the attitude of a Party towards the general question of the limits of criminal jurisdiction under international law.

Article 12

The present Convention does not affect the principle that the offences to which it refers shall in each State be defined, prosecuted and punished in conformity with its domestic law.

Article 13

The Parties to the present Convention shall be bound to execute letters of request relating to offences referred to in the Convention in accordance with their domestic law and practice.

The transmission of letters of request shall be effected:

(1) By direct communication between the judicial authorities; or
(2) By direct communication between the Ministers of Justice of the two States, or by direct communication from another competent authority of the State making the request to the Minister of Justice of the State to which the request is made; or
(3) Through the diplomatic or consular representative

of the State making the request in the State to which the request is made; this representative shall send the letters of request direct to the competent judicial authority or to the authority indicated by the Government of the State to which the request is made, and shall receive direct from such authority the papers constituting the execution of the letters of request.

In cases 1 and 3 a copy of the letters of request shall always be sent to the superior authority of the State to which application is made.

Unless otherwise agreed, the letters of request shall be drawn up in the language of the authority making the request, provided always that the State to which the request is made may require a translation in its own language, certified correct by the authority making the request.

Each Party to the present Convention shall notify to each of the other Parties to the Convention the method or methods of transmission mentioned above which it will recognise for the letters of request of the latter State.

Until such notification is made by a State, its existing procedure in regard to letters of request shall remain in force.

Execution of letters of request shall not give rise to a claim for reimbursement of charges or expenses of any nature whatever other than expenses of experts.

Nothing in the present article shall be construed as an undertaking on the part of the Parties to the present Convention to adopt in criminal matters any form or methods of proof contrary to their own domestic laws.

Article 14

Each Party to the present Convention shall establish or maintain a service charged with the co-ordination and centralisation of the results of the investigation of offences referred to in the present Convention.

Such services should compile all information calculated to facilitate the prevention and punishment of the offences referred to in the present Convention and should be in close contact with the corresponding services in other States.

Article 15

To the extent permitted by domestic law and to the extent to which the authorities responsible for the services referred to in article 14 may judge desirable, they shall furnish to the authorities responsible for the corresponding services in other States the following information:

(1) Particulars of any offence referred to in the present Convention or any attempt to commit such offence;

(2) Particulars of any search for any prosecution, arrest, conviction, refusal of admission or expulsion of persons guilty of any of the offences referred to in the present Convention, the movements of such persons and any other useful information with regard to them.

The information so furnished shall include descriptions of the offenders, their fingerprints, photographs, methods of operation, police records and records of conviction.

Article 16

The Parties to the present Convention agree to take or to encourage, through their public and private educational, health, social, economic and other related services, measures for the prevention of prostitution and for the rehabilitation and social adjustment of the victims of prostitution and of the offences referred to in the present Convention.

Article 17

The Parties to the present Convention undertake, in connection with immigration and emigration, to adopt or maintain such measures as are required, in terms of their obligations under the present Convention, to check the traffic in persons of either sex for the purpose of prostitution;

In particular they undertake:

(1) To make such regulations as are necessary for the protection of immigrants or emigrants, and in particular, women and children, both at the place of arrival and departure and while *en route;*

(2) To arrange for appropriate publicity warning the public of the dangers of the aforesaid traffic;

(3) To take appropriate measures to ensure supervision of railway stations, airports, seaports and *en route,* and of other public places, in order to prevent international traffic in persons for the purpose of prostitution;

(4) To take appropriate measures in order that the appropriate authorities be informed of the arrival of persons who *appear, prima facie,* to be the principals and accomplices in or victims of such traffic.

Article 18

The Parties to the present Convention undertake, in accordance with the conditions laid down by domestic law, to have declarations taken from aliens who are prostitutes, in order to establish their identity and civil status and to discover who has caused them to leave their State. The information obtained shall be communicated to the authorities of the State of origin of the said persons with a view to their eventual repatriation.

Article 19

The Parties to the present Convention undertake, in accordance with the Conditions laid down by domestic law and without prejudice to prosecution or other action for violations thereunder and so far as possible:

(1) Pending the completion of arrangements for the repatriation of destitute victims of international traffic in persons for the purpose of prostitution, to make suitable provisions for their temporary care and maintenance;

(2) To repatriate persons referred to in article 18 who desire to be repatriated or who may be claimed by persons exercising authority over them or whose expulsion is ordered in conformity with the law. Repatriation shall take place only after agreement is reached with the State of destination as to identity and nationality as well as to the place and date of arrival at frontiers. Each Party to the present Convention shall facilitate the passage of such persons through its territory.

Where the persons referred to in the preceding paragraph cannot themselves repay the cost of repatriation and have, neither spouse, relatives nor guardian to pay for them, the cost of repatriation, as far as the nearest frontier or port of embarkation or airport in the direction of the State of origin shall be borne by the State where they are in residence, and the cost of the remainder of the journey shall be borne by the State of origin.

Article 20

The Parties to the present Convention shall, if they have not already done so, take the necessary measures for the supervision of employment agencies in order to prevent persons seeking employment, in particular women and from being exposed to the danger of prostitution.

Article 21

The Parties to the present Convention shall communicate to the Secretary-General of the United Nations such laws and regulations as have already been promulgated in their States, and thereafter annually such laws and regulations as may be promulgated, relating to the subjects of the present Convention, as well as all measures taken by them concerning the application of the Convention. The information received shall be published periodically by the Secretary-General and sent to all Members of the United Nations and to non-member States to which the present Convention is officially communicated in accordance with article 23.

Article 22

If any dispute shall arise between the Parties to the present Convention relating to its interpretation or application and if such dispute cannot be settled by other means, the dispute shall, at the request of any one of the Parties to the dispute, be referred to the International Court of Justice.

Article 23

The present Convention shall be open for signature on behalf of any Member of the United Nations and also on behalf of any other State to which an invitation has been addressed by the Economic and Social Council.

The present Convention shall be ratified and the instruments, of ratification shall be deposited with the Secretary-General of the United Nations.

The States mentioned in the first paragraph which have not signed the Convention may accede to it.

Accession shall be effected by deposit of an instrument of accession with the Secretary-General of the United Nations.

For the purposes of the present Convention the word "State" shall include all the colonies and Trust Territories of a State signatory or acceding to the Convention and all territories for which such State is internationally responsible.

Article 24

The present Convention shall come into force on the ninetieth day following the date of deposit of the second instrument of ratification or accession.

For each State ratifying or acceding to the Convention after the deposit of the second instrument of ratification or accession, the Convention shall enter into force ninety days after the deposit by such State of its instrument of ratification or accession.

Article 25

After the expiration of five years from the entry into force of the present Convention, any Party to the Convention may denounce it by a written notification addressed to the Secretary-General of the United Nations.

Such denunciation shall take effect for the Party making it one year from the date upon which it is received by the Secretary-General of the United Nations.

Article 26

The Secretary-General of the United Nations shall inform all Members of the United Nations and non-member States referred to in article 23:

(a) Of signatures, ratifications and accessions received in accordance with article 23;

(b) Of the date on which the present Convention will come into force in accordance with article 24;

(c) Of denunciations received in accordance with article 25.

Article 27

Each Party to the present Convention undertakes to adopt, in accordance with its Constitution, the legislative or other measures necessary to ensure the application of the Convention.

Article 28

The provisions of the present Convention shall supersede in the relations between the Parties thereto the provisions of the international instruments referred to in subparagraphs

1, 2, 3 and 4 of the second paragraph of the Preamble, each of which shall be deemed to be terminated when all the Parties thereto shall have become Parties to the present Convention.

FINAL PROTOCOL

Nothing in the present Convention shall be deemed to prejudice any legislation which ensures, for the enforcement of the provisions for securing the suppression of the traffic in persons and of the exploitation of others for purposes of prostitution, stricter conditions than those provided by the present Convention.

The provisions of articles 23 to 26 inclusive of the Convention shall apply to the present Protocol.

CONVENTION ON THE POLITICAL RIGHTS OF WOMEN

Opened for Signature and Ratification by General Assembly Resolution 640 (VII) of 30 December 1953

Entry Into Force: 7 July 1954, in Accordance with Article VI

The Contracting Parties,

Desiring to implement the principle of equality of rights for men and women contained in the Charter of the United Nations,

Recognizing that everyone has the right to take part in the government of his country directly or indirectly through freely chosen representatives, and has the right to equal access to public service in his country, and desiring to equalise the status of men and women in the enjoyment and exercise of political rights, in accordance with the provisions of the Charter of the United Nations and of the Universal Declaration of Human Rights,

Having resolved to conclude a Convention for this purpose,

Hereby agree as hereinafter provided:

Article I

Women shall be entitled to vote in all elections on equal terms with men, without any discrimination.

Article II

Women shall be eligible for election to all publicly elected bodies, established by national law, on equal terms with men, without any discrimination.

Article III

Women shall be entitled to hold public office and to exercise all public functions, established by national law, on equal terms with men, without any discrimination.

Article IV

1. This Convention shall be open for signature on behalf of any Member of the United Nations and also on behalf of any other State to which an invitation has been addressed by the General Assembly.

2. This Convention shall be ratified and the instruments of ratification shall be deposited with the Secretary-General of the United Nations.

Article V

1. This Convention shall be open for accession to all States referred to in paragraph 1 of article IV.

2. Accession shall be effected by the deposit of an instrument of accession with the Secretary-General of the United Nations.

Article VI

1. This Convention shall come into force on the ninetieth day following the date of deposit of the sixth instrument of ratification or accession.

2. For each State ratifying or acceding to the Convention after the deposit of the sixth instrument of ratification or accession the Convention shall enter into force on the ninetieth day after deposit by such State of its instrument of ratification or accession.

Article VII

In the event that any State submits a reservation to any of the articles of this Convention at the time of signature, ratification or accession, the Secretary-General shall communicate the text of the reservation to all States which are or may become Parties to this Convention. Any State which objects to the reservation may, within a period of ninety days from the date of the said communication (or upon the date of its becoming a Party to the Convention), notify the Secretary-General that it does not accept it. In such case, the Convention shall not enter into force as between such State and the State making the reservation.

Article VIII

1. Any State may denounce this Convention by written notification to the Secretary-General of the United Nations. Denunciation shall take effect one year after the date of receipt of the notification by the Secretary-General.

2. This Convention shall cease to be in force as from the date when the denunciation which reduces the number of Parties to less than six becomes effective.

Article IX

Any dispute which may arise between any two or more Contracting States concerning the interpretation or application of this Convention, which is not settled by negotiation, shall at the request of any one of the parties to the dispute be referred to the International Court of Justice for decision, unless they agree to another mode of settlement.

Article X

The Secretary-General of the United Nations shall notify all Members of the United Nations and the non-member States contemplated in paragraph 1 of article IV of this Convention of the following:

(a) Signatures and instruments of ratification received in accordance with article IV;

(b) Instruments of accession received in accordance with article V;

(c) The date upon which this Convention enters into force in accordance with article VI;

(d) Communications and notifications received in accordance with article VII;

(e) Notifications of denunciation received in accordance with paragraph 1 of article VIII;

(f) Abrogation in accordance with paragraph 2 of article VIII.

Article XI

1. This Convention, of which the Chinese, English, French, Russian and Spanish texts shall be equally authentic, shall be deposited in the archives of the United Nations.

2. The Secretary-General of the United Nations shall transmit a certified copy to all Members of the United Nations and to the non-member States contemplated in paragraph 1 of article IV.

CONVENTION ON THE NATIONALITY OF MARRIED WOMEN

Opened for Signature and Ratification by General Assembly Resolution 1040 (XI) of 29 January 1957

Entry Into Force: 11 August 1958, in Accordance with Article 6

The Contracting States,

Recognizing that, conflicts in law in practice with reference to nationality arise as a result of provisions concerning the loss or acquisition of nationality by women as a result of marriage, of its dissolution or of the change of nationality by the husband during marriage,

Recognizing that, in article 15 of the Universal Declaration of Human Rights, the General Assembly of the United Nations has proclaimed that "everyone has the right to a nationality" and that "no one shall be arbitrarily deprived of his nationality nor denied the right to change his nationality",

Desiring to co-operate with the United Nations in promoting universal respect for, and observance of, human rights and fundamental freedoms for all without distinction as to sex,

Hereby agree as hereinafter provided:

Article 1

Each Contracting State agrees that neither the celebration nor the dissolution of a marriage between one of its nationals and an alien, nor the change of nationality by the husband during marriage, shall automatically affect the nationality of the wife.

Article 2

Each Contracting State agrees that neither the voluntary acquisition of the nationality of another State nor the renunciation of its nationality by one of its nationals shall prevent the retention of its nationality by the wife of such national.

Article 3

1. Each Contracting State agrees that the alien wife of one of its nationals may, at her request, acquire the nationality of her husband through specially privileged naturalisation procedures; the grant of such nationality may be subject to such limitations as may be imposed in the interests of national security or public policy.

2. Each Contracting State agrees that the present Convention shall not be construed as affecting any legislation or judicial practice by which the alien wife of one of its nationals may, at her request, acquire her husband's nationality as a matter of right.

Article 4

1. The present Convention shall be open for signature and ratification on behalf of any State Member of the United Nations and also on behalf of any other State which is or hereafter becomes a member of any specialised agency of the United Nations, or which is or hereafter becomes a Party to the Statute of the International Court of Justice, or any other State to which an invitation has been addressed by the General Assembly of the United Nations.

2. The present Convention shall be ratified and the instruments of ratification shall be deposited with the Secretary-General of the United Nations.

Article 5

1. The present Convention shall be open for accession to all States referred to in paragraph I of article 4.

2. Accession shall be effected by the deposit of an instrument of accession with the Secretary-General of the United Nations.

Article 6

1. The present Convention shall come into force on the ninetieth day following the date of deposit of the sixth instrument of ratification or accession.

2. For each State ratifying or acceding to the Convention after the deposit of the sixth instrument of ratification or accession, the Convention shall enter into force on the ninetieth day after deposit by such State of its instrument of ratification or accession.

Article 7

1. The present Convention shall apply to all non-self-governing, trust, colonial and other non-metropolitan territories for the international relations of which any Contracting State is responsible; the Contracting State concerned shall, subject to the provisions of paragraph *2* of the present article, at the time of signature, ratification or accession declare the non-metropolitan territory or territories to which the Convention shall apply *ipso facto* as a result of such signature, ratification or accession.

2. In any case in which, for the purpose of nationality, a non-metropolitan territory is not treated as one with the metropolitan territory, or in any case in which the previous consent of a non-metropolitan territory is required by the constitutional laws or practices of the Contracting State or of the non-metropolitan territory for the application of the Convention to that territory, that Contracting State shall endeavour to secure the needed consent of the non-metropolitan territory within the period of twelve months from the date of signature of the Convention by that Contracting State, and when such consent has been obtained the Contracting State shall notify the Secretary-General of the United Nations. The present Convention shall apply to the territory or territories named in such notification from the date of its receipt by the Secretary-General.

3. After the expiry of the twelve-month period mentioned in paragraph 2 of the present article, the Contracting States concerned shall inform the Secretary-General of the results of the consultations with those non-metropolitan territories for whose international relations they are responsible and whose consent to the application of the present Convention may have been withheld.

Article 8

1. At the time of signature, ratification or accession, any State may make reservations to any article of the present Convention other than articles 1 and 2.

2. If any State makes a reservation in accordance with paragraph 1 of the present article, the Convention, with the exception of those provisions to which the reservation relates, shall have effect as between the reserving State and the other Parties. The Secretary-General of the United Nations shall communicate the text of the reservation to all States which are or may become Parties to the Convention. Any State Party to the Convention or which thereafter becomes a Party may notify the Secretary-General that it does not agree to consider itself hound by the Convention with respect to the State making the reservation. This notification must be made, in the case of a State already a Party, within ninety days from the date of the communication by the Secretary-General; and, in the case of a State subsequently becoming a Party, within ninety days from the date when the instrument of ratification or accession is deposited. In the event that such a notification is made, the Convention shall not be deemed to be in effect as between the State making the notification and the State making the reservation.

3. Any State making a reservation in accordance with paragraph 1 of the present article may at any time withdraw the reservation, in whole or in part, after it has been accepted, by a notification to this effect addressed to the

Secretary-General of the United Nations. Such notification shall take effect on the date on which it is received.

Article 9

1. Any Contracting State may denounce the present Convention by written notification to the Secretary-General of the United Nations. Denunciation shall take effect one year after the date of receipt of the notification by the Secretary-General.

2. The present Convention shall cease to be in force as from the date when the denunciation which reduces the number of Parties to less than six becomes effective.

Article 10

Any dispute which may arise between any two or more Contracting States concerning the interpretation or application of the present Convention which is not settled by negotiation, shall, at the request of any one of the parties to the dispute, be referred to the International Court of Justice for decision, unless the parties agree to another mode of settlement.

Article 11

The Secretary-General of the United Nations shall notify all States Members of the United Nations and the non-member States contemplated in paragraph 1 of article 4 of the present Convention of the following:

(a) Signatures and instruments of ratification received in accordance with article 4;

(b) Instruments of accession received in accordance with article 5;

(c) The date upon which the present Convention enters into force in accordance with article 6;

(d) Communications and notifications received in accordance with article 8;

(e) Notifications of denunciation received in accordance with paragraph 1 of article 9;

(f) Abrogation in accordance with paragraph 2 of article 9.

Article 12

1. The present Convention, of which the Chinese, English, French, Russian and Spanish texts shall be equally authentic, shall be deposited in the archives of the United Nations.

2. The Secretary-General of the United Nations shall transmit a certified copy of the Convention to all States Members of the United Nations and to the non-member States contemplated in paragraph 1 of article 4.

INTERNATIONAL CONVENTION AGAINST APARTHEID IN SPORTS

Adopted and Opened for Signature and Ratification by General Assembly Resolution 40/64 of 10 December 1985

The States Parties to the Present Convention,

Recalling the provisions of the Charter of the United Nations, in which all Members pledged themselves to take joint and separate action, in cooperation with the Organisation, for the achievement of universal respect for, and observance of, human rights and fundamental freedoms for all without distinction as to race, sex, language or religion,

Considering that the Universal Declaration of Human Rights proclaims that all human beings are born free and equal in dignity and rights and that everyone is entitled to all the rights and freedoms set forth in the Declaration without distinction of any kind, particularly in regard to race, colour or national origin,

Observing that, in accordance with the International Convention on the Elimination of All Forms of Racial

Discrimination, States Parties to that Convention particularly condemn racial segregation and *apartheid* and undertake to prevent, prohibit and eradicate all practices of this nature in all fields,

Observing that the General Assembly of the United Nations has adopted a number of resolutions condemning the practice *of apartheid in* sports and has affirmed its unqualified support for the Olympic principle that no discrimination be allowed on the grounds of race, religion or political affiliation and that merit should be the sole criterion for participation in sports activities,

Considering that the International Declaration against *Apartheid* in Sports, which was adopted by the General Assembly on 14 December 1977, : solemnly affirms the necessity for the speedy elimination of *apartheid* in sports,

Recalling the provisions of the International Convention on the Suppression and Punishment of the Crime *of Apartheid and* recognizing, in particular, that participation in sports exchanges with teams selected on the basis of *apartheid* directly abets and encourages the commission of the crime of *apartheid,* as defined in that Convention,

Resolved to adopt all necessary measures to eradicate the practice of *apartheid* in sports and to promote international sports contacts based on the Olympic principle,

Recognizing that sports contact with any country practising *apartheid in* sports condones and strengthens *apartheid* in violation of the Olympic principle and thereby becomes the legitimate concern of all Governments,

Desiring to implement the principles embodied in th International Declaration against *Apartheid* in Sports and to secure the earliest adoption of practical measures to that end,

Convinced that the adoption of an International Convention against *Apartheid* in Sports would result in more effective measures at the international and national levels, with a view to eliminating *apartheid* in sports,

Have agreed as follows:

Article 1

For the purposes of the present Convention:

(a) The expression *"apartheid"* shall mean a system of institutionalised racial segregation and discrimination for the purpose of establishing and maintaining domination by one racial group of persons over another racial group of persons and systematically oppressing them, such as that pursued by South Africa, and "apartheid in sports" shall mean the application of the policies and practices of such a system in sports activities, whether organised on a professional or an amateur basis;

(b) The expression "national sports facilities" shall mean any sports facility operated within the framework of a sports programme conducted under the auspices of a national government;

(c) The expression "Olympic principle" shall mean the principle that no discrimination be allowed on the grounds of race, religion or political officiation;

(d) The expression "sports contracts" shall mean any contract concluded for the organisation, promotion, performance or derivative rights, including servicing, of any sports activity;

(e) The expression "sports bodies" shall mean any organisation constituted to organise sports activities at the national level, including national Olympic committees, national sports federations or national governing sports. committees;

(f) The expression "team" shall mean a group of sportsmen organised for the purpose of participating in sports activities in competition with other such organised groups;

(g) The expression "sportsmen" shall mean men and women who participate in sports activities on an individual or team basis, as well as managers, coaches, trainers and other officials whose functions are essential for the operation of a team.

Article 2

States Parties strongly condemn *apartheid* and undertake to pursue immediately by all appropriate means the policy of eliminating the practice of *apartheid* in all its forms from sports.

Article 3

States Parties shall not permit sports contact with a country practising *apartheid* and shall take appropriate action to ensure that their sports bodies, teams, and individual sportsmen do not have such contact.

Article 4

States Parties shall take all possible measures to prevent sports contact with a country practising *apartheid* and shall ensure that effective means exist for bringing about compliance with such measures.

Article 5

States Parties shall refuse to provide financial or other assistance to enable their sports bodies, teams and individual sportsmen to participate in sports activities in a country or with teams or individual sportsmen selected on the basis of *apartheid*.

Article 6

Each State Party shall take appropriate action against its sports bodies, teams and individual sportsmen that participate in sports activities in a country practising *apartheid* or with teams representing a country practising apartheid, which in particular shall include:

(a) Refusal to provide financial or other assistance for any purpose to such sports bodies, teams and individual sportsmen;

(b) Restriction of access to national sports facilities by such sports bodies, team's and individual sportsmen;

(c) Non-enforceability of all sports contracts which involve sports activities in a country practising *apartheid* or with teams or individual sportsmen selected on the basis of *apartheid;*

(d) Denial and withdrawal of national honours or awards in sports to such teams and individual sportsmen;

(e) Denial of official receptions in honour of such teams or sportsmen.

Article 7

States Parties shall deny visas and/or entry to representatives of sports bodies, teams and individual sportsmen representing a country practising *apartheid.*

Article 8

States Parties shall take all appropriate action to secure the expulsion of a country practising *apartheid* from international and regional sports bodies.

Article 9

States Parties shall take all appropriate measures to prevent international sports bodies from imposing financial or other penalties on affiliated bodies which, in accordance with United Nations resolutions, the provisions of the present Convention and the spirit of the Olympic principle, refuse to participate in sports with a country practising *apartheid.*

Article 10

1. States Parties shall use their best endeavours to ensure universal compliance with the Olympic principles of non-discrimination and the provisions of the present Convention.

2. Towards this end, States Parties shall prohibit entry into their countries of members of teams and individual sportsmen participating or who have participated in sports competitions in South Africa and shall prohibit entry into their countries of representatives of sports bodies, members of teams and individual sportsmen who invite on their own initiative sports bodies, teams and sportsmen officially representing a country practising *apartheid* and participating under its flag. States Parties may also prohibit entry of representatives of sports bodies, members of teams or individual sportsmen who maintain sports contacts with sports bodies, teams or sportsmen representing a country practising *apartheid* and participating under its flag. Prohibition of entry should not violate the regulations of the relevant sports federations which support the elimination of *apartheid* in sports and shall apply only to participation in sports activities.

3. States Parties shall advise their national representatives to international sports federations to take all possible and practical steps to prevent the participation of the sports bodies, teams and sportsmen referred to in paragraph 2 above in international sports competitions and shall, through their representatives in international sports organisations, take every possible measure:

(a) To ensure the expulsion of South Africa from all federations in which it still holds membership as well as to deny South Africa, reinstatement to membership in any federation from which it has been expelled;

(b) In case of national federations condoning sports exchanges; with a country practising apartheid, to impose sanctions against such national federations including, if necessary, expulsion from the relevant international sports organisation and exclusion of their representatives from participation in international sports competitions.

4. In cases of flagrant violations of the provisions of the present Convention, States Parties shall take appropriate action as they deem fit, including, where necessary, steps aimed at the exclusion of the responsible national sports governing bodies, national sports federations or sportsmen of the, countries concerned from international sports competition.

5. The provisions of the present article relating specifically to South Africa shall cease to apply when the system *of apartheid is* abolished in that country.

Article 11

1. There shall be established a Commission against *Apartheid in* Sports (hereinafter referred to as "the Commission") consisting of fifteen members of high moral character and committed to the struggle against *apartheid,* particular attention being paid to participation of persons having experience in sports administration, elected by the States Parties from among their nationals, having regard to the most equitable geographical distribution and the representation of the principal legal systems.

2. The members of the Commission shall be elected by secret ballot from a list of persons nominated by the States Parties. Each State Party may nominate one person from among its own nationals.

3. The initial election shall be held six months after the date of the entry into force of the present Convention. At least three months before the date of each election, the Secretary-General of the United Nations shall address a letter to the States Parties inviting them to submit their nominations within two months. The Secretary-General shall prepare a list in alphabetical order of all persons thus nominated, indicating the States Parties which have nominated them, and shall submit it to the States Parties.

4. Elections of the members of the Commission shall be

held at a meeting of States Parties convened by the Secretary-General at United Nations Headquarters. At that meeting, for which two thirds of the States Parties shall constitute a quorum, the persons elected to the Commission shall be those nominees who obtain the largest number of votes and an absolute majority of the votes of the representatives of States Parties present and voting.

5. The members of the Commission shall be elected for a term of four years. However, the terms of nine of the members elected at the first election shall expire at the end of two years; immediately after the first election, the names of these nine members shall be chosen by lot by the Chairman of the Commission.

6. For the filling of casual vacancies, the State Party whose national has ceased to function as a member of the Commission shall appoint another person from among its nationals, subject to the approval of the Commission.

7. States Parties shall be responsible for the expenses of the members of the Commission while they are in performance of Commission duties.

Article 12

1. States Parties undertake to submit to the Secretary-General of the United Nations, for consideration by the Commission, a report on the legislative, judicial, administrative or other measures which they have adopted to give effect to the provisions of the present Convention within one year of its entry into force and thereafter every two years. The Commission may request further information from the States Parties.

2. The Commission shall report annually through the Secretary-General to the General Assembly of the United Nations on its activities and may make suggestions and general recommendations based on the examination of the reports and information received from the States Parties.

Such suggestions and recommendations shall be reported to the General Assembly together with comments, if any, from States Parties concerned.

3. The Commission shall examine, in particular, the implementation of the provisions of article 10 of the present Convention and make recommendations on action to be undertaken.

4. A meeting of States Parties shall be convened by the Secretary-General at the request of a majority of the States Parties to consider further action with respect to the implementation of the provisions of article 10 of the present Convention. In cases of flagrant violation of the provisions of the present Convention, a meeting of States Parties shall be convened by the Secretary-General at the request of the Commission.

Article 13

1. Any State Party may at any time declare that it recognises the competence of the Commission to receive and examine complaints concerning breaches of the provisions of the present Convention submitted by States Parties which have also made such a declaration. The Commission may decide on the appropriate measures to be taken in respect of breaches.

2. States Parties against which a complaint has been made, in accordance with paragraph 1 of the present article, shall be entitled to be represented and take part in the proceedings of the Commission.

Article 14

1. The Commission shall meet at least once a year.

2. The Commission shall adopt its own rules of procedure.

3. The secretariat of the Commission shall be provided by the Secretary-General of the United Nations.

4. The meetings of the Commission shall normally be held at United Nations Headquarters.

5. The Secretary-General shall convene the initial meeting of the Commission.

Article 15

The Secretary-General of the United Nations shall be the depositary of the present Convention.

Article 16

1. The present Convention shall be open for signature at United Nations Headquarters by all States until its entry into force.

2. The present Convention shall be subject to ratification, acceptance or approval by the signatory States.

Article 17

The present Convention shall be open for accession by all States.

Article 18

1. The present Convention shall enter into force on the thirtieth day after the date of deposit with the Secretary-General of the United Nations of the twenty-seventh instrument of ratification, acceptance, approval or accession.

2. For each State ratifying, accepting, approving or acceding to the present Convention after its entry into force, the Convention shall enter into force on the thirtieth day after the date of deposit of the relevant instrument.

Article 19

Any dispute between States Parties arising out of the interpretation, application or implementation of the present Convention which is not settled by negotiation shall be brought before the International Court of Justice at the request and with the mutual consent of the States Parties to the dispute, save where the Parties to the dispute have agreed on some other form of settlement.

Article 20

1. Any State Party may propose an amendment or revision to the present Convention and file it with the depositary. The Secretary-General of the United Nations shall thereupon communicate the proposed amendment or revision to the States Parties with a request that they notify him whether they favour a conference of States Parties for the purpose of considering and voting upon the proposal. In the event that at least one third of the States Parties favour such a conference, the Secretary-General shall convene the conference under the auspices of the United Nations. Any amendment or revision adopted by the majority of the States Parties present and voting at the conference shall be submitted to the General Assembly of the United Nations for approval.

2. Amendments or revisions shall come into force when they have been approved by the General Assembly and accepted by a two-thirds majority of the States Parties, in accordance with their respective constitutional processes.

3. When amendments or revisions come into force, they shall be binding on those States Parties which have accepted them, other States Parties still being bound by the provisions of the present Convention and any earlier amendment or revision which they have accepted.

Article 21

A State Party may withdraw from the present Convention by written notification to the depositary. Such withdrawal shall take effect one year after the date of receipt of the notification by the depositary.

Article 22

The present Convention has been concluded in Arabic, Chinese, English, French, Russian and Spanish, all texts being equally authentic.

CONVENTION ON THE RIGHTS OF THE CHILD

Adopted and Opened for Signature, Ratification and Accession by General Assembly Resolution 44/25 of 20 November 1989

Entry Into Force: 2 September 1990, in Accordance with Article 49

Preamble

The States Parties to the Present Convention,

Considering that, in accordance with the principles proclaimed in the Charter of the United Nations, recognition of the inherent dignity and of the equal and inalienable rights of all members of the human family is the foundation of freedom, justice and peace in the world.

Bearing in mind that the peoples of the United Nations have, in the Charter, reaffirmed their faith in fundamental human rights and in the dignity and worth of the human person, and have determined to promote social progress and better standards of life in large freedom,

Recognising that the United Nations has, in the Universal Declaration of Human Rights and in the International Covenants on Human Rights, proclaimed and agreed that everyone is entitled to all the rights and freedoms set forth therein, without distinction of any kind, such as race, colour, sex, language, religion, political or other opinion, national or social origin, property, birth or other status,

Recalling that, in the Universal Declaration of Human Rights, the United Nations has proclaimed that childhood is entitled to special care and assistance,

Convinced that the family, as the fundamental group of society and the natural environment for the growth and well-being of all its members and particularly children, should be afforded the necessary protection and assistance so that it can fully assume its responsibilities within the community,

Recognising that the child, for the full and harmonious development of his or her personality, should grow up in a family environment, in an atmosphere of happiness, love and understanding,

Considering that the child should be fully prepared to live an individual life in society, and brought up in the spirit of the Ideals proclaimed in the Charter of the United Nations, and in particular in the spirit of peace, dignity, tolerance, freedom, equality and solidarity,

Bearing in mind that the need to extend particular care to the child has been stated in the Geneva Declaration of the Rights of the Child of 1924 and in the Declaration of the Rights of the Child adopted by the General Assembly on 20 November 1959 and recognised in the Universal Declaration of Human Rights, in the International Covenant on Civil and Political Rights (in particular in articles 23 and 24), in the International Covenant on Economic, Social and Cultural Rights (in particular in article 10) and in the statutes and relevant instruments of specialised agencies and international organisations concerned with the welfare of children.

Bearing in mind that, as indicated in the Declaration of the Rights of the Child, "the child, by reason of his physical and mental immaturity, needs special safeguards and care, including appropriate legal protection, before as well as after birth,"

Recalling the provisions of the Declaration on Social and Legal Principles relating to the Protection and Welfare of Children, with Special Reference to Foster Placement and Adoption Nationally and Internationally; the United Nations Standard Minimum Rules for the Administration of Juvenile Justice (The Beijing Rules); and the Declaration on the Protection of Women and Children in Emergency and Armed Conflict,

Recognising that, in all countries in the world, there are children living in exceptionally difficult conditions, and that such children need special consideration,

Taking due account of the importance of the traditions and cultural values of each people for the protection and harmonious development of the child,

Recognising the importance of internal co-operation for improving the living conditions of children in every country, in particular in the developing countries,

Have agreed as follows:

PART I

Article 1

For the purposes of the present Convention, a child means every human being below the age of eighteen years unless under the law applicable to the child, majority is attained earlier.

Article 2

1. State Parties shall respect and ensure the rights set forth in the present Convention to each child within their jurisdiction without discrimination of any kind, irrespective of the child's or his or her parent's or legal guardian's race, colour, sex, language, religion, political or other opinion, national, ethnic or social origin, property, disability, birth or other status.

2. States Parties shall take all appropriate measures to ensure that the child is protected against all forms of discrimination or punishment on the basis of the status, activities, expressed opinions, or beliefs of the child's parents, legal guardians, or family members.

Article 3

1. In all actions concerning children, whether undertaken by public or private social welfare institutions, courts of law, administrative authorities or legislative bodies, the best interests of the child shall be a primary consideration.

2. States Parties undertake to ensure the child such protection and care as is necessary for his or her well-being, taking into account the rights and duties of his or her parents, legal guardians, or other individuals legally responsible for him or her, and, to this end, shall take all appropriate legislative and administrative measures.

3. Sates Parties shall ensure that the institutions, services and facilities responsible for the care or protection of children shall conform with the standards established by competent authorities, particularly in the areas of safety, health, in the number and suitability of their staff, as well as competent supervision.

Article 4

States Parties shall undertake all appropriate legislative, administrative, and other measures for the implementation of the rights recognised in the present Convention. With regard to economic, social and cultural rights, States Parties shall undertake such measures to the maximum extent of their available resources and, where needed, within the framework of international co-operation.

Article 5

States Parties shall respect the responsibilities, rights and duties of parents or, where applicable, the members of the extended family or community as provided for by local custom, legal guardians or other persons legally responsible for the child, to provide, in a manner consistent with the evolving capacities of the child, appropriate direction and guidance in the exercise by the child of the rights recognised in the present Convention.

Article 6

1. States Parties recognise that every child has the inherent right to life.

2. States Parties shall ensure to the maximum extent possible the survival and development of the child.

Article 7

1. The child shall be registered immediately after birth and shall have the right from birth to a name, the right to acquire a nationality and, as far as possible, the right to know and be cared for by his or her parents.

2. States Parties shall ensure the implementation of these rights in accordance with their national law and their obligations under the relevant international instruments in this field, in particular where the child would otherwise be stateless.

Article 8

1. States Parties under take to respect the right of the child to preserve his or her identity, including nationality, name and family relations as recognised by law without unlawful interference.

2. Where a child is illegally deprived of some or all of the elements of his or her identity, states Parties shall provide appropriate assistance and protection, with a view to re-establishing speedily his or her identity.

Article 9

1. States Parties shall ensure that a child shall not be separated from his or her parents against their will, except when competent authorities subject to judicial review determine, in accordance with applicable law and procedures, that such separation is necessary for the best interests of the child. Such determination may be necessary in a particular case such as one involving abuse or neglect of the child by

the parents, or one where the parents are living separately and a decision must be made as to the child's place of residence.

2. In any proceedings pursuant to paragraph 1 of the present article. all interested parties shall be given an opportunity to participate in the proceedings and make their views known.

3. States Parties shall respect the right of the child who is separated from one or both parents to maintain personal relations and direct contact with both parents on a regular basis, except if it is contrary to the child's best interests.

4. Where such separation results from any action initiated by a State Party, such as the detention, imprisonment, exile, deportation or death (including death arising from any cause while the person is in the custody of the State) of one or both parents or of the child, that State Party shall, upon request, provide the parents or of the child, that State Party shall, upon request, provide the parents, the child or, if appropriate, another member of the family with the essential information concerning the whereabouts of the absent member(s) of the family unless the provision of the information would be detrimental to the well-being of the child. States Parties shall further ensure that the submission of such a request shall of itself entail no adverse consequences for the person(s) concerned.

Article 10

1. In accordance with the obligation of State Parties under article 9, paragraph 1, applications by a child or his or her parents to enter or leave a State Party for the purpose of family reunification shall be dealt with by States Parties) in a positive, humane and expeditious manner. States Parties shall further ensure that the submission of such a request shall entail no adverse consequences for the applicants and for the members of their family.

2. A child whose parents reside in different States shall have the right to maintain on a regular basis, save in exceptional circumstances personal relations and direct contacts with both parents. Towards that end and in accordance with the obligation of States Parties under article 9, paragraph 1, States Parties shall respect the right of the child and his or her parents to leave any country, including their own, and to enter their own country. The right to leave any country shall be subject only to such restrictions as are prescribed by law and which are necessary to protect the national security, public order (*order public*), public health or morals or the rights and freedoms of others and are consistent with the other rights recognised in the present Convention.

Article 11

1. States Parties shall take measures to combat the illicit transfer and non-return of children abroad.

2. To this end, States Parties shall promote the conclusions of bilateral or multilateral agreements or accession to existing agreements.

Article 12

1. State Parties shall assure to the child who is capable of forming his or her own views the right to express those views freely in all matters affecting the child, the views of the child being given due weight in accordance with the age and maturity of the child.

2. For this purpose, the child shall in particular be provided the opportunity to be heard in any judicial and administrative proceedings affecting the child, either directly, or through a representative or an appropriate body, in a manner consistent with the procedural rules of national law.

Article 13

1. The child shall have the right to freedom of expression;

this right shall include freedom to seek, receive and impart information and ideas of all kinds, regardless of frontiers, either orally, in writing or in print, in the from of art, or through any other media of the child's choice.

2. The exercise of this right may be subject to certain restrictions, but these shall only be such as are provided by law and are necessary:

(a) For respect of the rights or reputations of others; or

(b) For the protection of national security or of public order (*order public*), or of public health or morals.

Article 14

1. States Parties shall respect the right of the child to freedom of thought, conscience and religion.

2. States Parties shall respect the rights and duties of the parents and, when applicable, legal guardians, to provide direction to the child in the exercise of his or her right in a manner consistent with the evolving capacities of the child.

3. Freedom to manifest one's religion or beliefs may be subject only to such limitations as are prescribed by law and are necessary to protect public safety, order, health or morals,or the fundamental rights and freedoms of others.

Article 15

1. States Parties recognise the rights of the child to freedom of association and to freedom of peaceful assembly.

2. No restrictions may be placed on the exercise of these rights other than those imposed in conformity with the law and which are necessary in in a democratic society in the interests of national security or public safety, public order (*order public*), the protection of public health or morals or the protection of the rights and freedoms of others.

Article 16

1. No child shall be subject to arbitrary or unlawful interference with his or her privacy, family, home or correspondence, nor to unlawful attacks on his or her honour and reputation.

2. The child has the right to the protection of the law against such interference or attacks.

Article 17

States Parties recognise the important function performed by the mass media and shall ensure that the child has access to information and material from a diversity of national and international sources, especially those aimed at the promotion of his or her social, spiritual and moral well-being and physical and mental health. To this end, States Parties shall:

(a) Encourage the mass media to disseminate information and material of social and cultural benefit to the child and in accordance with the spirit of article 29;

(b) Encourage international co-operation in the production, exchange and dissemination of such information and material from a diversity of cultural, national and international sources;

(c) Encourage the production and dissemination of children's books;

(d) Encourage the mass media to have particular regard to the linguistic needs of the child who belongs to a minor it group or who is indigenous;

(e) Encourage the development of appropriate guidelines for he protection of the child from information and material injurious to his or her well-being, bearing in mind the provisions of article 13 and 18.

Article 18

1. States Parties shall use their best efforts to ensure recognition of the principle that both parents have common responsibilities for the upbringing and development of the child. Parents or, as the case may be, legal guardians, have the primary responsibility for the upbringing and development of the child. The best interests of the child will be their basic concern.

2. For the purpose of guaranteeing and promotion the rights set forth in the present Convention, States Parties shall render appropriate assistance to parents and legal guardians in the performance of their child-rearing responsibilities and shall ensure the development of institutions, facilities and services for the care of children.

3. States parties shall take all appropriate measures to ensure that children of working parents have the right to benefit from child-care service and facilities for which they are eligible.

Article 19

1. Sates Parties shall take all appropriate legislative, administrative, social and educational measures to protect the child from all forms of physical or mental violence, injury or abuse neglect or negligent treatment, maltreatment or exploitation, including sexual abuse, while in the care of parent(s), legal guardian(s) or any other person who has the care of the child.

2. Such protective measures should, as appropriate, include effective procedures for the establishment of social programmes to provide necessary support for the child and for those who have the care of the child, as well as for other forms of prevention and for identification, reporting, referral, investigation treatment and follow-up of instances of child maltreatment described heretofore, and, as appropriate, for judicial involvement.

Article 20

1. A child temporarily or permanently deprived of his or her family environment, or in whose own best interests cannot be allowed to remain in that environment, shall be entitled to special protection and assistance provided by the State.

2. States Parties shall in accordance with their national laws ensure alternative care for such a child.

3. Such care could include, *inter alia,* foster placement, ***kafalah*** of Islamic law, adoption or if necessary placement in suitable institutions for the care of children. When considering solutions, due regard shall be paid to the desirability of continuity in a child's upbringing and to the child's ethnic, religious, cultural and linguistic background.

Article 21

States Parties that recognise and/or permit the system of adoption shall ensure that the best interests of the child shall be the paramount consideration and they shall:

(a) Ensure that the adoption of a child is authorised only by competent authorities who determine, in accordance with applicable law and procedures and on the basis of all pertinent and reliable information, that the adoption is permissible in view of the child's status concerning parents, relatives and legal guardians and that, if required, the persons concerned have given their informed consent to the adoption on the basis of such counselling as may be necessary;

(b) Recognise that inter-country adoption may be considered as an alternative means of child's care, if the child cannot be placed in a foster or an adoptive family or cannot in any suitable manner be cared for in the child's country of origin;

(c) Ensure that the child concerned by inter-country adoption enjoys safeguards and standards equivalent to those existing in the case of national adoption;

(d) Take all appropriate measures to ensure that, in inter-country adoption, the placement does not result in improper financial gain for those involved in it;

(e) Promote, where appropriate, the objectives of the present article by concluding bilateral or multilateral arrangement or agreements, and endeavour, within this framework, to ensure that the placement of the child in another country is carried out by competent authorities or organs.

Article 22

1. States Parties shall take appropriate measures to ensure that a child who is seeking refugee status or who is considered a refugee in accordance with applicable international or domestic law and procedures shall, whether unaccompanied or accompanied by his or her parents or by another person, receive appropriate protection and humanitarian assistance in the enjoyment of applicable rights set forth in the present Convention and in other international human rights or humanitarian instruments to which the said State are Parties.

2. For this purpose, States Parties shall provide, as they consider appropriate, co-operation in any efforts by the United Nations and other competent intergovernmental organisations or non-governmental organisations co-operating with the United Nations to protect and assist such a child and to trace the parents or other members of the family of any refugee child in order to obtain information necessary for reunification with his or her family. In cases where no parents or other members of the family can be found, the child shall be accorded the same protection as any other child permanently or temporarily deprived of his or her family environment for any reason, as set forth in the present Convention.

Article 23

1. States Parties recognise that a mentally or physically disabled child should enjoy a full and decent life, in conditions which ensure dignity, promote self-reliance and facilitate the child's active participation in the community.

2. States Parties recognise the right of the disabled child to special care and shall encourage and ensure the extension, subject to available resources, to the eligible child and those responsible for his or her care, of assistance for which application is made and which is appropriate to the child's condition and to the circumstances of the parents or others caring for the child.

3. Recognising the special needs of a disabled child, assistance extended in accordance with paragraph 2 of the present article shall be provided free of charge, whenever possible, taking into account the financial resources of the parents or others caring for the child, and shall be designed to ensure that the disabled child has effective access to and receives education, training, health care services, rehabilitation services, preparation for employment and recreation opportunities in a manner conducive to the child's achieving the fullest possible social integration and individual development, including his or her cultural and spiritual development.

4. States Parties shall promote, in the spirit of international co-operation, the exchange of appropriate information in the field of preventive health care and of medical, psychological and functional treatment of disabled children, including dissemination of and access to information concerning methods of rehabilitation, education and vocational services, with the aim of enabling States Parties to improve their capabilities and skills and to widen their experience in these areas. In this regard, particular account shall be taken of the needs of developing countries.

Article 24

1. States Parties recognise the right of the child to the enjoyment of the highest attainable standard of health and to facilities for the treatment of illness and rehabilitation of health. States Parties shall strive to ensure that no child is deprived of his or her right of access to such health care services.

2. States Parties shall pursue full implementation of this right and, in particular,shall take appropriate measures:

(a) To diminish infant and child morality;

(b) To ensure the provision of necessary medical assistance and health care to all children with emphasis on the development of primary health care;

(c) To combat disease and malnutrition, including within the frame-work of primary health care, through,*inter alia,* the application of readily available technology and through the provision of adequate nutritious foods and clean drinking-water, taking into consideration the dangers and risks of environmental pollution;

(d) To ensure appropriate pre-natal and post natal health care for mothers;

(e) To ensure that all segments of society, in particular parents and children, are informed, have access to education and are supported in the use of basic knowledge of child health and nutrition, the advantages of breast-feeding, hygiene and environmental sanitation and the prevention of accident;

(f) To develop preventive health care, guidance for parents and family planning education and services.

3. States Parties shall take all effective and appropriate measures with a view to abolishing tradition practices prejudicial to the health of children.

4. States Parties undertake to promote and encourage international co-operation with a view to achieving progressively the full realisation of the right recognised in the present article. In this regard, particular account shall be taken of the needs of developing countries.

Article 25

States Parties recognise the right of a child who has been placed by the competent authorities for the purposes of care, protection or treatment of his or her physical or mental health, to a periodic review of the treatment provided to the child and all other circumstances relevant to his or her placement.

Article 26

1. States Parties shall recognise for every child the right to benefit from social security, including social insurance, and shall take the necessary measures to achieve the full realisation of this right in accordance with their national law.

2. The benefits should, where appropriate, be granted, taking into account the resources and the circumstances of the child and persons having responsibility for the maintenance of the child, as well as any other consideration relevant to an application for benefits made by or on behalf of the child.

Article 27

1. States Parties recognise the right of every child to a standard of living adequate for the child's physical, mental, spiritual, moral and social development.

2. The parent(s) or others responsible for the child have the primary responsibility to secure, within their abilities and financial capacities, the conditions of living necessary for the child's development.

3. States Parties, in accordance with national conditions and within their means, shall take appropriate measures to assist parents and others responsible for the child to implement this right and shall in case of need provide material assistance and support programmes, particularly with regard to nutrition, clothing and housing.

4. States Parties shall take all appropriate measures of secure the recovery of maintenance for the child from the parents or other persons having financial responsibility for the child, both within the State Party and from abroad. In particular, where the person having financial responsibility for the child lives in a State different from that of the child, States Parties shall promote the accession to international agreements or the conclusion of such agreements, as well as the making of other appropriate arrangements.

Article 28

1. States Parties recognise the right of the child to education, and with a view to achieving this right progressively and on the basis of equal opportunity, they shall, in particular;

(a) Make primary education compulsory and available free to all;

(b) Encourage the development of different forms of secondary education, including general and vocational education, make them available and accessible to every child, and take appropriate measures such as the introduction of free education and offering financial assistance in case of need;

(c) Make higher education accessible to all on the basis of capacity by every appropriate means;

(d) Make educational and vocational information and guidance available and accessible to all children;

(e) Take measures to encourage regular attendance at schools and the reduction of drop-out rates.

2. States Parties shall take all appropriate measures to ensure that school discipline is administered in a manner consistent with the child's human dignity and in conformity with the present Convention.

3. States Parties shall promote and encourage international co-operation in matters relating to education, in particular with a view to contributing to the elimination of ignorance and illiteracy throughout the world and facilitating access to scientific and technical knowledge and modern teaching methods. In this regard, particular account shall be taken of the needs of developing countries.

Article 29

1. State Parties agree that the education of the child shall be directed to:

(a) The development of the child's personality, talents and mental and physical abilities to their fullest potential;

(b) The development of respect for human rights and fundamental freedoms, and for the principles enshrined in the Charter of the United Nations;

(c) The development of respect for the child's parents, his or her own cultural identity, language and values, for the national values of the country in which the child is living, the country from which he or she may originate, and for civilisations different from his or her own;

(d) The preparation of the child for responsible life in a free society, in the spirit of understanding, peace, tolerance, equality of sexes, and friendship among all peoples, ethnic, national and religious groups and persons of indigenous origin;

(e) The development of respect for the natural environment.

2. No part of the present article or article 28 shall be construed so as to interfere with the liberty of individuals and bodies to establish and direct educational institutions, subject always to the observance of the principle set forth in paragraph 1 of the present article and to the requirements that the education given in such institutions shall conform to such minimum standards as may be laid down by the State.

Article 30

In those States in which ethnic, religious or linguistic minorities or persons of indigenous origin exist, a child belonging to such a minority or who is indigenous shall not be denied the right, in community with other members of his or her group, to enjoy his or her own culture, to profess and practise his or her own religion, or to use his or her own language.

Article 31

1. States Parties recognise the right of the child to rest and leisure, to engage in play and recreational activities appropriate to the age of the child and to participate freely in cultural life and the arts.

2. States Parties shall respect and promote the right of the child to participate fully in cultural and artistic life and shall encourage the provision of appropriate and equal opportunities for cultural, artistic, recreational and leisure activity.

Article 32

1. States Parties recognise the right of the child to be protected from economic exploitation and from performing any work that is likely to be hazardous or to interfere with the child's education, or to be harmful to the child's health or physical, mental, spiritual, moral or social development.

2. States Parties shall take legislative, administrative, social and educational measures to ensure the implementation

of the present article. To this end, and having regard to the relevant provisions of other international instruments, States Parties shall in particular:

(a) Provide for a minimum age or minimum ages for admission to employment;
(b) Provide for appropriate regulation of the hours and conditions of employment;
(c) Provide for appropriate penalties or other sanctions to ensure the effective enforcement of the present article.

Article 33

States Parties shall take all appropriate measures, including legislative, administrative, social and educational measures, to protect children from the illicit use of narcotic drugs and psychotropic substances as defined in the relevant international treaties, and to prevent the use of children in the illicit production and trafficking of such substances.

Article 34

States Parties undertake to protect the child from all forms of sexual exploitation and sexual abuse. For these purposes, States Parties shall in particular take all appropriate national, bilateral and multilateral measures to prevent:

(a) The inducement or coercion of a child to engage in any unlawful sexual activity;
(b) The exploitative use of children in prostitution or other unalwful sexual practices;
(c) The exploitative use of children in pornographic performances and materials.

Article 35

States Parties shall take all appropriate national, bilateral and multilateral measures to prevent the abduction of, the sale of or traffic in children for any purpose or in any form.

Article 36

States Parties shall protect the child against all other forms of exploitation prejudicial to any aspects of the child's welfare.

Article 37

States Parties shall ensure that:

(a) No child shall be subjected to torture or other cruel, inhuman or degrading treatment or punishment. Neither capital punishment nor life imprisonment without possibility of release shall be imposed for offences committed by persons below eighteen years of age;

(b) No child shall be deprived of his or her liberty unlawfully or arbitrarily. The arrest, detention or imprisonment of a child shall be in conformity with the law and shall be used only as a measure of last resort and for the shortest appropriate period of time;

(c) Every child deprived of liberty shall be treated with humanity and respect for the inherent dignity of the human person, and in a manner which takes into account the needs of persons of his or her age. In particular, every child deprived of liberty shall be separated from adults unless is considered in the child's best interest not to do so and shall have the right to maintain contract with his or her family through correspondence and visits, save in exceptional circumstances;

(d) Every child deprived of his or her liberty shall have the right to prompt access to legal and other appropriate assistance, as well as the right to challenge the legality of the deprivation of his or her liberty before a court or other competent, independent and impartial authority, and to a prompt decision on any such action.

Article 38

1. States Parties undertake to respect and to ensure respect for rules of international humanitarian law applicable to them in armed conflicts which are relevant to the child.

2. Sates Parties shall take all feasible measures to ensure that persons who have not attained the age of fifteen years do not take a direct part in hostilities.

3. States Parties shall refrain from recruiting any person who has not attained the age of fifteen years into their armed forces. In recruiting among those persons who have attained the age of fifteen years but who have not attained the age of eighteen years, States Parties shall endeavour to give priority to those who are oldest.

4. In accordance with their obligations under international humanitarian law to protect the civilian population in armed conflicts, Sates parties shall take all feasible measures to ensure protection and care of children who are affected by an armed conflict.

Article 39

States Parties shall take all appropriate measures to promote physical and psychological recovery and social reintegration of a child victim of any from of neglect, exploitation, or abuse; torture or any other from of cruel, inhuman or degrading treatment or punishment; or armed conflicts. Such recovery and reintegration shall take place in an environment which fosters the health, self-respect and dignity of the child.

Article 40

1. States Parties recognise the right of every child alleged as, accused of or recognised as having infringed the penal law to be treated in a manner consistent with the promotion of the child's sense of dignity and worth which reinforces the child's respect for the human rights and fundamental freedoms of others and which takes into account

the child's age and the desirability of promoting the child's reintegration and the child's assuming a constructive role in society.

2. To this end, and having regard to the relevant provisions of international instruments, States Parties shall, in particular, ensure that:

(a) No child shall be alleged as, be accused of, or recognised as having infringed the penal law by reason of acts or omissions that were not prohibited by national or international law at the time they were committed;

(b) Every child alleged as or accused of having infringed the penal law has atleast the following guarantees:

  (i) To be presumed innocent until proven guilty according to law;

  (ii) To be informed promptly and directly of the charges against him or her, and, if appropriate, through his or her parents or legal guardians, and to have legal or other appropriate assistance in the preparation and presentation of his or her defence;

  (iii) To have the matter determined without delay by a competent, independent and impartial authority or judicial body in a fair hearing according to law, in the presence of legal or other appropriate assistance and, unless it is considered not to be in the best interest of the child, in particular, taking into account his or her age or situation, his or her parents or legal guardians;

  (iv) Not to be compelled to give testimony or to confess guilt; to examine or have examined adverse witnesses and to obtain the participation and examination of witnesses on his or her behalf under conditions of equality;

(v) If considered to have infringed the penal law, to have this decision and any measures imposed in consequence thereof reviewed by a higher competent, independent and impartial authority or judicial body according to law;

(vi) To have the free assistance of an interpreter if the child cannot understand or speak the language used;

(vii) To have his or her privacy fully respected at all sages of the proceedings.

3. States Parties shall seek to promote the establishment of laws, procedures, authorities and institutions specifically applicable to children alleged as, accused of, or recognised as having infringed the penal law, and, in particular;

(a) The establishment of a minimum age below which children shall be presumed not to have the capacity to infringe the penal law;

(b) Whenever appropriate and desirable,measures for dealing with such children without resorting to judicial proceedings, providing that human rights and legal safeguards are fully respected.

4. A variety of dispositions, such as care, guidance and supervision orders; counselling; probation; foster care; education and vocational training programmes and other alternatives to institutional care shall be available to ensure that children are dealt with in a manner appropriate to their well being and proportionate both to their circumstances and the offence.

Article 41

Nothing in the present Convention shall affect any provisions which are more conducive to the realisation of the rights of the child and which may be contained in:

(a) The law of a Sate party; or

(b) International law in force for that State.

PART II

Article 42

States Parties undertake to make the principles and provisions of the Convention widely known, by appropriate and active means, to adults and children alike.

swArticle 43

1. For the purpose of examining the progress made by State Parties in achieving the realisation of the obligations undertaken in the present Convention, there shall be established a Committee on the Rights of the Child, which shall carry out the functions hereinafter provided.

2. The Committee shall consist of ten experts of high moral standing and recognised competence in the field covered by this Convention. The members of the Committee shall be elected by States Parties from among their nationals and shall serve in their personal capacity, consideration being given to equitable geographical distribution, as well as to the principal legal system.

3. The members of the Committee shall be elected by secret ballot from a list of persons nominated by States Parties. Each State Party may nominate one person from among its own nationals.

4. The initial election to the Committee shall be held no later than six months after the date of the entry into force of the present Convention and thereafter every second year. At least four months before the date of each election, the Secretary-General of the United Nations shall address a letter to States Parties inviting them to submit their nominations within two months. The Secretary-General shall subsequently prepare a list in alphabetical order of all persons thus nominated, indicating States Parties which

have nominated them, and shall submit it to the States Parties to the parent Convention.

5. The elections shall be held at meetings of States Parties convened by the Secretary-General at United Nations Headquarters. At those meetings, for which two thirds of States Parties shall constitute a quorum, the persons elected to the Committee shall be those who obtain the largest number of votes and an absolute majority of the votes of the representatives of States Parties present and voting.

6. The members of the Committee shall be elected for a term of four years. They shall be eligible for re-election if renominated. The term of five of the members elected at the first election shall expire at the end of two years; immediately after the first election the names of these five members shall be chosen by lot by the Chairman of the meeting.

7. If a member of the Committee dies or resigns or declares that for any other cause he or she can no longer perform the duties of the Committee, the State Party which nominated the member/shall appoint another expert from among its nationals to serve for the remainder of the term, subject to the approval of the Committee.

8. The Committee shall establish its own rules of procedure.

9. The Committee shall elect its officers for a period of two years.

10. The meetings of the Committee shall normally be held at United Nations Headquarters or at any other convenient place as determined by the Committee. The Committee shall normally meet annually. The duration of the meetings of the Committee shall be determined, and reviewed, if necessary, by a meeting of the States Parties to the present Convention, subject to the approval of the General Assembly.

11. The Secretary-General of the United Nations shall provide the necessary staff and facilities for the effective performance of the functions of the Committee under the present Convention.

12. With the approval of the General Assembly, the members of the committee established under the present Convention shall received emolument from United Nations resources on such terms and conditions as the Assembly may decide.

Article 44

1. States Parties undertake to submit to the Committee, through the Secretary-General of the United Nations, reports on the measures they have adopted which give effect to the rights recognised herein and on the progress made on the enjoyment of those rights:

(a) Within two years of the entry into force of the Convention for the State Party concerned;
(b) Thereafter every five years.

2. Reports made under the present article shall indicate factors and difficulties, if any, affecting the degree of fulfilment of the obligations under the present Convention. Reports shall also contain sufficient information to provide the Committee with a comprehensive understanding of the implementation of the Convention in the country concerned.

3. A State Party which has submitted a comprehensive initial report to the Committee need not, in its subsequent reports submitted in accordance with paragraph 1 (b) of the present article, repeat basic information previously provided.

4. The Committee may request from States Parties further information relevant to the implementation of the Convention.,

5. The Committee shall submit to the General Assembly,

through the Economic and Social Council, every two years, reports on its activities.

6. States Parties shall make their reports widely available to the public in their own countries.

Article 45

In order to foster the effective implementation of the Convention and to encourage international co-operation in the field covered by the Convention:

(a) The specialised agencies, the United Nations Children's Fund, and other United Nations organs shall be entitled to be represented at the consideration of the implementation of such provisions of the present Convention as fall within the scope of their mandate. The Committee may invite the specialised agencies, the United Nations Children's Fund and other competent bodies as it may consider appropriate to provide expert advice on the implementation of the Convention in areas falling within the scope of their respective mandates. The Committee may invite the specialised agencies, the United Nations Children's Fund, and other United Nations organs to submit report on the implementation of the Convention in areas falling within the scope of their activities;

(b) The Committee shall transmit, as it may consider appropriate, to the specialised agencies, the United Nations Children's Fund and other competent bodies, an reports from State Parties that contain a request, or indicate a need, for technical advice or assistance, along with the Cor mittee's observations and suggestions, if any, on these requests or indications;

(c) The Committee may recommend to the General Assembly to request the Secretary-General to undertake on its behalf studies on specific issues relating to the rights of the child;

(d) The Committee may make suggestions and general recommendations based on information received pursuant to articles 44 and 45 of the present Convention. Such suggestions and general recommendations shall be transmitted to any State Party concerned and reported to the General Assembly, together with comments, if any, from States Parties.

PART III

Article 46

The present Convention shall be open for signature by all States.

Article 47

The present Convention is subject to ratification. Instruments of ratification shall be deposited with the Secretary-General of the United Nations.

Article 48

The present Convention shall remain open for accession by any State. The instruments of accession shall be deposited with the Secretary-General of the United Nations.

Article 49

1. The present Convention shall enter into force on the thirtieth day following the date of deposit with the Secretary-General of the United Nations of the twentieth instrument of ratification or accession.

2. For each State ratifying on acceding to the Convention after the deposit of the twentieth instrument of ratification or accession, the Convention shall enter into force on the thirtieth day after the deposit by such State of its instrument of ratification or accession.

Article 50

1. Any Sate Party may propose an amendment and file

it with the Secretary-General of the United Nations. The Secretary-General shall thereupon communicate the proposed amendment to State Parties, with a request that they indicate whether they favour a conference of States Parties for the purpose of considering and voting upon the proposals. In the event that, of the States Parties favour such a conference, the Secretary-General shall convene the conference under the auspices of the United Nations. Any amendment adopted by a majority of States parties present and voting at the conference shall be submitted to the General Assembly for approval.

2. An amendment adopted in accordance with paragraph 1 of the present article shall enter into force when it has been approved by the General Assembly of the United Nations and accepted by a two-thirds majority of States Parties.

3. When an amendment enters into force, it shall be binding on those States Parties which have accepted it, other States parties still being bound by the provisions of the present Convention and any earlier amendments which they have accepted.

Article 51

1. The Secretary-General of the United Nations shall receive and circulate to all States the text of reservations made by States at the time of ratification or accession.

2. A reservation incompatible with the object and purpose of the present Convention shall not be permitted.

3. Reservations may be withdrawn at any time by notification to that effect addressed to the Secretary-General of the United Nations,who shall then inform all States. Such Notification shall take effect on the date on which it is received by the Secretary-General.

Article 52

A State Party may denounce the present Convention

by written notification to the Secretary-General of the United Nations. Denunciation becomes effective one year after the date of receipt of the notification by the Secretary-General.

Article 53

The Secretary-General of the United Nations is designated as the depositary of the present Convention.

Article 54

The original of the present Convention, of which the Arabic, Chinese, English, French, Russian and Spanish texts are equally authentic, shall be deposited with the Secretary-General of the United Nations.

In *Witness Thereof* the undersigned plenipotentiaries, being duly authorised there to by their respective Governments, have signed the present "Convention."

CONVENTION ON THE ELIMINATION OF ALL FORMS OF DISCRIMINATION AGAINST WOMEN

Adopted and Opened for Signature, Ratification and Accession by General Assembly resolution 34/180 of 18 December 1979

Entry Into Force: 3 September 1981, in Accordance with Article 27 (1)

The States Parties to the Present Convention,

Noting that the Charter of the United Nations reaffirms faith in fundamental human rights, in the dignity and worth of the human person and in the equal rights of men and women,

Noting that the Universal Declaration of Human Rights affirms the principle of the inadmissibility of discrimination and proclaims that all human beings are born free and equal in dignity and rights and that everyone is entitled to all the rights and freedoms set forth therein, without distinction of any kind, including distinction based on sex,

Noting that the States Parties to the International Covenants on Human Rights have the obligation to ensure the equal rights of men and women to enjoy all economic, social, cultural, civil and political rights,

Considering the international conventions concluded under the auspices of the United Nations and the specialised agencies promoting equality of rights of men and women,

Noting also the resolutions, declarations and recommendations adopted by the United Nations and the specialised agencies promoting equality of rights of men and women,

Concerned, however, that despite these various instruments extensive discrimination against women continues to exist,

Recalling that discrimination against women violates the principles of equality of rights and respect for human dignity, is an obstacle to the participation of women, on equal terms with men, in the political, social, economic and cultural life of their countries, hampers the growth of the prosperity of society and the family and makes more difficult the full development of the potentialities of women in the service of their countries and of humanity,

Concerned that in situations of poverty women have the least access to food, health, education, training and opportunities for employment and other needs,

Convinced that the establishment of the new international economic order based on equity and justice will contribute significantly towards the promotion of equality between men and women,

Emphasizing that the eradication of apartheid, all forms

of racism, racial discrimination, colonialism, neocolonialism, aggression, foreign occupation and domination and interference in the internal affairs of States is essential to the full enjoyment of the rights of men and women,

Affirming that the strengthening of international peace and security, the relaxation of international tension, mutual cooperation among all States irrespective of their social and economic systems, general and complete disarmament, in particular nuclear disarmament under strict and effective international control, the affirmation of the principles of justice, equality and mutual benefit in relations among countries and the realisation of the right of peoples under alien and colonial domination and foreign occupation to self-determination and independence, as well as respect for national sovereignty and territorial integrity, will promote social progress and development and as a consequence will contribute to the attainment of full equality between men and women,

Convinced that the full and complete development of a country, the welfare of the world and the cause of peace require the maximum participation of women on equal terms with men in all fields,

Bearing in mind the great contribution of women to the welfare of the family and to the development of society, so far not fully recognised, the social significance of maternity and the role of both parents in the family and in the upbringing of children, and aware that the role of women in procreation should not be a basis for discrimination but that the upbringing of children requires a sharing of responsibility between men and women and society as a whole,

Aware that a change in the traditional role of men as well as the role of women in society and in the family is needed to achieve full equality between men and women,

Determined to implement the principles set forth in the Declaration on the Elimination of Discrimination against Women and, for that purpose, to adopt the measures required for the elimination of such discrimination in all its forms and manifestations,

Have agreed on the following:

PART I

Article 1

For the purposes of the present Convention, the term "discrimination against women" shall mean any distinction, exclusion or restriction made on the basis of sex which has the effect or purpose of impairing or nullifying the recognition, enjoyment or exercise by women, irrespective of their marital status, on a basis of equality of men and women, of human rights and fundamental freedoms in the political, economic, social, cultural, civil or any other field.

Article 2

States Parties condemn discrimination against women in all its forms, agree to pursue by all appropriate means and without delay a policy of eliminating discrimination against women and, to this end, undertake;

(a) To embody the principle of the equality of men and women in their national constitutions or other appropriate legislation if not yet incorporated therein and to ensure, through law and other appropriate means, the practical realisation of this principle;

(b) To adopt appropriate legislative and other measures, including sanctions where appropriate, prohibiting all discrimination against women;

(c) To establish legal protection of the rights of women on an equal basis with men and to ensure through competent national tribunals and other public institutions the effective protection of women against any act of discrimination;

(d) To refrain from engaging in any act or practice of discrimination against women and to ensure that public authorities and institutions shall act in conformity with this obligation;

(e) To take all appropriate measures to eliminate discrimination against women by any person, organisation or enterprise;

(f) To take all appropriate measures, including legislation, to modify or abolish existing laws, regulations, customs and practices which constitute discrimination against women;

(g) To repeal all national penal provisions which constitute discrimination against women.

Article 3

States Parties shall take in all fields, in particular in the political, social, economic and cultural fields, all appropriate measures, including legislation, to ensure the full development and advancement of women, for the purpose of guaranteeing them the exercise and enjoyment of human rights and fundamental freedoms on a basis of equality with men.

Article 4

1. Adoption by States Parties of temporary special measures aimed at accelerating de facto equality between men and women shall not be considered discrimination as defined in the present Convention, but shall in no way entail as a consequence the maintenance of unequal or separate standards; these measures shall be discontinued when the objectives of equality of opportunity and treatment have been achieved.

2. Adoption by States Parties of special measures, including those measures contained in the present

Convention, aimed at protecting maternity shall not be considered discriminatory.

Article 5

States Parties shall take all appropriate measures:

(a) To modify the social and cultural patterns of conduct of men and women, with a view to achieving the elimination of prejudices and customary and all other practices which are based on the idea of the inferiority or the superiority of either of the sexes or on stereotyped roles for men and women;

(b) To ensure that family education includes a proper understanding of maternity as a social function and the recognition of the common responsibility of men and women in the upbringing and development of their children, it being understood that the interest of the children is the primordial consideration in all cases.

Article 6

States Parties shall take all appropriate measures, including legislation, to suppress all forms of traffic in women and exploitation of prostitution of women.

PART II

Article 7

States Parties shall take all appropriate measures to eliminate discrimination against women in the political and public life of the country and, in particular, shall ensure to women, on equal terms with men, the right:

(a) To vote in all elections and public referenda and to be eligible for election to all publicly elected bodies;

(b) To participate in the formulation of government policy and the implementation thereof and to hold public office and perform all public functions at all levels of government;

(c) To participate in non-governmental organisations and associations concerned with the public and political life of the country.

Article 8

States Parties shall take all appropriate measures to ensure to women, on equal terms with men and without any discrimination, the opportunity to represent their Governments at the international level and to participate in the work of international organisations.

Article 9

1. States Parties shall grant women equal rights with men to acquire, change or retain their nationality. They shall ensure in particular that neither marriage to an alien nor change of nationality by the husband during marriage shall automatically change the nationality of the wife, render her stateless or force upon her the nationality of the husband.

2. States Parties shall grant women equal rights with men with respect to the nationality of their children.

PART III

Article 10

States Parties shall take all appropriate measures to eliminate discrimination against women in order to ensure to them equal rights with men in the field of education and in particular to ensure, on a basis of equality of men and women:

(a) The same conditions for career and vocational guidance, for access to studies and for the achievement of diplomas in educational establishments of all categories in rural as well as in urban areas; this equality shall be ensured in preschool, general, technical, professional and higher technical education, as well as in all types of vocational training;

(b) Access to the same curricula, the same examinations, teaching staff with qualifications of the same standard and school premises and equipment of the same quality;

(c) The elimination of any stereotyped concept of the roles of men and women at all levels and in all forms of education by encouraging coeducation and other types of education which will help to achieve this aim and, in particular, by the revision of textbooks and school programmes and the adaptation of teaching methods;

(d) The same opportunities to benefit from scholarships and other study grants;

(e) The same opportunities for access to programmes of continuing education, including adult and functional literacy programmes, particularly those aimed at reducing, at the earliest possible time, any gap in education existing between men and women;

(f) The reduction of female student drop-out rates and the organisation of programmes for girls and women who have left school prematurely;

(g) The same opportunities to participate actively in sports and physical education;

(h) Access to specific educational information to help to ensure the health and well-being of families, including information and advice on family planning.

Article 11

1. States Parties shall take all appropriate measures to eliminate discrimination against women in the field of employment in order to ensure, on a basis of equality of men and women, the same rights, in particular:

(a) The right to work as an inalienable right of all human beings;

(b) The right to the same employment opportunities, including the application of the same criteria for selection in matters of employment;

(c) The right to free choice of profession and employment, the right to promotion, job security and all benefits and conditions of service and the right to receive vocational training and retraining, including apprenticeships, advanced vocational training and recurrent training;

(d) The right to equal remuneration, including benefits, and to equal treatment in respect of work of equal value, as well as equality of treatment in the evaluation of the quality of work;

(e) The right to social security, particularly in cases of retirement, unemployment, sickness, invalidity and old age and other incapacity to work, as well as the right to paid leave;

(f) The right to protection of health and to safety in working conditions, including the safeguarding of the function of reproduction.

2. In order to prevent discrimination against women on the grounds of marriage or maternity and to ensure their effective right to work, States Parties shall take appropriate measures:

(a) To prohibit, subject to the imposition of sanctions, dismissal on the grounds of pregnancy or of maternity leave and discrimination in dismissals on the basis of marital status;

(b) To introduce maternity leave with pay or with comparable social benefits without loss of former employment, seniority or social allowances;

(c) To encourage the provision of the necessary supporting social services to enable parents to combine family obligations with work responsibilities and participation in public life, in particular through promoting the establishment and development of a network of childcare facilities.

(d) To provide special protection to women during pregnancy in types of work proved to be harmful to them.

3. Protective legislation relating to matters covered in this article shall be reviewed periodically in the light of scientific and technological knowledge and shall be revised, repealed or extended as necessary.

Article 12

1. States Parties shall take all appropriate measures to eliminate discrimination against women in the field of health care in order to ensure, on a basis of equality of men and women, access to health care services, including those related to family planning.

2. Notwithstanding the provisions of paragraph 1 of this article. States Parties shall ensure to women appropriate services in connection with pregnancy, confinement and the post-natal period, granting free services where necessary, as well as adequate nutrition during pregnancy and lactation.

Article 13

States Parties shall take all appropriate measures to eliminate discrimination against women in other areas of economic and social life in order to ensure, on a basis of equality of men and women, the same rights, in particular:

(a) The right to family benefits;

(b) The right to bank loans, mortgages and other forms of financial credit;

(c) The right to participate in recreational activities, sports and all aspects of cultural life.

Article 14

1. States Parties shall take into account the particular

problems faced by rural women and the significant roles which rural women play in the economic survival of their families, including their work in the non-monetised sectors of the economy, and shall take all appropriate measures to ensure the application of the provisions of the present Convention to women in rural areas.

2. States Parties shall take all appropriate measures to eliminate discrimination against women in rural areas in order to ensure, on a basis of equality of men and women, that they participate in and benefit from rural development and, in particular, shall ensure to such women the right:

(a) To participate in the elaboration and implementation of development planning at all levels;
(b) To have access to adequate health-care facilities, including information, counselling and services in family planning;
(c) To benefit directly from social security programmes;
(d) To obtain all types of training and education, formal and non-formal, including that relating to functional literacy, as well as, *inter alia,* the benefit of all community and extension services, in order to increase their technical proficiency;
(e) To organise self-help groups and cooperatives in order to obtain equal access to economic opportunities through employment or self-employment;
(f) To participate in all community activities;
(g) To have access to agricultural credit and loans, marketing facilities, appropriate technology and equal treatment in land and agrarian reform as well as in land resettlement schemes;
(h) To enjoy adequate living conditions, particularly in relation to housing, sanitation, electricity and water supply, transport and communications.

PART IV

Article 15

1. States Parties shall accord to women equality with men before the law.

2. States Parties shall accord to women, in civil matters, a legal capacity identical to that of men and the same opportunities to exercise that capacity. In particular, they shall give women equal rights to conclude contracts and to administer property and shall treat them equally in all stages of procedure in courts and tribunals.

3. States Parties agree that all contracts and all other private instruments of any kind with a legal effect which is directed at restricting the legal capacity of women shall be deemed null and void.

4. States Parties shall accord to men and women the same rights with regard to the law relating to the movement of persons and the freedom to choose their residence and domicile.

Article 16

1. States Parties shall take all appropriate measures to eliminate discrimination against women in all matters relating to marriage and family relations and in particular shall ensure, on a basis of equality of men and women:

(a) The same right to enter into marriage;

(b) The same right freely to choose a spouse and to enter into marriage only with their free and full consent;

(c) The same rights and responsibilities during marriage and at its dissolution;

(d) The same rights and responsibilities as parents, irrespective of their marital status, in matters relating to their children; in all cases the interests of the children shall be paramount;

(e) The same rights to decide freely and responsibly on the number and spacing of their children and to have access to the information, education and means to enable them to exercise these rights;

(f) The same rights and responsibilities with regard to guardianship, wardship, trusteeship and adoption of children, or similar institutions where these concepts exist in national legislation; in all cases the interests of the children shall be paramount;

(g) The same personal rights as husband and wife, including the right to choose a family name, a profession and an occupation;

(h) The same rights for both spouses in respect of the ownership, acquisition, management, administration, enjoyment and disposition of property, whether free of charge or for a valuable consideration.

2. The betrothal and the marriage of a child shall have no legal effect, and all necessary action, including legislation, shall be taken to specify a minimum age for marriage and to make the registration of marriages in an official registry compulsory.

PART V

Article 17

1. For the purpose of considering the progress made in the implementation of the present Convention, there shall be established a Committee on the Elimination of Discrimination against Women (hereinafter referred to as the Committee) consisting, at the time of entry into force of the Convention, of eighteen and, after ratification of or accession to the Convention by the thirty-fifth State Party, of twenty-three experts of high moral standing and competence in the field covered by the Convention. The experts shall be elected by States Parties from among their nationals and shall serve in their personal capacity, consideration being given to equitable geographical

distribution and to the representation of the different forms of civilisation as well as the principal legal systems.

2. The members of the Committee shall be elected by secret ballot from a list of persons nominated by States Parties. Each State Party may nominate one person from among its own nationals.

3. The initial election shall be held six months after the date of the entry into force of the present Convention. At least three months before the date of each election the Secretary-General of the United Nations shall address a letter to the States Parties inviting them to submit their nominations within two months. The Secretary-General shall prepare a list in alphabetical order of all persons thus nominated, indicating the States Parties which have nominated them, and shall submit it to the States Parties.

4. Elections of the members of the Committee shall be held at a meeting of States Parties convened by the Secretary-General at United Nations Headquarters. At that meeting, for which two thirds of the States Parties shall constitute a quorum, the persons elected to the Committee shall be those nominees who obtain the largest number of votes and an absolute majority of the votes of the representatives of States Parties present and voting.

5. The members of the Committee shall be elected for a term of four years. However, the terms of nine of the members elected at the first election shall expire at the end of two years; immediately after the first election the names of these nine members shall be chosen by lot by the Chairman of the Committee.

6. The election of the five additional members of the Committee shall be held in accordance with the provisions of paragraphs 2, 3 and 4 of this article, following the thirty-fifth ratification or accession. The terms of two of the additional members elected on this occasion shall expire at the end of two years, the names of these two members

having been chosen by lot by the Chairman of the Committee.

7. For the filling of casual vacancies, the State Party whose expert has ceased to function as a member of the Committee shall appoint another expert from among its nationals, subject to the approval of the Committee.

8. The members of the Committee shall, with the approval of the General Assembly, receive emoluments from United Nations resources on such terms and conditions as the Assembly may decide, having regard to the importance of the Committee's responsibilities.

9. The Secretary-General of the United Nations shall provide the necessary staff and facilities for the effective performance of the functions of the Committee under the present Convention.

Article 18

1. States Parties undertake to submit to the Secretary-General of the United Nations, for consideration by the Committee, a report on the legislative, judicial, administrative or other measures which they have adopted to give effect to the provisions of the present Convention and on the progress made in this respect:

(a) Within one year after the entry into force for the State concerned;

(b) Thereafter at least every four years and further whenever the Committee so requests.

2. Reports may indicate factors and difficulties affecting the degree of fulfilment of obligations under the present Convention.

Article 19

1. The Committee shall adopt its own rules of procedure.

2. The Committee shall elect its officers for a term of two years.

Article 20

1. The Committee shall normally meet for a period of not more than two weeks annually in order to consider the reports submitted in accordance with article 18 of the present Convention.

2. The meetings of the Committee shall normally be held at United Nations Headquarters or at any other convenient place as determined by the Committee.

Article 21

1. The Committee shall, through the Economic and Social Council, report annually to the General Assembly of the United Nations on its activities and may make suggestions and general recommendations based on the examination of reports and information received from the States Parties. Such suggestions and general recommendations shall be included in the report of the Committee together with comments, if any, from States Parties.

2. The Secretary-General of the United Nations shall transmit the reports of the Committee to the Commission on the Status of Women for its information.

Article 22

The specialised agencies shall be entitled to be represented at the consideration of the implementation of such provisions of the present Convention as fall within the scope of their activities. The Committee may invite the specialised agencies to submit reports on the implementation of the Convention in areas falling within the scope of their activities.

PART VI

Article 23

Nothing in the present Convention shall affect any provisions that are more conducive to the achievement of equality between men and women which may be contained:

(a) In the legislation of a State Party; or

(b) In any other international convention, treaty or agreement in force for that State.

Article 24

State Parties undertake to adopt all necessary measures at the national level aimed at achieving the full realisation of the rights recognised in the present Convention.

Article 25

1. The present Convention shall be open for signature by all States.

2. The Secretary-General of the United Nations is designated as the depositary of the present Convention.

3. The present Convention is subject to ratification. Instruments of ratification shall be deposited with the Secretary-General of the United Nations.

4. The present Convention shall be open to accession by all States. Accession shall be effected by the deposit of an instrument of accession with the Secretary-General of the United Nations.

Article 26

1. A request for the revision of the present Convention may be made at any time by any State Party by means of a notification in writing addressed to the Secretary-General of the United Nations.

2. The General Assembly of the United Nations shall decide upon the steps, if any, to be taken in respect of such a request.

Article 27

1. The present Convention shall enter into force on the thirtieth day after the date of deposit with the Secretary-General of the United Nations of the twentieth instrument of ratification or accession.

2. For each State ratifying the present Convention or acceding to it after the deposit of the twentieth instrument of ratification or accession, the Convention shall enter into force on the thirtieth day after the date of the deposit of its own instrument of ratification or accession.

Article 28

1. The Secretary-General of the United Nations shall receive and circulate to all States the text of reservations made by States at the time of ratification or accession.

2. A reservation incompatible with the object and purpose of the present Convention shall not be permitted.

3. Reservations may be withdrawn at any time by notification to this effect addressed to the Secretary-General of the United Nations, who shall then inform all States thereof. Such notification shall take effect on the date on which it is received.

Article 29

1. Any dispute between two or more States Parties concerning the interpretation or application of the present Convention which is not settled by negotiation shall, at the request of one of them, be submitted to arbitration. If within six months from the date of the request for arbitration the parties are unable to agree on the organisation of the arbitration, any one of those parties may refer the dispute to the International Court of Justice by request in conformity with the Statute of the Court.

2. Each State Party may at the time of signature or ratification of the present Convention or accession thereto declare that it does not consider itself bound by paragraph 1 of this article. The other States Parties shall not be bound by that paragraph with respect to any State Party which has made such a reservation.

3. Any State Party which has made a reservation in

accordance with paragraph 2 of this article may at any time withdraw that reservation by notification to the Secretary-General of the United Nations.

Article 30

The present Convention, the Arabic, Chinese, English, French, Russian and Spanish texts of which are equally authentic, shall be deposited with the Secretary-General of the United Nations.

In Witness Whereof the undersigned, duly authorised, have signed the present Convention.

PROTOCOL AMENDING THE SLAVERY CONVENTION SIGNED AT GENEVA ON 25 SEPTEMBER 1926

Approved by General Assembly Resolution 794 (VIII) of 23 October 1953

Entry Into Force: 7 December 1953, in Accordance with Article III

The States Parties to the Present Protocol,

Considering that under the Slavery Convention signed at Geneva on 25 September 1926 (hereinafter called "the Convention") the League of Nations was invested with certain duties and functions, and

Considering that it is expedient that these duties and functions should be continued by the United Nations,

Have agreed as follows:

Article I

The States Parties to the present Protocol undertake that as between themselves they will, in accordance with the provisions of the Protocol, attribute full legal force and effect to and duly apply the amendments to the Convention set forth in the annex to the Protocol.

Article II

1. The present Protocol shall be open for signature or acceptance by any of the States Parties to the Convention to which the Secretary-General has communicated for this purpose a copy of the Protocol.

2. States may become Parties to the present Protocol by:

(a) Signature without reservation as to acceptance;
(b) Signature with reservation as to acceptance, followed by acceptance;
(c) Acceptance.

3. Acceptance shall be effected by the deposit of a formal instrument with the Secretary-General of the United Nations.

Article III

1. The present Protocol shall come into force on the date on which two States shall have become Parties thereto, and shall thereafter come into force in respect of each State upon the date on which it becomes a Party to the Protocol.

2. The amendments set forth in the annex to the present Protocol shall come into force when twenty-three States shall have become Parties to the Protocol, and consequently any State becoming a Party to the Convention, after the amendments thereto have come into force, shall become a Party to the Convention as so amended.

Article IV

In accordance with paragraph 1 of Article 102 of the Charter of the United Nations and the regulations pursuant thereto adopted by the General Assembly, the Secretary-General of the United Nations is authorised to effect registration of the present Protocol and of the amendments made in the Convention by the Protocol on the respective dates of their entry into force and to publish the Protocol and the amended text of the Convention as soon as possible after registration.

Article V

The present Protocol, of which the Chinese, English, French, Russian and Spanish texts are equally authentic, shall be deposited in the archives of the United Nations Secretariat. The texts of the Convention to be amended in accordance with the annex being authentic in the English and French languages only, the English and French texts of the annex shall be equally authentic, and the Chinese, Russian and Spanish texts shall be translations. The Secretary-General shall prepare certified copies of the Protocol, including the annex, for communication to States Parties to the Convention, as well as to all other States Members of the United Nations. He shall likewise prepare for communication to States including States not Members of the United Nations, upon the entry into force of the amendments as provided in article III, certified copies of the Convention as so amended.

In Witness Whereof the undersigned, being duly authorised thereto by their respective Governments, signed the present Protocol on the date appearing opposite their respective signatures.

Done at the Headquarters of the United Nations, New York, this seventh day of December. one thousand nine hundred and fifty-three.

Annex to the Protocol amending the Slavery Convention signed at Geneva on 25 September 1926

In *article 7* "the Secretary-General or the United Nations" shall be substituted for "the Secretary-General of the League of Nations".

In *article 8* "the International Court of Justice" shall be substituted for the "Permanent Court of International Justice", and "the Statute of the International Court of

Justice" shall be substituted for "the Protocol of December 16th, 1920, relating to the Permanent Court of International Justice".

In the first and second paragraphs of *article 10* "the United Nations" shall be substituted for "the League of Nations".

The last three paragraphs *of article 11* shall be deleted and the following substituted:

"The present Convention shall be open to accession by all States including States which are not Members of the United Nations, to which the Secretary-General of the United Nations shall have communicated a certified copy of the Convention.

"Accession shall be effected by the deposit of a formal instrument with the Secretary-General of the United Nations, who shall give notice thereof to all States Parties to the Convention and to all other States contemplated in the present article, informing them of the date on which each such instrument of accession was received in deposit."

In *article 12* "the United Nations" shall be substituted for "the League of Nations".

OPTIONAL PROTOCOL TO THE INTERNATIONAL COVENANT ON CIVIL AND POLITICAL RIGHTS

Adopted and opened for signature, ratification and accession by General Assembly resolution 2200 A (XXI) of 16 December 1966

Entry into Force: 23 March 1976, in Accordance with article 9

The States Parties to the present Protocol,

Considering that in order further to achieve the purposes of the International Covenant on Civil and Political Rights (hereinafter referred to as the Covenant) and the implementation of its provisions it would be appropriate to enable the Human Rights Committee set up in part IV of the Covenant (hereinafter referred to as the Committee) to receive and consider, as provided in the present Protocol, communications from individuals claiming to be victims of violations of any of the rights set forth in the Covenant,

Have agreed as follows:

Article 1

A State Party to the Covenant that becomes a Party to the present Protocol recognises the competence of the Committee to receive and consider communications from individuals subject to its jurisdiction who claim to be victims of a violation by that State Party of any of the rights set forth in the Covenant. No communication shall be received by the Committee if it concerns a State Party to the Covenant which is not a Party to the present Protocol.

Article 2

Subject to the provisions of article 1, individuals who claim that any of their rights enumerated in the Covenant have been violated and who have exhausted all available domestic remedies may submit a written communication to the Committee for consideration.

Article 3

The Committee shall consider inadmissible any communication under the present Protocol which is anonymous, or which it considers to be an abuse of the right of submission of such communications or to be incompatible with the provisions of the Covenant.

Article 4

1. Subject to the provisions of article 3, the Committee shall bring any communications submitted to it under the present Protocol to the attention of the State Party to the

present Protocol alleged to be violating any provision of the Covenant.

2 Within six months, the receiving State shall submit to the Committee written explanations or statements clarifying the matter and the remedy, if any, that may have been taken by the State.

Article 5

1. The Committee shall consider communications received under the present Protocol in the light of all written information made available to it by the individual and by the State Party concerned.

2. The Committee shall not consider any communication from an individual unless it has ascertained that:

(a) The same matter is not being examined under another procedure of international investigation or settlement;

(b) The individual has exhausted all available domestic remedies. This shall not be the rule where the application of the remedies is unreasonably prolonged.

3. The Committee shall hold closed meetings when examining communications under the present Protocol.

4. The Committee shall forward its views to the State Party concerned and to the individual.

Article 6

The Committee shall include in its annual report under article 45 of the Covenant a summary of its activities tinder the present Protocol.

Article 7

Pending the achievement of the objectives of resolution 1514 (XV) adopted by the General Assembly of the United

Nations on 14 December 1960 concerning the Declaration on the Granting of Independence to Colonial Countries and Peoples, the provisions of the present Protocol shall in no way limit the right of petition granted to these peoples by the Charter of the United Nations and other international conventions and instruments under the United Nations and its specialised agencies.

Article 8

1. The present Protocol is open for signature by any State which has signed the Covenant.

2. The present Protocol is subject to ratification by any State which has ratified or acceded to the Covenant. Instruments of ratification shall be deposited with the Secretary-General of the United Nations.

3. The present Protocol shall be open to accession by any State which has ratified or acceded to the Covenant.

4. Accession shall be effected by the deposit of an instrument of accession with the Secretary-General of the United Nations.

5. The Secretary-General of the United Nations shall inform all States which have signed the present Protocol or acceded to it of the deposit of each instrument of ratification or accession.

Article 9

1. Subject to the entry into force of the Covenant, the present Protocol shall enter into force three months after the date of the deposit with the Secretary-General of the United Nations of the tenth instrument of ratification or instrument of accession.

2. For each State ratifying the present Protocol or acceding to it after the deposit of the tenth instrument of ratification or instrument of accession, the present Protocol shall enter into force three months after the date of the

deposit of its own instrument of ratification or instrument of accession.

Article 10

The provisions of the present Protocol shall extend to all parts of federal States without any limitations or exceptions.

Article 11

1. Any State Party to the present Protocol may propose an amendment and file it with the Secretary-General of the United nations. The Secretary-General shall thereupon communicate any proposed amendments to the States Parties to the present Protocol with a request that they notify him whether they favour a conference of States Parties for the purpose of considering and voting upon the proposal. In the event that at least one-third of the States Parties favour such a conference, the Secretary-General shall convene the conference under the auspices of the United Nations. Any amendment adopted by a majority of the States parties present and voting at the conference shall be submitted to the General Assembly of the United Nations for approval.

2. Amendments shall come into force when they have been approved by the General Assembly of the United Nations and accepted by a two-thirds majority of the States Parties to the present Protocol in accordance with their respective constitutional processes.

3. When amendments come into force, they shall be binding on those States Parties which have accepted them, other States Parties still being bound by the provisions of the present Protocol and any earlier amendment which they have accepted.

Article 12

1. Any State Party may denounce the present Protocol at any time by written notification addressed to the Secretary-General of the United Nations. Denunciation shall take

effect three months after the date of receipt of the notification by the Secretary-General.

2. Denunciation shall he without prejudice to the continued application of the provisions of the present Protocol to any communication submitted under article 2 before the effective date of denunciation.

Article 13

Irrespective of the notifications made under article 8, paragraph 5, of the present Protocol, the Secretary-General of the United Nations shall inform all States referred to in article 48, paragraph 1, of the Covenant of the following particulars:

(a) Signatures, ratifications and accessions under article 8;
(b) The date of the entry into force of the present Protocol under Article 9 and the date of the entry into force of any amendments under article 11,
(c) Denunciations under article 12.

Article 14

1. The present Protocol, of which the Chinese, English, French, Russian and Spanish texts are equally authentic, shall be deposited in the archives of the United Nations.

2. The Secretary-General of the United Nations shall transmit certified copies of the present Protocol to all States referred to in article 48 of the Covenant.

Declaration by the Government of India

Whereas the International Covenant on Economic, Social and Cultural Rights and the International Covenant on Civil and Political Rights were adopted by the General Assembly of the United Nations in Resolution 2200 (XXI) of 16 December 1966, which Covenants are reproduced in the Annexure to this Document;

And Whereas it Is fit and expedient to accede to the aforesaid Covenants subject to the following Declarations:

Declaration

I. With reference to Articles 4 and 8 of the International Covenant Economic, Social and Cultural Rights and Article I of the International Covenant on Civil and Political Rights, the Government of the Republic of India declares that the words "the right of self-determination" appearing in those articles apply only to the peoples under foreign domination and that these words do not apply to sovereign independent States or to a section of a people or nation—which is the essence of national integrity.

II. With reference to Article 9 of International Covenant on Civil and Political Rights, the Government of the Republic of India takes the position that the provisions of the article shall be so applied as to be in consonance with the provisions of clauses (3) to (7) of Article 22 of the Constitution of India. Further under the Indian Legal System, there is no enforceable right to compensation for persons claiming to be victims of unlawful arrest or detention against the State.

III. With respect to Article 13 of the International Covenant on Civil and Political Rights, the Government of the Republic of India reserves the right to apply its law relating to foreigners.

IV. With reference to Articles 4 & 8 of the International Covenant on Economic, Social and Cultural Rights, and Articles 12, 19(3), 21 and 22 of the International Covenant on Civil and Political Rights the Government of the Republic of India declares that the provisions of the said articles shall be so applied as to be in conformity with the provisions of Article 19 of the Constitution of India.

V. With reference to Article 7 (c) of the International Covenant on Economic, Social and Cultural Rights, the Government of the Republic of India declares the provisions of the said article shall be so applied as to be in conformity with the provision of Article 19 of the Constitution of India.

Now, Therefore, Be It Known that the Government of the Republic of India, having seen and considered the said Covenants, do hereby accede to the same, subject to the aforementioned Declarations.

In Testimony Whereof I, Neelam Sanjiva Reddy, President Of India, have signed these Covenants and affixed hereunto my Seal at New Delhi this the sixth day of Chaitra of the Saka year one thousand nine hundred and one corresponding to the twenty seventh day of March of the Year one thousand nine hundred and seventy nine A.D. in the Thirtieth year of the Republic of India.

Sd/-

(Neelam Sanjiva Reddy)
President of India

Deposited with the
U.N. on 10-04-1979

Select Bibliography

A. Curtis Wilgus, ed., *South American Dictators,* Washington, D.C.: George Washington University Press, 1937.

Action, H.B. Symposium on rights. *Proceedings of the Aristotelian Society,* Supp. Volume 24, 1950; 107-8.

Agarwal, R.S. *Human Rights in Modern World.* New Delhi, Chetna, 1978. pp. 122.

Ahmad, I. International efforts in the field of human rights: An evaluation. *Indian Journal of Politics,* 1980.

Albert Carr, *Juggernaut: The Path of Dictatorships,* New York: Viking Press, 1939.

Alfred Cobban, *Dictatorship, Its History and Theory,* New York: Charles Scribner's Sons, 1939.

Alston, P. Human rights and the new international development strategy. *Bulletin of Peace Proposals,* 1979.

American Jewish Committee. *World Charter for Human Rights.* New Delhi, 1946.

Arendt, Hannah. *Human Conditions.* Garden City. New York, Doubleday, 1959.

Barnes, Leonard. Rights of dependent peoples. In *Human Rights.* Ed. by UNESCO. London, 1950; 242-45.

Batra, T.S. *Human Rights—A Critique.* New Delhi, Metropolitan, 1979. pp. 350.

Beckett. Human rights. *Transactions of the Grotius Society,* 34, 1949.

Bhagat, B.R. Human rights: A survey of recent developments. *Foreign Affairs Reports* 32 (6-7) Jun-Jul. 1983; 86-122.

Bilder, R. Rethinking international human rights: Some basic questions *Wisconsin Law Review*, 1969; 171-217.

Bokser, Ben Zion. Ethics of the Fathers. In *Great Expressions of Human Right's*. Ed. by R.M. MacIver. New York, 1950; 43-50.

Brown, Stuart M. Inalienable rights. *Philosophical Review* 64, 1955; 192-211.

Buckley, Ken. *All About Citizens' rights*. Melbourne, Nelson, 1976.

Buergenthal, Thomas. International and regional human rights law and institutions; Some examples of their interactions. *Texas International Law Journal,* 12, 1977; 331-50.

Bull, H. University of human rights. *Journal of International Studies,* August, 1979.

Carr, E.H. Rights of man. In *Human Rights*. Ed. by Unesco. London Allan Wingate; 1950; 19-23.

Cartwright, Hilary. International action for the protection of human rights. In *Rights and Wrongs*. Ed. by C.R. Hill. Middlesex, 1969; 146-80.

Castel, J.G. International year for human rights. *Canadian Bar Review,* 46, 1968.

Chan, Wing-tsit. "Within the four seas all are brothers.". In *Great Expressions of Human Rights*. Ed by R.M. MacIver New York, 1950; 19-28.

Chandrachud, Y.V. Range and rationale of human rights. *Akashvani,* 14 Feb. 1982; 2-4.

Chattopadhyaya, Amal. Human rights—some ominous signs. *Amrita Bazar Patrika,* 11 Dec 1979.

Claude, Richard P. ed. *Comparative Human Rights*. Baltimore, 1976.

Count Carlo Sforza, "Totalitarian War and the Fate of Democracy," *Annals of the American Academy of Political and Social Science*, CXVI (July, 1941), pp. 65-72.

Cranston, Maurice. *What are Human Rights?* New York, Taplinger, 1973.

Cushman, Robert Eugene. *Excess Condemnation*. Doctoral dissertation. New York, Apleton, 1917, pp. 323.

De Madariaga, Don Salvador. Rights of man or human relations? In *Human rights.* Ed. by Unesco, London, Alan Wingate, 1950; 47-53.

Diana Spearman, *Modern Dictatorship* (New York: Columbia University Press, 1939). Significant for its emphasis upon socio-phychological characteristics of modern dictatorships, and its psychological analysis of leadership and autocracy.

Dimbleby, Jonathan. Acts of man. *New Statesman,* 94, July 1977.

Dominguez, Jorge I. Assessing Human rights conditions. In Jorge I. Dominguez. *etc. Enhancing Global Human Rights,* New York, McGraw-Hill, 1979; 21-116.

Dominguez, Jorge I. ed. et al. *Enhancing Global Human Rights.* New York, McGraw-Hill, 1980.

E.E. Kellett, *The Story of Dictatorship* (New York: E.P. Dutton and Co., 1937). A concise treatment of selected dictatorships from ancient times to the present.

Eide, Asbjorn. *Human rights in the world society.* Earl M. New York, Coleman, 1980.

Fritz Morstein Marz, "Propaganda and Dictatorship," *Annals of the American Academy of Political and Social Science,* CLXXIX (May, 1935), pp. 211-218.

G.M. Gilbert, *Tne Psychology of Dictatorship,* (New York: Ronald Press, 1950). Based on an examination of the leaders of Nazi Germany.

Guiseppe A. Borgese Goliath: *The March of Fascism* (New York: Viking Press, 1937). A penetrating analysis of Mussolini's dictatorship.

Guy Stanton Ford, ed., *Dictatorship in the Modern World* (Minneapolis: University of Minnesota Press 1939). A collection of valuable studies of the various dictatorships in the world.

H.D. Lasswell, "Garrison State," *American Journal of Sociology,* XLVI (January, 1941), pp. 455-468.

H.S. Spencer, "Dictatorship," *Encyclopaedia of the Social Sciences,* V (New York: The Macmillan Co., 1931), pp. 133-316.

Hans Kohn, *Revolutions and Dictatorships* (Cambridge, Mass.: Harvard University Press, 1939). Presents an interesting comparison of Communist and Fascist philosophies.

Hassan. P. Word arbitrary as used in the universal declaration of human rights Illegal or unjust? *Harvard International Law Journal.* 10, 1969.

Henkin, Louis. *Rights of Man Today.* Boulder, Westview Press, 1978.

Herbert W. Schneider and Shepard B. Clough, *Making Fascists* (Chicago: University of Chicago Press, 1929). An early but still useful study of indoctrination and civic training in Fascist Italy.

Hill, C. R. *ed. Rights and Wrongs; Some Essays on Human Rights.* Middlesex, Penguin Books, 1969. pp. 188.

Holcomb, A. *Human Rights in the Modern World.* New York, 1948.

Hondius, Frits. *Second Generation of Human Rights.* Strasbourg, Jul. 1979.

Human rights in the *World Community.* Washington, U.S. House of Representatives, 93rd Congress, 2nd Session, Committee on Foreign Affairs. n.d.

Huxley, Aldous. Rights of man and the facts of the human situation. In *Human Rights.* Ed. by UNESCO. London, 1950.

Impact of the Universal Declaration of Human Rights. New York, UN Department of Social Affairs, 1951.

J.O. Hertzler, "The Causal and Contributory Factors of Dictatorship." *Sociology and Social Research,* XXIV (September-October, 1939), pp. 3-21.

J.R. Angell, "The Future of Intellectual Freedom," *American Scholar*, VIII (Autumn, (1939), pp. 468-487.

James H. Mersil, "Georges Sorel's Last Myth," *Journal of Politics,* XII, 1 (February, 1950), pp. 52-65.

John Gunther, *Inside Europe* (New York: Harper and Brothers, 1939). A journalistic but useful account of European political personalities and conditions.

John. R. Tunis, "The Dictators Discover Sport," *Foreign Affairs,* XIV (July, 1936), pp. 606-617.

Joyce, James Avery. Human rights: A new dimension. *Contemporary Review,* Sep 1976.

Karl Loewenstein, "Autocracy versus Democracy in Contemporary Europe," *American Political Science Review,* XXIX (August, 1935), pp. 571-593.

Konrad Heiden, *Der Fuehrer* (Boston: Houghton Mifflin Co., 1944). The best study of Hitler.

L.S. Stavrianos, "Schooling Under the Dictators," *Current History,* XLIV (September, 1936), pp. 139-146.

Lyons, David. Apology for rights. *Corneil Review,* 3 Spr 1978; 24-32.

Merle Fainsod, *How Russia is Ruled* (Cambridge, Mass.: Harvard University Press, 1935). One the best of the many books dealing with contemporary Soviet regime.

Nariman, F.S. Recent trends in the field of human rights. In *Seminar on Human Rights.* Allahabad, 1980; 124-37.

Owen. David, *Human Rights.* London, Jonathan Cape, 1978; p. 154.

P.E. Corbett, *"The Casuistry of Dictatorship,"* World Politics, III (July, 1951), pp. 539-544.

Painter, Sidney. Magna Carta. *American Historical Review,* 53, 1948.

R.V. Daniels, "The State and Revolution: A Case Study in the Genesis and Transformation of the Communist Ideology," *The American Slavic and East European Review*, XII (February, 1953), pp. 22-43.

Robson, William (1976). *Welfare State and Welfare* Society. London: George Allen and Unwin.

S.H. Pathak, *Social Welfare: An Evolutionary and Developmental Perspective,* (New-Delhi, Macmillan, 1981), p. 152.

S.H. Pathak, "Social Development and Social Work - Some Unsolved Issues" Nayak and Siddiqui (ed) *Social Work and Social Development* (New Delhi, Gitanjali Publication, 1989) pp. 7-8.

Warner, W. Boehm, *Objectives of The Social Work Curriculum in the Future Curriculum Study* 1. (New York, Council on Social Work Education. 1959) p. 54.

Weinberger, Paul, ed. (1974). *Perspectives on Social Welfare.* New York: Macmillan.

Wilensky and Lebeaux, *Industrial Society and Social Welfare,* New York, Free Press 1965), p. 138 quoted by Pothak, Social Welfare, p. 159-160.

Index

A

Abdul Gaffar, 36
Affluent countries, 44
African countries, 30
AIPRF, 100
All India Peoples Resistance Forum, 99
Amnesty International, 25, 29
Amnesty report, 21
Aristotle, 15
Axis Powers, 2

B

Bentham, 31
Bill of Rights, 2
British Rule, 48

C

Certiorari, 20
Chad, 28
Charter of the United Nations, 31
Civil Rights, 127
 and Political Rights, 3, 5, 297
Clemenceau, 33
Committee,
 on the Elimination of Discrimination, 282
 on the Elimination of Racial Discriminat, 128
 on the Rights of the Child, 264
Constitution of India, 2
Correctional Administration, 102
Crime of Genocide, 42
Criminal Justice System, 102
Criminal Procedure Code, 52
Cultural life, 271
Cultural rights, 127
Cyprus, 35

D

D.D. Raphel, 26
Decalogue, 18
Declaration of Rights of Man and Citizen, 2
Development strategies, 45
Directive Principles of State Policy, 7
Draconian powers, 30

E

Economic, Social and Cultural Rights, 4
El Salvador, 28
Eleanor Roosevelt, 19

European Court of Human Rights, 36

F

Fawcett, 26
Fundamental Freedoms, 2, 274
Fundamental obligations, 126

G

General Assembly of the United Nations, 295
General Assembly, 23, 268
Genscher, 21
Georges Clemenceau, 33
German thesis, 29
Glimpses of Human Rights, 15
Glorious Revolution of 1688, 16
GNP, 45

H

Habeas Corpus, 20
Helsinki Accords, 31
Helsinki Conference, 24
Human rights, 110, 121, 123, 124, 125, 128, 140, 141, 147, 150, 151, 155, 158, 168, 174, 177, 178, 183, 270, 273, 274, 292
  and Criminal Justice Administration, 47
  Committee, 5, 6
  Courts, 69
Hungary, 35

I

India, 21
Indian Constitution, 48, 49, 50, 51, 53
Indian Legal System, 297
Initial election, 129
Institute of International Law, 2
Institutionalisation of Human Rights, 16
International,
  Convention of the Elimination of All, 22
  Court of Justice, 291
  Covenant on Civil and Political Right, 3, 291
  Covenant on Economic, 297, 298
  Covenants on Human Rights, 271
  Covenants on Human Rights, 19
  Covenants, 24
  Human Rights Law, 37
  Labour Organisation, 22, 42
Islamic Law, 47

J

Jamaica, 19

K

Kantian, 27

L

League of Nations, 34
Locke, 16

M

Magna Carta, 2
Mandamus, 20
Maoist Communit Centre, 99
Members of Legislatures, 102
Minorities Treaties, 34
Muslim Rule, 47

N

National Capital Territory, 75
Natural Law, 16
Natural Right, 1, 48
Neelam Sanjiva Reddy, 298
NGOs, 100
NHRC, 68, 69
Nowheresville, 17

O

Optional Protocol (1966), 3
Optional Protocol, 5

P

Pakistan, 28, 30
Panderewski, 33
Paul Sieghart, 36
Peaceful assembly, 127
Peter Beneson, 35
Plato, 15
Pope, 16
Proclamation of Tehran, 4
Progressive nations, 20
Prohibition, 20
Protection of Human Rights Act, 1993, 3

Q

Quo warranto, 20

R

Right,
- to Bail, 51
- to nationality, 127
- to Protection, 51
- to Silence, 51

Romans, 15
Roosevelt, 23
Rousseau, 15, 16, 27, 41

S

Social and Cultural Rights, 298
Sophists, 15
South Africa, 35
Spain, 35
Supreme Court of India, 6, 20
Supreme Court of India, 6

T

T.A.D.A., 68, 82
Ten Commandments, 18

Tobago, 19

Trinidad, 19

U

U.N. Charter, 37

U.N. Commission on Human Rights, 24

U.N. Declaration of Human Rights, 23

U.N.O., 5, 7

UNESCO, 42

United Nations, 4, 19, 23, 24, 31, 32, 33, 129, 271, 291

Headquarters, 265, 266

Organisation, 4

United States, 3

Declaration of Independence, 2

Universal Declaration of Human Rights, 3, 7, 19, 23, 26, 42, 43, 104, 105, 271

Universal Declaration of Rights (1948); 7, 8

V

Vienna, 33

W

World Bank, 45

World War I, 34

U

Y.V Chandrachud, 28

●●●